One Patch of Grass

ANDREW LINKER

DEDICATION

In memory of my father, Joseph Linker, who always took me to the ball-games when I was a kid. He also enjoyed a good Garcia Y Vega cigar.

In honor of Michelle and Annie, the home team.

Collin Cureageous

A portion of the proceeds from each book sale will be donated to the Fund for the Care & Cure of Collin Kratzer, my 3-year-old godson from Harrisburg who is fighting brain cancer. If you would like to learn more about Collin's remarkable journey and his on-going care, please visit the following websites:

www.facebook.com/CollinCureageous
http://littleprinceyfellow.blogspot.com
http://www.cancer.net/patient/Cancer+Types/Medulloblastoma+-+Childhood

TABLE OF CONTENTS

One Patch of Grass

Foreword

By Dave Trembley

In 1987, professional baseball returned to Harrisburg after a 35-year absence. The Senators would occupy City Island that season and end up winning the Eastern League championship.

Looking back on that first season, many memories come to mind. It isn't often that one has the opportunity to convey those thoughts in a public

DAVE TREMBLEY

manner and when I was approached by Andy Linker to share some of my recollections about my time in Harrisburg, the wheels starting turning in my mind.

Twenty-five years later, it all seems like yesterday. When I was named the manager of the ballclub, I knew nothing about the history of baseball in Harrisburg, much less about the people who lived there.

I soon found out in the winter before heading to spring training in Bradenton, Florida, just how excited the entire community was for the return of baseball and how they were eagerly awaiting the arrival of the team.

That spring training was filled with anticipation. Most of the players had spent the year before in Nashua, New Hampshire – a last-place team with poor attendance and little community support. The baseball facilities there were less than ideal and the thought of going to a new environment where they were wanted had everyone looking forward to getting the season under way.

We had been told by the Harrisburg media attending the first spring training that the players would love being in Harrisburg. None of us knew the extent of that sense of pride and passion until we arrived in early April.

Dave Trembley, right, and GM Rick Redd with the 1987 championship banner

The Welcome Dinner that first evening was an electric environment with an overflow crowd. It seemed like home. Everyone was so genuine; they made us instantly feel comfortable.

The Senators' front office, headed by general manager Rick Redd, was an outstanding young group of tireless workers with a real sense of community spirit. The mayor, Steve Reed, made us all feel welcome in the city.

Opening Day was like a movie. The stadium was jammed. The fans were on their feet the entire game … it was like winning the World Series. I knew then how lucky we were to be in Harrisburg.

The wins were hard to come by early that first season, but the fans kept coming out to the ballpark. We all felt a certain sense of responsibility, and the players were determined to turn the season around. We kept at it with long practices and, at times, some heart-to-heart discussions about doing our best. The players bought into it.

We realized this would be the one and only time when we could all make a mark on not only that first season but for the years to come.

That summer the stadium was filled, and the energy and excitement was beyond what any of us had ever imagined. This was Harrisburg's team. The people were phenomenal in their support for the players. The year ended with some nail-biting games as we won the Eastern League crown. We all wanted to win not so much for ourselves but for the people of Harrisburg. They treated us like family.

To this day, I still speak to many of the players from that ballclub. They all say it was the best year of their lives.

In retrospect, I can't adequately tell you how much of an impact those three seasons I spent in Harrisburg had on my life. Friendships that were established then are as strong as ever now. We all have grown to appreciate our time together during those seasons.

The focus now is making sure baseball continues to be an integral part of the community, as well as never forgetting what it took to make it what it is today.

I am proud to say I spent time in Harrisburg as the manager of the Senators. It allowed so many good things to happen in my life, and I wouldn't trade the experience for anything. Here's to baseball in Harrisburg, the fans and the players who have made it all possible.

Enjoy the book.

AUTHOR'S NOTE: Dave Trembley was the Senators' manager from 1987 to 1989. Trembley brought to Harrisburg a passion for teaching the fundamentals of baseball to his players. He never lost any of that enthusiasm as he traveled around the minor leagues for 20 years before finally being rewarded in 2007 with a spot in the majors as Baltimore's bullpen coach. By midseason, the reward turned into the ultimate promotion as Trembley became Baltimore's manager and ran the Orioles for three years. As the Senators entered their 25th anniversary season in 2012, Trembley was beginning his second season as the Atlanta Braves' field director, teaching fundamentals to a new generation of ballplayers with the same energy he once brought to City Island.

Introduction

More than 1,500 'burgs, 'villes and cities across the country have fielded minor league baseball teams since 1890. All have had their tales of Hall of Famers, quirky characters and championship seasons. Some may have had more Hall of Fame players than Harrisburg and others may have had weirder stories or won more titles.

None, though, share Harrisburg's claim of having so many weird and wondrous moments occur on the same patch of grass for more than a century.

Give or take a couple of feet here or there in elevation, the field on City Island, which sits in the Susquehanna River equidistant from Pennsylvania's capital city and its west shore, has not moved since the Harrisburg Ponies first played there in 1890.

Over the decades, the island's grandstands have burned down, flooded or simply worn away. Each time, they were rebuilt. But the field itself has remained in its original orientation – facing away from the city and toward the more affluent West Shore, and 260 miles downriver from Cooperstown, New York, the home of baseball's Hall of Fame and the start of the Susquehanna River at Otsego Lake.

Long before the players of the Senators' modern era arrived in 1987 on City Island, their 63-acre home was known by a handful of names, including Forster's Island, Hargast Island, Maclay's Island, Island Park and – perhaps foreshadowing the woebegone 1952 team – Turkey Island.

Prospects today play on the same ground once occupied by Chief Bender, Josh Gibson and Willie Mays at the start of their Hall of Fame careers. Jim Thorpe, Oscar Charleston and Satchel Paige also played on the same field.

So did outfielder Horace McBride, infielder Elbert Isreal and 16-year-old Lefty Hefflefinger – stars in their time, even if none of them ever reached the majors.

The island as it looked on Opening Day 1987, when baseball came back to the 'burg

One Patch of Grass chronicles the lives and careers of some of the more memorable people to pass through the island. A few would reach the Hall of Fame; others had modest careers in the majors.

These pages also tell of clowns, convicts and championships. Of trailblazers and heroes. Of some men who tried to steal the game from Harrisburg, and of some others who were not allowed to play it at the highest levels, merely because of the color of their skin.

And now the disclaimer:

One Patch of Grass is not meant to be an exhaustive be-all, end-all, year-by-year, inning-by-inning, mayfly-by-mayfly account of the history of baseball played on Harrisburg's City Island since 1890.

To present this work as anything other than an informal accounting of one town's journey through professional baseball would be disingenuous. History is simply too fluid. No one can truly account for everything.

Over the years, for example, no one has been able to prove that Babe Ruth "called" his home run off Cubs pitcher Charlie Root in Game Three of the 1932 World Series at Wrigley Field. Players involved in the game disagreed for decades about what really happened that day.

There are similar disagreements about a ball the Babe hit four years earlier on City Island during an exhibition game between the Senators and the Yankees. Newspaper accounts suggest the ball landed in the second row of trees beyond the right field wall. Others claimed for years that the blast was even more majestic and was last seen headed toward the other side of the river.

No one knows for sure.

But that's the beauty of baseball. There is a lot we don't know and, in the grand scheme of things, we don't care. Still, we love rehashing those moments, some of which happened decades before most of us were born.

Those moments are what this book is about.

Pregame Stretch

Spring training 1999, and it's blistering hot.

Just like every other spring training.

You dread moving. Movement means exertion and exertion means a further loss of the energy you no longer have.

You pray for a passing cloud to block out the unforgiving sun, if only for a moment. But you're not going to get that cloud, and you know it.

You're a minor league ballplayer stuck in Jupiter, Florida, where it's broiling and it's not even 11 in the morning. You have already bathed in Sun Block 50 and you still feel the burn. Forget about visualization. You can think all you want about snow, but all you wind up with is an image of the North Pole on fire.

You're parched. You crave a beer; you settle for water.

With the inescapable humidity enveloping the back fields behind newly built Roger Dean Stadium, you find yourself sleeping with your eyes open. As prayers for cloud cover – not to mention the beer – go unanswered, you hear the rumble of 130 pairs of cleats pounding the macadam path next to you. The noise brings some relief from the monotony of training camp. It's lunchtime.

Lunchtime on the back fields of Jupiter's complex is filled with mostly anonymous ballplayers. These players, property of the Montreal Expos, were well known back home, but that was in high school and college. Most of them now are treated as cattle, curtly called by their last names by a coach with a stopwatch around his neck, a sweat-drenched roster in his hand and, quite often with some of them, an agenda. A few of the instructors seem to enjoy getting on these minor leaguers – especially the younger players – because, if nothing else, they never possessed the talents of those they now teach. They also never had the same walking around money or the kinds of tricked-up rides waiting for them in the parking lot.

16

Not that any of that enters into the minds of the players, who do whatever the instructors demand. Disobedience is not a good option; no one wants to get released. Each hopes to one day play in the majors, but none of them truly cares if that day comes with the Expos or with any of the 29 other teams in the big leagues.

On this day in late March 1999, no one notices their work on the back fields, except for maybe a couple of sportswriters and a handful of itinerant workers who are handing the players prepackaged sandwiches, a piece of fruit and a sports drink.

The players find a place to sit and eat. They split into groups of two to 10, sharing yet another meal under the sun-filled sky that burns through Florida in March.

Every conversation is the same. Every routine is the same – from 11:30 a.m., when lunch starts, to 12:30 or so, when the players start preparing for that afternoon's game against a team from another organization with players whose days are just as monotonous.

Talk invariably centers on the women you met last night and the ones you hope to meet tonight. If the family is in town, the conversation may drift toward critiquing the newest stores that moved into the newest shopping centers near the newest housing developments popping up everywhere in nouveau riche spring training sites such as Jupiter.

Every day, there is quasi encouragement for teammates who you, quite frankly, want to see fail, or at least stumble enough so you can pass them on your way up the minor league food chain.

As a marginal player you run the numbers in your head. One hundred jobs for four teams from Class A to AAA and there are 130-plus players in camp. You know a lot of players are going to be released before the end of the training camp, if not later that day. You could be one of them.

So if the guy next to you at lunch – the guy who just happens to play your position – starts choking on that prepackaged sandwich, that's OK. He wants the same to happen to you. Nothing personal. Just business.

There is one exception among the players, the one who eats by himself and talks to no one. Idle conversations are of no interest to Milton Bradley, just as the pending roster cuts are no concern.

All Bradley wants on this day is to continue his daily routine of eating alone. He enjoys spending his lunchtimes lounging in the coaches' golf cart. There, under the cart's canopy, Bradley takes refuge from the sun.

Coaches don't like players sitting in their golf carts. No one, though, dares chase away the 20-year-old center fielder, fearing Bradley is a pressure cooker who can shift from cool to meltdown in a matter of seconds.

Bradley knows the coaches won't bother him during lunch. If peace and solitude can be found in the golf cart, so be it. Let Milton have it.

MILTON BRADLEY

Lunchtime also happens to be the best time for sportswriters to talk with minor leaguers. It's not like the farmhands are going anywhere, since their clubhouse is just far enough away to keep them from retreating there between lunch and the afternoon game.

Besides, most players secretly enjoy being interviewed at lunch. For one thing, chatting with reporters is a break from an umpteenth dead-end conversation with another player who wants to take away his job. Secondly, being interviewed is nearly the same as being special again, like back in those BMOC days.

Besides, best to be interviewed in the here and now, because by next week you could be out of baseball, waiting on tables or loading boxes into oversized brown trucks.

None of this is in Bradley's plans.

Neither apparently is conversation, as Bradley hunkers down in the golf cart, keeping everyone – teammates, instructors and, most of all, sportswriters – away. His eyes, what little of them you can see under his pulled down cap, convey two words.

Get lost.

On this day, the Sphinx in spikes props his feet on the golf cart's dashboard, lunch in his lap, game face already screwed on.

Watching from 15 feet away are Doug Sisson, who is about to embark on the strangest season of his life as Bradley's manager in Class AA Harrisburg, and Rick Sweet, Montreal's minor league field coordinator.

Also watching is a sportswriter looking for someone to interview. Seeing Bradley sitting by himself and seemingly available, the writer approaches Sisson and Sweet, and asks if they think Bradley would chat for a few minutes.

Both laugh.

"Go ahead and ask, vulture," Sweet says, using his pet nickname for sports writers.

"Hey," Sisson whispers as the writer takes his first step toward the golf cart, "let us know how it turns out."

Sisson and Sweet smile, because they believe they already know the outcome – especially Sisson, who spent half of the 1998 season with Bradley in the Class A Florida State League.

Both expect another meltdown from the 6-foot, 215-pound Bradley. Actually, they hope for it; managers and coaches secretly enjoy seeing their players use sportswriters for floss. And, having heard of Bradley's reputation, the writer expects the same thing.

All three are surprised when Bradley sticks out his hand, offers the writer a seat in the cart and starts talking about everything.

About his family, growing up in gritty neighborhoods of Los Angeles, getting selected by the Expos in the second round of the 1996 amateur draft.

About his $363,000 signing bonus, much of which would be stolen by his former agent, and of the enormous physical talents that separate him from his teammates. About how nobody in the lower end of Montreal's farm system can match his combination of speed and power on offense or his range and arm on defense.

About poking fingers into the face mask of an umpire only a few months earlier, an incident that led to his banishment from the prospect-oriented Maryland Fall League. About routinely ticking off teammates, coaches and managers. About being a loner.

Bradley is cordial and candid as he chats about how the misdeeds of his past continue to dog him in the present.

Who knew? Under the angry veneer is a seemingly rational, articulate person who actually answers the questions asked of him, rather than dispensing the same clichés that players – especially minor leaguers – are taught to give the media.

"When I first came to the Expos, I got in trouble," Bradley says. "I was yelling at coaches. I wouldn't run hard. Then, I saw that this is a gift given to me, to go out and be able to play baseball. I needed to take advantage of everything I had and to play the game the right way."

When Bradley loses his composure – as he frequently would do in the summer of 1999 and in the seasons since – he pushes himself to the edge, as if he enjoys seeing how far he can dangle his career over the precipice.

When he keeps his composure, few are more gifted on a baseball field than Bradley. But no one knows how he will respond on a given day.

Will he be great or grating?

Finally, after 20 minutes, he politely excuses himself and rises out of the golf cart to warm up for that afternoon's game against the St. Louis Cardinals' Class AA affiliate.

Bradley again sticks out his hand, smiles and says, "Thanks, I enjoyed it. Talk to you later."

This day in late March would be the preamble to the 1999 season in Harrisburg, a season unlike any of the dozen preceding it since professional baseball had returned to Harrisburg in 1987 – and certainly unlike any other summer of baseball since the game was first played on City Island in 1890.

By the time Bradley joined them, the Senators of the 1990s had already become to the minor leagues what the New York Yankees had been to the majors for nearly a century.

Four times from 1993 to 1998, the Senators won the Class AA Eastern League championship. The 1999 team, with Bradley at the top of the order, would be trying for a league-record fourth straight title on City Island.

That pursuit, the quest to add to Harrisburg's already rich baseball history, is going to take place 1,100 miles north of Jupiter, Florida.

On a patch of grass in the middle of the Susquehanna River.

Until then, Milton Bradley had never seen City Island.

Turned out, he would never forget the place.

1st INNING

Here Comes "Jeeee-sus!"

Ten minutes, maybe.

That would be all the time granted for an audience with the almighty, and those 10 minutes would be shared by five sports writers and a radio broadcaster.

Each had been hoping for an opportunity to conduct an interview, but instead ended up being compressed – along with the competition – into one lone time slot so that each of the four local television stations could have its own five minutes for an interview. A few more minutes were set aside for an exclusive "one-on-one" with the local newspaper.

These were the ground rules.

And don't dare try to ask for more.

There would be no deviations.

That was the edict put forth on April 6, 2010 by Terry Byrom, the Harrisburg Senators' director of media relations. On this mild Tuesday afternoon, a beleaguered Byrom dealt with a challenge like none other in his first five seasons as the team's front man and radio voice. In seasons past, he only needed to handle the local newspaper and four TV crews for the Senators' first preseason workout on City Island. There had been no special requests then.

On this day, though, Byrom had to deal with a media turnout four times larger than usual, and each outlet wanted something from him.

Patience waning, Byrom's face grew longer by the minute. He seemed flustered.

Then again, he had never had to introduce a god to the media.

In this case, the deity stood 6-foot-4, weighed 230 pounds, sported a little billy goat of a beard and came with a blemish on his left cheek.

No one particularly cared about his looks. The much ballyhooed Stephen Strasburg was arriving on City Island with a Heaven-blessed right arm that cranked out fastballs timed in excess of 100 mph.

Strasburg was baseball's top pitching prospect in 2010, its most hyped pitching prospect since Mark Prior turned pro out of the University of Southern California in 2001.

Strasburg was scheduled to make his professional debut the following Sunday in Altoona, Pa., where the Senators would open their 24th season since rejoining the Class AA Eastern League in 1987.

Only one other game in modern franchise history had been as greatly anticipated. That came Opening Day on the island in 1987, when pro baseball returned to Harrisburg after a 35-year absence.

Only one other player had been met with such interest and awe – and that was 120 years earlier when Frank Grant, one of baseball's premier players in the late 19th century, was brought to the island by horse, carriage and hype to join the Harrisburg Ponies.

On that day, Grant was met by enthusiastic masses lining the new People's Bridge that led from downtown to the island. Not knowing quite how to react to adulation from total strangers, the man who many felt was the finest black ballplayer of his day simply doffed his cap in appreciation.

Strasburg was greeted not by adoring fans but by a gaggle of gawking media. Knowing exactly how to react, he skillfully responded with ready-made answers to the questions he knew he might face.

But that was when Strasburg finally got around to answering them. He was running way behind, thereby rendering Byrom's carefully crafted interview schedule useless.

Jason Bristol, the Emmy Award-winning sports director from Harrisburg's CBS affiliate, was among the first scheduled for an interview.

He spent more time shaking his head, pursing his lips and pointing to his watch than he would get talking to Strasburg.

"This is supposed to be my time now," Bristol said. "Where is he?"

Alas, Strasburg was busily trying to find his glove.

When the 21-year-old Californian finally stepped out of the dugout and onto the field he was promptly led by Byrom and a front-office underling to the first waiting TV camera. After five minutes there, Strasburg was led to the next TV interview, followed by a third and fourth.

The writers came last.

As Strasburg was shepherded from one interview to the next, his two dozen new teammates sat in the dugout and watched, left to entertain themselves while waiting for the dog-and-pony show to end and their workout to begin.

Occasionally one of them was pulled from the dugout to be asked a perfunctory question or two about the upcoming season before being asked more questions about – who else? – Stephen Strasburg.

This was how the Senators' front office – with guidance from the Washington Nationals, their major league affiliate – handled the early moments of Strasburg's introduction to his new city, and to the local media covering him.

Strasburg, though, already was well known.

He had been a collegiate All-American at San Diego State, a member of the United States' Olympic baseball team in 2008 and the first overall pick of the 2009 amateur draft.

Only a few weeks before showing up in Harrisburg, Strasburg experienced his first major league spring training with the Nationals.

He already was known to his prospective teammates there, too. Upon first seeing Strasburg pitch in camp at Viera, Florida, Nationals center fielder Nyjer Morgan announced in awe to all, *"Jeeee-sus!"*

So much for blending in.

"It's to be expected," Strasburg nonchalantly said. "Not too many guys have had this kind of hype coming out of the draft, so I just have to live with it and keep things simple."

But how was that possible, especially when chatty teammates refer to you as "Jeeee-sus," and the media continue asking you to comment on that throughout camp?

The question again was broached on his first round of interviews in Harrisburg.

"Not that again," Strasburg said softly. "Now, there's no hype there, is there? ... (Morgan) was just messing with me a little bit."

Truth be known, Strasburg had welcomed Morgan's comment.

"It was good," he admitted, "because it made me feel comfortable."

With the Senators, Strasburg was ready to embark on a career that would quickly take him to the major leagues, where he would win every game he pitched, appear annually in the All-Star Game and become the first unanimous selection to the Hall of Fame.

Or so said the pundits.

And why not? While at San Diego State, Strasburg had become a bigger celebrity than the team's coach – and the city's most iconic sports figure – Hall of Fame outfielder Tony Gwynn.

"I'm just trying to fit in here," Strasburg said to the group of writers who had waited nearly an hour for their audience with him on the island.

"I'm just trying to go with the flow."

An almost impossible task.

Outside of wearing the same uniform and playing for the same organization, Strasburg and his new Harrisburg teammates had little in common, and likely never would.

None of them had been the first overall pick of the annual amateur draft, as Strasburg had been in 2009.

None of them had been in a position to command anything remotely close to the $15.1 million contract Strasburg received late in the summer of 2009 from the Nationals, who waited for the spring of 2010 to start him on his professional career with their Class AA affiliate on City Island.

And certainly none of them had ever been considered a perennial All-Star, future Cy Young Award winner and – dare it be said? – Hall of Famer before ever playing in a pro game.

None of his teammates could claim his All-American status, or a spot on the 2008 Olympic team, or having been on countless magazine covers. Nor could Strasburg's first pro pitching coach, Randy Tomlin, the onetime Harrisburg left-hander and Pittsburgh Pirate who in 2010 was beginning his third season working with the Senators' staff.

During his playing career a couple of decades earlier, Tomlin had been the virtual anti-Strasburg. He was a 5-foot-9, 179-pound lefty who relied on changing speeds, nibbling at corners and fielders behind him making plays.

Tomlin's plans for handling Strasburg were simple: Watch, enjoy and dispatch glowing reports about the right-hander to the home office.

"Stephen's a great pitcher now," Tomlin said in the spring of 2010. "He understands the stuff he has. I can try to help him with the experience I have in the game, like game management and what it's going to take for him to pitch in the big leagues as far as adjustments and game situations. I can help him with stuff like that."

Great expectations accompanied Stephen Strasburg to City Island in 2010

The rest of the stuff – the ultimate combination of a ridiculously fast 100-mph fastball and a timing-killer 79-mph changeup – could not be taught.

Strasburg knew it.

Tomlin knew it.

Everyone else knew it.

If the pundits are right, Strasburg will turn out to be greater than any of the seven Hall of Famers who once summered on the island – Hughie Jennings, Frank Grant, Vic Willis, Billy Hamilton, Chief Bender, Oscar Charleston and Ben Taylor.

Greater than Spottswood Poles, the outfielder who was so good in the early 1900s that he often was called the "black Ty Cobb."

Greater than Vladimir Guerrero, the right fielder who obliterated Eastern League pitching in 1996 while leading the Senators to the first of four straight Class AA Eastern League titles.

These were the yardsticks from Harrisburg's past by which Strasburg would be judged for as long as he played on City Island.

Not that Strasburg had ever heard of City Island before seeing it, or knew of the storied teams and Hall of Famers who had played there since 1890.

"I'm just concerned with what I'm doing now," Strasburg said, then diplomatically added, "but it's obviously cool to play in parks where there's been a lot of history."

Before he would add to the island's history, Strasburg had to endure the team's annual preseason media day, which included a local radio announcer shoving a slip of paper into Strasburg's right hand and asking him to read three lines into a tape recorder.

"This is Stephen Strasburg, and you're listening to Senators baseball on 1460, The Ticket."

"Senators baseball on 1460, The Ticket."

"I'm Stephen Strasburg, and this is Senators baseball on 1460, The Ticket."

Strasburg did everything in one take with perfect elocution and returned the slip of paper to the radio man, whose work was done for the day.

And just how many similar non-compensated plugs had he given over the last couple of years?

Strasburg rolled his eyes.

"Too many."

By now, Strasburg had grown accustomed to being steered from one interview to another, asked the same non-probing questions for the umpteenth time and coming up with variations of the same answers.

"It would be nice to get settled in," he said, "but you guys (in the media) have a job to do, too. I understand that. You guys have to fill up that piece of paper, so I'll do my best to help you."

On his terms.

What the media quickly learned in 2010 – first at Class AA Harrisburg, then Triple-A Syracuse and, ultimately, Washington in the major leagues – were the "Strasburg Rules."

After the initial crush at media day on the island, Strasburg never again conducted a one-on-one interview while playing in Harrisburg. He was made available to the media only after the games he pitched – and that availability was confined to an orchestrated press conference monitored by the Nationals.

Just like on media day, there would be no deviations. Reporters knew better than to ask for more.

Not that Strasburg seemed to care.

"I don't think too many people look at newspapers anymore," Strasburg said mere moments after telling the writers that he appreciated their jobs.

He then admitted he was among those who no longer relied on newspapers for information.

"My dad does all of that," Strasburg said. "He does the reading. He keeps me updated. I try to keep away from all of that stuff."

That stuff would include his $15.1 million contract, which became a lightning rod for disgruntled fans in Harrisburg who thought that for the money Strasburg was being paid he should have been willing to give them an autograph or two or 12.

Strasburg frustrated some fans even before the season started by arriving late to the team's preseason banquet and, once there, segregating himself from the majority of the fans.

That was by design.

"Our players don't typically generate mob interest," said Senators team president Kevin Kulp. "Our players can go to the batting cage with the back gate open and nobody is going to hound them, but with a guy like Strasburg everything changes."

The front office's approach to a home game became two-fold: Use Strasburg's presence as the carrot to sell tickets to as many fans as possible but, once that was accomplished, keep those same fans from smothering him with requests for autographs, photos and locks of his hair.

"It's so rare that a guy comes here with that much notoriety," Kulp said. "Usually, you don't know who these guys are until they're long gone. You can say, 'Oh, Ryan Howard was here,' but he was just Ryan Howard then. Unless it's a major league rehab appearance, you never have this much interest.

"This is one of those things where we have to be smart about the situations we put him in, so that he can do his job," Kulp said. "We just can't throw him to the wolves. I can't treat him like every other player, because people aren't going to treat him like every other player."

During his brief time in Harrisburg, Strasburg was vilified for not giving out more autographs. The same fate would befall Bryce Harper, the 18-year-old outfielder who was mercilessly hounded by autograph seekers after joining the Senators midway through the 2011 season.

Both signed autographs, but not as many – or as readily – as some fans demanded.

The Nationals understandably wanted to limit outside contact with Strasburg and later Harper, preferring that their top two prospects concentrate more on their craft while in Harrisburg.

"It's a job coming here every day," Strasburg said before his inevitable promotion to a higher league after only five starts for the Senators in 2010.

Not that you can truly blame players for being cynical when it comes to handing out autographs, since what they sign tonight could be up for auction on eBay by tomorrow morning, if not sooner.

Nationals jerseys signed by Strasburg sold for $200 or more on eBay; signed baseball cards routinely went for more than $250. One single-issued card issued by Topps for its Bowman series attracted 84 bidders on eBay before selling for $16,403 – $400 more than the cost in 2010 for a year's tuition at Penn State's main campus.

Within two months of his arrival in Harrisburg, there were 3,056 Strasburg-related items for sale on eBay. At the time, his items were only 34 fewer than the total for Hall of Famer and noted recluse Sandy Koufax, and two more than those posted for Tim Lincecum, the two-time reigning Cy Young Award winner.

The profit-taking mentality of some eBay-driven fans also extended to the Senators' front office, which twice got caught up in the hype – first with Strasburg and then a year later with Harper.

Senators general manager Randy Whitaker openly and understandably gushed about the special T-shirts to be ordered, the customized jerseys to be produced and, of course, the money to be made.

"We didn't build anything around Strasburg," Whitaker said. "This just kind of happened. Now, did we do anything to adjust the merchandise in our store? Darn right we did."

To further hype Strasburg, the password for the wireless Internet signal to the press box at the start of the 2010 season was changed to "100mphfastball."

"After he leaves here," mused one press box wag, "they'll probably change it to 'Tryingtogetto500.' "

On May 1– the eve of Strasburg's final 2010 start on the island – Senators public address announcer Chris Andree read from a script prepared by the front office.

"We invite you back tomorrow afternoon for a 2 p.m. game with Stephen Strasburg on the mound. Your chance to see the 2009 Number One draft pick. Limited tickets are available. ... It seems like a big day tomorrow."

Andree read the announcement six times that night, not the least bit worried how Strasburg's less-publicized teammates felt about playing subordinates to Strasburg's stardom.

"They tolerate it, because they realize he's legit and he's not going to be around here for long," Andree said. "Besides, what are they going to do? Call him out?"

The Nationals decided Strasburg needed only five starts for Harrisburg, where he went 3-1 with a 1.64 ERA and 27 strikeouts in just 22 innings. He was even better at Class AAA Syracuse, going 4-1 with a 1.08 ERA in six starts while striking out 38 in just 33 and one-third innings.

Strasburg's major league debut came June 8, 2010, when he made the Pittsburgh Pirates look like the Class AAA team they were often accused of resembling.

The Nationals drew a crowd of 40,315 that night as Strasburg struck out 14, walked none and allowed only two runs on four hits over seven innings.

Every strikeout was called by Bob Costas for the MLB Network, with Jim Kaat and John Smoltz – two pretty fair pitchers in their time – dissecting Strasburg's every step, tic and pitch.

Strasburg's night began with a standing ovation and ended the same way. More standing O's followed as Strasburg, who spent less than two months with Harrisburg and Syracuse, continued to fill Nationals Park.

Autograph hunters on City Island gravitated to Stephen Strasburg in 2010 and 2011

In Strasburg's seven home starts in 2010, the Nationals averaged crowds of 33,446. For their other 74 home dates, their average was nearly 12,000 less at 21,540.

Major League Baseball would report that Strasburg's No. 37 Nationals jersey was the game's top-selling jersey in June 2010. MLB's bean counters said they believed Strasburg may have been the first player to top the list for jersey sales in his first month in the majors.

While everyone in the Nationals' front office was convinced that Strasburg as a rookie already physically possessed all the tools to be a perennial All-Star – not to mention box-office gold – others inside and outside the organization worried about his composure on the field.

What would happen, they wondered, when some batters actually got a hit or two off Strasburg?

Those who were concerned quickly received an answer.

In only his second major league start at Cleveland, Strasburg seemed more concerned with his landing spot on the pitcher's mound than he was by the Indians' lineup. He would get pushed around in other starts against Atlanta, Cincinnati and Florida.

No huge red flags; more like a white napkin with polka dots.

"Sometimes, his body language is awful," said one high-ranking Nationals official. "He's a baby. He lived at home when he was in college. Look, he's a great kid, but he's not very worldly."

At least one Hall of Famer – Bob Feller – thought Strasburg, at that early juncture of his career, was as much sizzle as substance.

"Call me when he wins his first 100," Feller told reporters after watching Strasburg's mound-pawing performance in Cleveland.

Feller could relate to Strasburg's enormous talent, though. He had been like Strasburg more than 50 years before Strasburg was born.

Feller, also a right-hander, went 5-3 in 14 appearances for the Indians as a 17-year-old rookie in 1936 and would have 31 career victories in the majors before his 20th birthday. Feller, too, knew how to fire a baseball, throwing as fast if not faster than Strasburg in an era before radar guns.

"If you start believing all that hype and attention, that's the end of your career," Feller said. "You can't believe all that. It's 24/7 now on hype, but there's nothing wrong with that. All sports are show business now. ... The game itself in all sports is almost incidental to what goes on around it in merchandising. It's a different world."

The perfect little world that Strasburg was supposed to have in the major leagues was suddenly and dramatically altered on Aug. 21, 2010 in Philadelphia.

With one out in the bottom of the fifth inning, Strasburg threw a 1-1 changeup to the Phillies' Domonic Brown, winced in pain and immediately began shaking his right arm.

Strasburg subsequently learned he had torn the ulnar collateral ligament in his pitching elbow.

What followed was Tommy John surgery, named for the Senators 2002 pitching coach who in the mid-1970s had his playing career revived with a then-experimental ligament transplant procedure to repair his damaged left arm.

Today the surgery is commonplace in baseball and often results in pitchers coming back as good as new. Sometimes it takes a year, sometimes two.

> *"Our players don't typically generate mob interest. Our players can go to the batting cage with the back gate open and nobody is going to hound them, but with a guy like Strasburg everything changes."*
>
> Senators team president Kevin Kulp

Strasburg returned to City Island on Sept. 1, 2011 – 362 days after his surgery, a remarkably short recovery time considering his rehab start for the Senators was preceded by five other tune-ups with Washington's Class A affiliates Hagerstown and Potomac, as well Triple-A Syracuse.

The night was like none other in the century-plus history of baseball on the island.

The chosen one was pitching again for the Senators, if only for one more time.

Future Hall of Famer Ivan Rodriguez, in Harrisburg on his own injury rehab assignment, was catching.

Not that the Senators needed any help selling tickets for the game.

They already had a large presale for fans wanting to see the return of a wildly popular, between-innings act known as "Cowboy Monkeys." The game also was held on one of the team's "Thirsty Thursdays," so beer was on sale for $2 a cup.

The combination of Strasburg pitching, Rodriguez catching, monkeys riding atop dogs chasing goats and cheap beer flowing led to a sellout crowd of 8,637 – the largest ever to watch a baseball game on the island.

Strasburg worked six shutout innings, allowing one hit while walking none and striking out four in Harrisburg's 10-0 victory over Portland. The victory clinched the Senators' first division title since 1997.

Fifty-four of Strasburg's 71 pitches were strikes. Thirty-seven of those pitches were clocked between 94 and 99 mph. Twelve of his pitches over the first three innings were called strikes as Portland's batters appeared content to take pitches so they could one day tell their wives and girlfriends how they stood tall against a god's thunderbolts.

The proudest Sea Dog may have been Dan Butler, whose double down the left-field line to lead off the sixth inning accounted for Portland's lone hit off Strasburg.

As it was, Strasburg did not allow a baserunner until there were two outs in the fifth inning. That's when Jeremy Hazelbaker reached base after his billowing jersey was clipped by a 97-mph fastball.

Had the pitch actually hit him, Hazelbaker might have ended up in the ER with fractured ribs.

The outing was the longest, and easily the best, of Strasburg's six rehab starts in 2011. In his five minor league tests prior to rejoining the Senators, Strasburg had struck out 25 and walked just three in 14 and one-third innings. That was good. He had also allowed eight earned runs in those five games for a 5.02 ERA. That was not so good.

After his final rehab start – just as it had been when he had first arrived on City Island 17 months earlier – Strasburg was escorted by public relations handlers to a makeshift press conference beneath the grandstand. Strasburg talked of his recovery and of what awaited him next in the majors.

"My work isn't done," he said. "I need to keep on grinding, finish the season strong and go into the offseason healthy and see what kind of pitcher I am in 2012. If these six innings are any indication, it's looking pretty good."

Given his abilities now and his projected path to success, that "pretty good" for Strasburg is better than most pitchers' "exceptionally good."

Even if he didn't admit it publicly, Strasburg embraced all of the attention – the demands from the media for his time, the requests from the fans for his scrawl on a baseball, the expectations from his teammates to lead them to the World Series.

Strasburg often was reminded as much by his college coach, Tony Gwynn – a first-ballot Hall of Famer and one of the game's greatest hitters.

"He said to me, 'Would you rather be batting .350 and having everybody want to talk to you or would you rather be batting .250 and not having anybody want to talk to you?' " Strasburg said.

"The bottom line is as a competitor you want to go out there and be successful. And, if you're successful, you have to deal with people, because people want to see who you are."

Tending to History

Raymond Boss watched his first game on Island Park in 1907, and never left. The man better known as "Bones" would become the ballpark's groundskeeper, and a witness to history.

Boss saw Jim Thorpe play on the Island in 1915 for a baseball team that split its season between Harrisburg and Newark, New Jersey.

He saw the incomparable Oscar Charleston and the talent-rich Harrisburg Giants of the Eastern Colored League play in the shadows of segregation during the mid-1920s.

He groomed the field for the Senators' 1928 exhibition game against Babe Ruth, Lou Gehrig and the rest of the New York Yankees. He did the same in the early 1940s for a minor leaguer from Newport, Pa., named Billy Cox, who later became one of the best fielding third basemen in major league history.

Finally, he cut the island's outfield grass where a fledging pro named Willie Mays played for Trenton in 1950.

"Island Park was quite a place once," Boss said after the old Senators folded in 1952. "I guess you could call it my second home; maybe my first. It's a shame it had to die."

Boss' home turf sat fallow for 35 years before University of Massachusetts political science professor Jerry Mileur moved his Class AA Eastern League team from Nashua, New Hampshire to Harrisburg.

Alas, Boss never saw the new Senators.

He died in 1968 – 19 years before professional baseball came back to Harrisburg. But depending upon how the wind blew and how the floodwaters behaved during those 19 years, Boss may well have been part of the Senators' return in 1987. After all, his ashes reportedly were scattered on City Island after his death.

So next time you are on City Island and the wind blows some dust in your eyes, think of Boss. Who knows; that speck of dust may be a bit of old "Bones" himself.

What's Bugging You?

Come summertime, they live and die by the millions on the island.

And we're not talking about the fans who had to watch the replacement players that permeated the Senators' dreadful lineup in 1995.

We're talking about mayflies.

If you have been to City Island for a night game, then you have seen them. They flock to the ballpark by the tens of thousands on warm nights, waiting until sundown before swarming near the lights above the field. Exactly how many are there is hard to estimate; it's not like they need tickets to get in. And, if you happen to wear anything light colored – say a white T-shirt – to the game, chances are good you will unwittingly take home a few mayflies on your clothes or in your hair.

Mayflies have been part of the island since, well, forever. They are an invaluable part of the ecological system, as the newly hatched mayflies make fine appetizers for the aquatic life in the Susquehanna River.

But what exactly is a mayfly?

Each mayfly – that's ephemeroptera in science-speak – has two sets of wings, can grow larger than an inch from head to tail, has a mouth but doesn't eat, mates while fluttering near the lights and, finally, dies.

All in 48 hours or less.

In between – at least for the ones on the island – mayflies have been known to send kids shrieking in horror by landing on their hair and to leave their fathers gasping in sorrow as another hovering insect dives into their beer.

Given the little buggers' life cycle, perhaps that's not the worst way to go.

Of Gummies and Geritol

Bryce Harper was two days removed from his sixth birthday when a highly touted 33-year-old Cuban refugee named Orlando Hernandez made his World Series debut on Oct. 18,1998 at Yankee Stadium.

Who knew that a few years later they would come within 12 months of being teammates on City Island?

When he joined the Senators on Aug. 15, 2010 as a 44-year-old relief pitcher Hernandez became Harrisburg's oldest player since pro baseball first came to the island in 1890 and the oldest to pitch competitively on the island since 50-something Satchel Paige came to Harrisburg in the 1950s.

Less than 11 months after Hernandez's arrival, Harper joined the Senators on July 4, 2011 as an 18-year-old outfielder who would be the youngest player in the team's modern era.

The two would have made quite the pair: Bengay meets Clearasil.

Since 1890, Harrisburg has had 31 players who were still teenagers with another 13 players who were 39 or older.

THE TOP 10 NEWBIES
   16, Robert "Lefty" Hefflefinger, pitcher, 1929 (born 1913)
   18, Elbie Fletcher, first baseman, 1934 (born March 18, 1916)
   18, Kohly Miller, shortstop, 1892 (born January 1874)
   18, Bob Keller, second baseman, 1935 (born Dec. 12, 1916)
   18, Rube Bressler, pitcher, 1913 (born Oct. 23, 1894)
   18, Bryce Harper, outfielder, 2011 (born Oct. 16, 1992)
   18, Walt Pennington, infielder, 1947 (born Oct. 4, 1928)
   18, Horace McBride, outfielder, 1927 (born Aug. 9, 1908)
   18, Frank Peticolas, pitcher, 1935 (born 1917)
   19, Vic Willis, pitcher, 1895 (born April 12, 1876)

THE TOP 10 GOLDEN OLDIES
   44, Orlando Hernandez, pitcher, 2010 (born Oct. 11, 1965)
   42, Andy Rush, pitcher, 1932 (born Dec. 26, 1889)
   42, Pop Schriver, catcher, 1907 (born July 18, 1865)
   41, Dutch Schesler, pitcher, 1941 (born June 1, 1900)
   41, Danny Taylor, outfielder, 1942 (born Dec. 23, 1900)
   40, Billy Hamilton, outfielder, 1906 (born Feb. 15, 1866)
   40, Bill Morrell, pitcher, 1933 (born April 9, 1893)
   40, Mickey LaLonge, catcher, 1924 (born April 18, 1884)
   40, Charlie O'Brien, catcher, 2000 (born May 1, 1960)
   39, Les Bell, infielder, 1941 (born Dec. 14, 1901)

2nd INNING

The Great Makeover

Opening Day was coming and much work still needed to be done on the stadium.

Nearly everything was new or upgraded. Anyone wearing a hardhat had a checklist. There were seats to number, concession stands to set up, novelties to stock and new toilets to flush for the first time.

The Senators' front office staff was scrambling in 2010 as March melted into April and the shiny new home that would be Harrisburg's latest stadium was not yet complete.

A different staff had faced similar challenges 23 years earlier as the city prepared for its first pro baseball team since 1952.

Back in 1987, RiverSide Stadium cost $1.8 million to build. The place was slapped together in just a few months after the owners of the Pittsburgh Pirates' Class AA franchise announced their team's pending move from Nashua, New Hampshire, to City Island.

When RiverSide opened it was considered a better-than-average ballpark. In reality, the place looked like it was built with an Erector Set that was missing a couple of pieces.

The support beams holding up the grandstand roof obstructed views from behind home plate. The lower box seats were made of hard plastic; the bleachers were equally uncomfortable slats of aluminum and wood. The men's rooms were adorned in early horse trough.

Yet none of that deterred Harrisburg mayor Stephen R. Reed from proclaiming the ballpark to be one of the "finest in the country."

Perhaps he meant to say the county.

Reed's beloved stadium, aluminum warts and all, was the cornerstone to the rejuvenation of City Island, a place Reed promised to overhaul when he was first elected mayor in 1981.

Reed vowed to build a stadium and bring a minor league franchise to the island, which would attract other businesses to the 63-acre parcel of land in the middle of the Susquehanna River.

Alas, RiverSide Stadium with its 5,200 seats was born too soon. Within two years of its opening, the place was outdated. Its rapid decline coincided with Baltimore's construction of Camden Yards, a project that started in 1989 and soon ignited a building boom that would jumpstart stadium construction throughout the major and minor leagues.

The construction craze largely was underwritten by tax dollars, but no such money was available to Harrisburg – not after the city just built a stadium that was young in age but passé from the start.

The Senators, despite their overwhelming success on the field during the 1990s, played in a cheerless metal shell that kept in the chill during cool April nights as reliably as it retained the heat throughout the broiling days of summer. You either froze or fried watching baseball on the island.

For years, Reed lobbied for a matching state grant for massive renovations to RiverSide, where the capacity over time expanded from 5,200 uncomfortable seats to 6,300 uncomfortable seats.

After $4.5 million of mostly cosmetic improvements over 20 years, the city finally received the funds in late 2008 to begin rebuilding a stadium that had been renamed Metro Bank Park.

"The old ballpark had a lot of charm in its own way," said team president Kevin Kulp. "At the time it was built in '87, it was the jewel of the Eastern League. That was as good as it got back then."

Then along came Camden Yards, and suddenly RiverSide began aging overnight like Dorian Gray's portrait.

"Our ballpark," Kulp said, "got old quick in terms of design and functionality."

A sparse crowd at old RiverSide Stadium for a chilly April game in 1988

The renovations took nearly 16 months, causing logistical inconveniences for players and fans alike, as much of the work was carried out during the 2009 season.

By the time the new ballpark was ready, Reed was out of office – upset in his 2009 bid for an unprecedented eighth term as mayor by a long-time political rival, City Council president Linda Thompson.

Also gone by Opening Day 2010 were all but a few reminders of the original stadium from 1987. The makeover had cannibalized RiverSide, leaving a new ballpark built upon the bones of the old one.

Total cost: $45 million – up 33 percent from the $34 million Reed had estimated years earlier.

The cost to house and keep the Senators since 1987 actually approached $60 million by 2010. Initial construction, updates and reconstruction totaled nearly $51 million; the cost for the city to buy the Senators in 1995 was an additional $6.7 million.

Much of this money was borrowed or siphoned from other city agencies. The city's habit of using credit to run up a tab extended well beyond the Senators. Reed had spearheaded financially doomed projects that included a trash incinerator that left the city with a $317 million debt by March 2012.

Reed also spent $30 million in public funds to build a Civil War museum, as well as $8.3 million to purchase artifacts for a Wild West museum that was never built.

While the shopping spree was bankrupting Pennsylvania's capital city and tarnishing Reed's legacy, the Senators' antiquated stadium received its $45 million facelift.

None of the Class AA Eastern League's 11 other ballparks cost nearly as much to build from scratch as Harrisburg spent to redo its stadium.

Two of the league's more critically acclaimed ballparks in the post-Camden Yards era – Canal Park in Akron, Ohio, and Blair County Ballpark in Altoona – cost $31 million and $12.5 million, respectively, to build in the late 1990s. The league's most recent stadium construction in Manchester, New Hampshire, cost $19 million when it was finished in 2005.

The only part of old RiverSide still showing after its makeover was the set of metal bleachers stretching down the right-field line. Their survival provided a sense of symmetry in that the only preexisting component of the stadium that opened in 1987 was the set of wooden bleachers down the left-field line.

"We built a new ballpark on top of the old bunker building," Kulp said. "That's kind of unique.

"It made us put things in certain places, so when you walk around the ballpark, you might ask, 'Why did they do this?' It has to do with the fact that we left everything underneath."

Portions of the new grandstands were built on top of the concrete dugouts that were part of the old stadium.

"We saved millions by using the existing foundation, the beams and whatever else was in place," he said. "It allowed us to spend more on the other bells and whistles around the ballpark."

The upgrades included more concession stands, bigger bathrooms and wider seats beneath a cantilevered roof that eliminated obstructed view seats. The light standards, the ones that had been so close to the field and the fans, were moved behind the grandstands and bleachers. The mayflies, like Icarus, would still climb to the top of the lights before crashing to earth. Only their final destination was behind the bleachers, not in somebody's cup of beer.

City Island's ballpark in 2010 after its $45 million makeover

There were also state-of-the-art message boards to complement one of the largest scoreboards in the minors, a boardwalk above the outfield wall and – a must for all new stadium construction – luxury boxes.

Some of the Senators' 21 rooftop suites offered commanding views of the city skyline to those paying up to $35,000 a year for the privilege, catered meals included.

"I can't say there is one thing about the old ballpark that I'm going to miss," said longtime Senators fan Jeanne Jacobs, whose father, Gordon "Buck" Jones, was the team's PA announcer in the early 1950s. "This is a very large improvement."

While the façade has changed over the years, the field itself has remained in the same location since the Harrisburg Ponies of 1890 became the first pro team to play on the island.

It was the same place in 1915 when Olympian Jim Thorpe played in the outfield for Harrisburg; in the 1920s when Oscar Charleston and Babe Ruth hit homers into the trees beyond the right field wall; in 1952 when Eleanor Engle became the first woman to sign a pro baseball contract; and in the 1990s when the Senators won five titles in a span of seven seasons.

There have been four ownership groups in the first quarter-century since the team relocated from New Hampshire in 1987 – Jerome Mileur, a professor of political science from the University of Massachusetts; a quartet of investors from suburban Philadelphia that clandestinely planned to move the team; the city itself with Reed as the de facto owner; and finally Michael Reinsdorf, the son of the owner of the American League's Chicago White Sox and the NBA's Chicago Bulls.

The longest tenure was that of the city, which was forced to buy the franchise in 1995 or watch the Senators move to Springfield, Massachusetts, after the 1996 season.

Unbeknownst to Reed, in the spring of 1995 the Senators' quartet of owners agreed to move to Springfield with a 10-year lease and a promise that a new stadium would be built.

When Reed learned of the chicanery, the mayor quickly, excitedly and profanely complained to the National Association, which governed minor league baseball. Officials there listened. Knowing Reed was right, they acted swiftly by giving the city of Harrisburg the option to buy the team from the Philadelphia Four.

So within nine months of buying the Senators from Mileur for $4.1 million with the intent of leaving Harrisburg, the owners decided to stiff Springfield and sell the Senators to Reed for $6.7 million – a record sum at the time for a Class AA franchise.

Not that Reed wanted to pay the money; he simply had no choice. If the city wanted to keep an Eastern League team on the island, it would have to buy its own.

Reed knew that RiverSide Stadium, with its deficiencies, had been grandfathered into the latest working agreement between Major League Baseball and its minor league affiliates. RiverSide's woefully undersized clubhouses and its primitive batting cage did not meet industry standards.

Reed also knew that because of those shortcomings Harrisburg, had it lost the Senators, would have been forced to spend millions to bring the stadium up to code before being considered for another team. His estimation was $6.5 million.

Reed had gone through too much in the early 1980s to get a team for Harrisburg only to turn around in the mid-90s and see it move away.

Reed remembered how *The Patriot-News* had derided his plans to re-build an island overgrown with weeds and overrun by the drug-dealing dregs of the city. The newspaper referred to the project as "Reed's Folly."

The scoreboard at RiverSide in 1987; sometimes it worked, sometimes not

Reed also remembered how the paper's sports editor, Nick Horvath Jr., said fans from the region's wealthier West Shore would never travel to the island and mingle with the less-affluent residents of the East Shore. Horvath gave the team a two- or three-year window of success before interest waned and the island would again be the desolate place it had become after the original Senators folded in 1952.

"Those of little faith – and there seemed to be a lot of them in those days – have been proven wrong," Reed said on the eve of the 2011 opener.

Old RiverSide was marginally ready for its first opener in 1987. Back then general manager Rick Redd and assistant GM Todd Vander Woude, along with their wives and other staff members, literally watched the dawn of the Senators' rebirth as they pulled an all-nighter to finish numbering the stadium's seats.

Reed credited the Senators' on-field success with generating interest early and the fans for sustaining that interest.

"The fans are the underlying strength and foundation on which baseball here is based," Reed said.

"If the fans didn't show up, as the cynics once suggested, if the fan support disappeared as the cynics said would happen, there would be no new ballpark today. There would not even be a franchise in Harrisburg today. It's that simple."

Following the Franchise

1980: Tom Kayser pays $35,000 for the Holyoke Millers, forefathers of to-day's Harrisburg Senators. Holyoke had been the Milwaukee Brewers' Class AA affiliate since 1977, when the franchise relocated after only one season as an Eastern League expansion team in Pittsfield, Massachusetts.

Nov. 3, 1981: Stephen R. Reed, a 32-year-old Democrat, is elected Harrisburg's mayor on a platform that includes bringing a minor league baseball team to

63-acre City Island. Within two years, he begins talking to EL president Charlie Eshbach about such a move.

1982: University of Massachusetts professor Jerome Mileur and longtime friends George Como and Ben Surner buy the Millers from Kayser for $85,000, switch major league affiliations from the Brewers to the Angels and move the team to Nashua, New Hampshire.

April 4, 1983: Eshbach tells Reed the Lynn Pirates

JEROME MILEUR   can relocate from Massachusetts to Harrisburg for the 1984 season. The deal quickly falls apart since Harrisburg has no stadium. At the same time, local businessmen Brad Shover and Jeffrey Kirkus join with Maryland-based Realtors Fred Shulley and Don Berkheimer to pursue a team for the island.

April 4, 1983: Lynn owner Mike Agganis says his team will move to Harrisburg. Five months later he changes his mind and moves to Burlington, Vermont.

Sept. 1, 1983: Reed launches a campaign to raise $1.1 million to build a stadium on City Island, then known as Island Park.

1984: Nashua switches major league affiliations from the Angels to the Pirates, with whom Nashua remains through the relocation in 1987 to City Island.

Sept. 23, 1985: Shover announces his group's purchase of the Newark (N.Y.) Orioles of the short-season, Class A New York-Penn League. Five weeks later, the league rejects Harrisburg as a location, saying the city is too far removed from its 11 other teams. Shover and Co. then look to buy the EL franchise in Glens Falls, New York, but are unsuccessful.

March 1, 1986: Shover says his group has the right-of-first-refusal to buy Mileur's team for $750,000. Mileur would claim otherwise later that year and retain the franchise as it moves from Nashua to Harrisburg. Spurned by Mileur, Shover buys the Philadelphia Phillies' Class A South Atlantic League team in Spartanburg, South Carolina.

April 30, 1986: Bidding begins for stadium construction on City Island.

May 1986: Mileur is convinced he needs to relocate after an advance ticket sale of only 150 forces him to cancel an exhibition game between Holyoke and its major league affiliate, the Pirates.

Aug. 12, 1986: Groundbreaking ceremonies take place for the stadium construction on City Island, although actual groundbreaking begins a year earlier.

Dec. 9, 1986: Eastern League owners approve Mileur's relocation of the Pirates' Class AA affiliate to Harrisburg with Houston businessmen Scott Carter and Cliff Wilson running the team in Mileur's absence.

Jan. 13, 1987: Rick Redd is named the Senators' first general manager with Todd Vander Woude his assistant. They open up shop in Harrisburg's City Government Center.

April 11, 1987: The Senators play the first game of their modern era and lose 11-5 on City Island to the Vermont Reds, who are still owned by Mike Agganis. The game begins after helicopters hover over the outfield to dry it after rain threatens Harrisburg's first scheduled game since 1952.

January 18, 1991: After four seasons as Pittsburgh's Class AA team, the Senators become the Montreal Expos' Eastern League affiliate. The Senators maintain the working agreement after the Expos relocate to Washington, D.C., in 2005.

June 18, 1992: Redd resigns as GM and is replaced by Vander Woude.

July 22, 1993: New York businessman Van Farber reaches a tentative agreement to buy the team from Mileur for $4 million.

April 26, 1994: The National Association rejects Farber as the Senators' new owner based on his finances.

July 8, 1994: Mileur agrees to sell the team to longtime minor league owner William L. Collins III for $3.5 million.

Sept. 23, 1994: The deal with Collins collapses. A few days later Mileur sells the Senators for $4.1 million to a group of investors from suburban Philadelphia. The group includes Nancy Stein, wife of Reading Phillies owner Craig Stein.

Oct. 5, 1994: Steven Resnick, the new managing partner, says the team will honor its City Island lease that runs through 2006 but ominously adds, "Nothing is forever."

Dec. 28, 1994: Major League Baseball approves the sale.

Dec. 29, 1994: Reports surface that Lehigh Valley officials are trying to lure the Senators to a proposed $10 million stadium to be built near Easton.

Feb. 1, 1995: Resnick concedes his group is considering moving the Senators after the 1996 season. Within two days local legislators plead with Gov. Tom Ridge to withhold a $5 million grant to Northampton County for a new stadium. Ridge announces he will release the grant to Northampton County providing officials there do not use the stadium to attract another team from within the state.

April 5, 1995: Resnick meets with officials from Springfield, Massachusetts, and quickly agrees to a 10-year lease, with plans to move the Senators there after the 1996 season. Two weeks later, Reed implores EL owners to block the move.

May 2, 1995: The Commonwealth of Massachusetts says it will kick in $10.3 million for Springfield's proposed $13.75 million stadium.

July 7, 1995: After asking the National Association for a chance to buy the Senators rather than lose them, the city of Harrisburg purchases the franchise for $6.7 million – a record at the time for a Class AA team. For their six-month investment of $4.1 million, Resnick and his partners earn a tidy 63.4 percent profit.

October 27, 2006: After 11 seasons as the Senators' de facto owner, Reed says the city is looking to sell the team. Prospective buyers include Cal Ripken Jr.

May 16, 2007: Michael Reinsdorf, the son of Chicago White Sox owner Jerry Reinsdorf, purchases the Senators for $13.25 million – a record price for an EL franchise and nearly twice as much as the city spent to buy the team in 1995.

October 11, 2007: Reinsdorf receives final OKs from the Eastern League, Minor League Baseball and Major League Baseball to acquire the team. He also agrees to a 29-year lease to keep the Senators in Harrisburg.

November 15, 2007: Vander Woude resigns after longtime assistant GM Mark Mattern is fired. Eleven days later, Randy Whitaker, the marketing director for Harrisburg's ABC television affiliate, is named GM.

July 3, 2008: Assistant GM Mark Clarke, a front office fixture since 1988, resigns. A few days later, longtime minor league operators Kevin Kulp and Bill Davidson are named team president and CEO, respectively.

September 1, 2008: The Senators end the season attracting only 164,182 fans for 66 home dates, marking the only time they failed to draw at least 200,000 in attendance since pro baseball returned to the island in 1987.

December 2008: Reed announces state funding finally is available to begin stadium renovations. The work starts in January 2009 and continues through Opening Night 2010. The final price: $45 million.

Building a Ballpark

The city of Harrisburg and the Senators invested 18 months and $45 million from 2008 to 2010 to rebuild Metro Bank Park (nee RiverSide Stadium).

The city initially needed less than six months and $1.8 million from the fall of 1986 to the spring of 1987 to erect the original RiverSide around a set of well-worn, wooden bleachers that remained from the 1952 season.

Not counting the paint used by harried office staffers to touch up the rails only hours before Opening Day on April 11, 1987, RiverSide's materials included:

60 tons of steel	60 tons of reinforced steel in concrete
60 tons of aluminum	1,200 cubic yards of concrete
2,500 pounds of wood	44,000 cubic yards of dirt
115,000 square feet of sod	4,000 linear feet of underground pipe

Jim Neidlinger delivers the Senators' first pitch April 11, 1987 on City Island

RiverSide Stadium Firsts

Whenever a new stadium opens, someone somewhere dutifully jots down everything that happens for the first time – from who throws the first pitch to who hits the first homer to which idiot in the press box is the first to spill mustard on his shirt. Some call it history, others call it minutiae. Either way, here are some factoids for your next bar bet.

FIRST GAME: April 11, 1987, Senators vs. Vermont..
FIRST PITCH: Jim Neidlinger, Harrisburg, 2:09 p.m., to John Bryant..
FIRST FINAL SCORE: 11-5 Vermont, April 11, 1987.
FIRST SENATORS WIN: 4-1 vs. Vermont, April 14, 1987.

HITTING

BATTER: John Bryant, Vermont, groundout (third baseman Dimas Gutierrez to first baseman Lance Belen), April 11, 1987. **SENATORS BATTER:** Jeff Cook, groundout (pitcher Glenn Spagnola to first baseman Greg Monda), April 11, 1987.

HIT: Chris Jones, Vermont, solo home run, 2nd inning (Jim Neidlinger), April 11, 1987. **SENATORS HIT:** Lance Belen, infield single vs. Vermont, 2nd inning (Glenn Spagnola), April 11, 1987.

RUN: Chris Jones, Vermont, 2nd inning (Jim Neidlinger), April 11, 1987. **SENATORS RUN:** Lance Belen vs. Vermont, 2nd inning (Glenn Spagnola), April 11, 1987.

47

DOUBLE: Joe Dunlap, Vermont, 3rd inning (Jim Neidlinger), April 11, 1987. **SENATORS DOUBLE:** Tom Prince vs. Vermont, 2nd inning (Steve Oliverio), April 14, 1987. **TRIPLE:** Tom Prince vs. Glens Falls, 7th inning (Mark Lee), April 15, 1987.

HOME RUN: Chris Jones, Vermont, 2nd inning (Jim Neidlinger), April 11, 1987. **SENATORS HOMER:** Crash Brown vs. Vermont, 4th inning (Glenn Spagnola), April 11, 1987.

GRAND SLAM: Joe Oliver, Vermont, 3rd inning (Jim Neidlinger), April 11, 1987. **SENATORS SLAM:** Ron Johns vs. Albany, 6th inning (Mauricio Garcia), June 17, 1987.

RBI: Chris Jones, Vermont, 2nd inning (Jim Neidlinger), April 11, 1987. **SENATORS RBI:** Brian Jones vs. Vermont, 2nd inning, (Glenn Spagnola) April 11, 1987.

STOLEN BASE: Crash Brown vs. Vermont, 2nd inning, April 14, 1987.

STRIKEOUT VICTIM: Marty Brown, Vermont, 1st inning (Jim Neidlinger), April 11, 1987. **WALK:** Glenn Spagnola, Vermont, 3rd inning (Jim Neidlinger), April 11, 1987.

SACRIFICE FLY: John Bryant, Vermont, 3rd inning (Rich Sauveur), April 14, 1987.

PINCH-HITTER: Ben Abner vs. Vermont, 5th inning (Glenn Spagnola), groundout, April 11, 1987. **PINCH-HIT:** Geno Gentile vs. Pittsfield, 7th inning (Dave Masters), single, April 28, 1987.

AL REYES

CYCLE: Bernie Tatis, Canton-Akron (16-2 Senators victory), Aug. 18, 1990 with single, double, flyout, strikeout, triple, homer. **SENATORS CYCLE:** Matt Stairs vs. New Britain (7-4 Senators loss), Aug. 23, 1991 with double, triple, homer, bunt single. **NATURAL CYCLE:** Geoff Blum vs. New Haven (3-2), Aug. 6, 1998, 4-for-4 with single, double, triple, home run.

WALK-OFF HIT: Brian Jones, 11th inning single vs. Glens Falls (Ramon Pena), April 15, 1987. **WALK-OFF HOMER:** Ed Yacopino vs. Hagerstown, 7th inning (Mike Linskey), Game 1 of DH, July 17, 1989. **WALK-OFF GRAND SLAM:** Antonio Grissom vs. Trenton, 9th inning (Bret Cederblad), Aug. 1, 1995.

FIELDING

ERROR: Marty Brown, Vermont third baseman, 2nd inning, April 11, 1987.

FIRST TRIPLE PLAY: Pittsfield, 5th inning, June 12, 1987 Jeff Cook lined out to left fielder Dwight Smith, who relayed to second baseman Rich Amaral to double up Dimas Gutierrez. Amaral then threw to first baseman Mark Grace to complete triple play on Tom Prince. **SENATORS TRIPLE PLAY:** vs. Bowie, 9th inning, May 16, 1994. Started by closer Al Reyes, who caught Bo Ortiz's low liner to the mound. Reyes threw to second baseman Mike Hardge to double up Brent Miller, with Hardge relaying the ball to first baseman Randy Wilstead before Hector Vargas could get back to the base.

PITCHING

RELIEF PITCHER: Chris Ritter vs. Vermont, 4th inning, April 11, 1987.

SAVE: Brett Gideon vs. Vermont, April 14, 1987.

SHUTOUT: April 14, 1987 vs. Vermont (1-0, 7 innings, Orlando Lind-Scott Neal).

NO-HITTER: Jason Grimsley, Reading (3-0 victory, 7 innings), Game 1 of DH, May 3, 1989. **SENATORS NO-HITTER:** Seung Song vs. Erie (2-1), April 28, 2003.

The Babe Goes Island Hopping

Dressed in a blue serge suit with a blue silk shirt and polka dot tie, Babe Ruth strolled into the governor's office on the morning of June 26, 1928, where he chatted up the honorable John S. Fisher for a few minutes.

According to a local reporter, the Babe smiled at the governor's stenographers and commented about the "feminine pulchritude in Harrisburg." And, the Babe being the Babe, he thoughtfully invited the ladies to see him play later that day.

Ruth, arguably baseball's greatest player, was as prodigious off the field as he was on it. He had it all. Home runs. Hot dogs. And even hotter stenos.

Whatever the Babe did, he did memorably, and nothing was different on that June day in 1928, when Ruth and the New York Yankees came to the island for an exhibition game against the Senators.

After arriving the night before by train following an exhibition game in Johnstown, Ruth and the Yankees stayed at the old Penn-Harris Hotel on the corner of Third and Walnut streets in downtown Harrisburg. As his teammates slept, ate breakfast, smoked cigarettes and generally lazed about the hotel lobby reading the morning paper, the snoozing Babe had his own agenda to attend to before joining them at the ballpark.

The visit to the island was the second for Ruth, who in 1919 blended into a fall crowd to watch the country's best high school football team, Harrisburg Tech, complete its 12-0 season.

By the time he returned nine years later, Ruth was the most famous athlete in the United States and, as such, was pampered by anyone and everyone around him.

After sleeping in until 11 a.m., Ruth – clad in purple pajamas – was greeted by a room service-delivered platter of ham, eggs and toast with a glass of sauerkraut juice. After inhaling breakfast, Ruth was off to meet the governor before embarking on a sightseeing trip through the city and a hurried goodwill visit to sick youngsters at Harrisburg Hospital.

At 1 p.m., Ruth was brought to the island to umpire a kids' game between a pair of local sandlot teams called the Aces and Deuces. While Ruth was calling balls and strikes for the tykes, the rest of the Yankees were taking cabs to the island, where they were besieged by hundreds of

> *As years passed, the height of Ruth's home run increased, while the length of its journey grew. Who knows? This year the ball may land just outside Chambersburg.*

autograph seekers. According to the Harrisburg *Telegraph*, Ruth signed more than 1,000 baseballs before the game against the Senators. Harrisburg player-manager Glenn Killinger, the onetime All-American quarterback at Penn State, was among those who had a baseball signed by the Babe.

By 2 p.m. the ballpark's wooden stands were filling with 3,000 fans. When the game started at 3, the crowd had swelled to a standing room-only total of 4,200. According to Harrisburg's *Evening News*, the Yankees took 60 percent of the gate receipts, giving them a cut of $2,676.

For the game, Ruth and Lou Gehrig switched positions; Gehrig went to right field with Ruth moving to first base.

The game was barely 30 minutes old when Ruth lined a fourth-inning fastball from right-hander Johnny Tillman into the second row of trees beyond the right-field wall. The solo homer halved the 2-0 lead the Senators had taken in the first inning on Ray Flood's two-run homer to center off right-hander Myles Thomas.

Historians quickly noted that Ruth's drive into the foliage was only the *second* longest hit on the island; Oscar Charleston of the all-black Harrisburg Giants had hit one a couple of years earlier over the third row of trees beyond the wall in right. Some old-timers later would claim the ball hit by Ruth was headed across the river and toward the Lemoyne bottleneck.

As years passed, the height of Ruth's home run increased, while the length of its journey grew. Who knows? This year the ball may land just outside Chambersburg.

When Ruth arrived on the island in 1928 he was leading the majors in homers with 28; Gehrig was second at 16. The Senators had 40 homers as a team – for the entire season.

In all, four future Hall of Famers were in the starting lineup that day for the Yankees – Ruth, Gehrig, center fielder Earle Combs and second baseman Tony Lazzeri.

Another future Hall of Famer, Leo Durocher, pinch-hit for the Yankees' Mark Koenig in the top of the seventh, then replaced him at shortstop in the bottom of the inning.

By the time the 90-minute exhibition had ended – ah, the good old days of quick games – the Yankees and Senators each had six runs, leaving home plate umpire Leo Houck to declare a tie. Not that anyone dared argue with Houck, the onetime middleweight from Lancaster who 41 years later was inducted into boxing's Hall of Fame.

Especially pleased by Houck's decision was Ruth, who as the ninth inning ended was chased off the field by an estimated 1,000 fans looking for a handshake, an autograph or a piece of Ruth's uniform. That the Babe was still inside that uniform was of little concern to the onrushing mob. As the crowd lost its collective mind, Ruth lost his cap.

The Babe, whose girth belied his speed, finally jumped into a waiting car and was whisked away to the Elks club. He and the rest of the Yankees caught the 7 p.m. train for Philadelphia, where the next day the Yankees beat Lefty Grove and the Athletics 7-4. A day later, the Yankees again beat the A's, this time 10-5 in a game featuring two Ruth homers – his 29th and 30th – en route to 54 for the season.

"I can't tell you how I hit 'em like I do," the pajama-clad Babe told a Harrisburg *Telegraph* reporter during breakfast.

"You have good days and bad days. Sometimes when I'm in a slump, I feel as if I couldn't touch a football and other times when things are going good, I think I could hit a pea."

Through the Years

For major league teams, the minors exist only for one reason: to separate the prospects from the wannabes. So long as they are not talking on the record, farm directors will gladly tell you they do not care if their affiliates lose 100 games, just so long as they develop a future All-Star or two for the big league team.

Over the years, the Senators have never suffered a 100-loss season, although two teams – the ones from 1952 and 2004 – came close by losing 94 and 90 games, respectively. As for future All-Stars, the Senators have nurtured plenty of them since 1931, when they formally began their first affiliation with Connie Mack's Philadelphia Athletics.

HARRISBURG'S MAJOR LEAGUE AFFILIATES

1931: Philadelphia A's, Class B New York-Penn League
1932-1935: Boston Braves, Class A New York-Penn League
1940-1942: Pittsburgh Pirates, Class B Interstate League
1946-1951: Cleveland Indians, Class B Interstate League
1952: Philadelphia A's, Class B Interstate League
1987-1990: Pittsburgh Pirates, Class AA Eastern League
1991-2004: Montreal Expos, Class AA Eastern League
2005 current: Washington Nationals, AA Eastern League

LEAGUES OF THEIR OWN

Harrisburg – whether it went by the name of the Ponies, Islanders, Giants or Senators – was affiliated with 16 leagues before settling into the Class AA Eastern League in 1987.

Inter-State Association, 1883	Tri-State League, 1904-1914
Eastern League, 1884	International League, 1915
Middle States League, 1889	New York State League, 1916-1917
Eastern Interstate League, 1890	Eastern Colored League, 1924-1927
Atlantic Association, 1890	New York-Penn League, 1924-1935
Pennsylvania State League, 1892-1895	Interstate League, 1940-1942
Atlantic League, 1900	Negro National League, 1943
Pennsylvania State League, 1901	Interstate League, 1946-1952

Eastern League, 1987-present

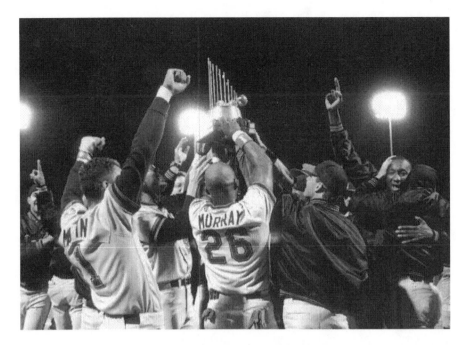

The 1993 Senators celebrate the Class AA Eastern League title they won in Canton, Ohio

We are the Champions

Since pro baseball arrived on City Island in 1890, Harrisburg has fielded 13 championship teams.

Some came in years with playoffs, others in years without them. Through 2011, Harrisburg's teams had reached the playoffs 13 other times, only to fall in the semifinals or finals. Their success doesn't quite match the decades-long dominance of the New York Yankees in the majors, but the Senators haven't exactly emulated the Chicago Cubs, either.

CHAMPIONSHIP SEASONS (with league playoffs)

1941, Interstate League, Class B (Les Bell, manager)
1946, Interstate, Class B (Les Bell, manager)
1987, Eastern, Class AA (Dave Trembley, manager)
1993, Eastern, Class AA (Jim Tracy, manager)
1996, Eastern, Class AA (Pat Kelly, manager)
1997, Eastern, Class AA (Rick Sofield, manager)
1998, Eastern, Class AA (Rick Sweet manager)
1999, Eastern, Class AA (Doug Sisson and Rick Sweet, managers)

REGULAR-SEASON CHAMPIONS (without playoffs)

1912, Tri-State, Class B (George Cockill, manager)

1914, Tri-State, Class B (George Cockill, manager)

1927, New York-Penn, Class B (Win Clark, manager)

1928, New York-Penn, Class B (Glenn Killinger, manager)

1931, New York-Penn, Class B (Joe Cobb, Eddie Onslow, managers)

REALLY CLOSE (losers in final round of league playoffs)

1894, Pennsylvania State, no classification (Jack Huston, manager)

1949, Interstate, Class B (Les Bell, manager)

1989, Eastern, Class AA (Dave Trembley, manager)

1991, Eastern, Class AA (Mike Quade, manager)

1994, Eastern, Class AA (Dave Jauss, manager)

2002, Eastern, Class AA (Dave Huppert, manager)

SORT OF CLOSE (losers in semifinals of league playoffs)

1942, Interstate, Class B (Danny Thomas, manager)

1947, Interstate, Class B (Les Bell, manager)

1950, Interstate, Class B (Les Bell, manager)

1992, Eastern , Class AA (Mike Quade, manager)

2000, Eastern, Class AA (Doug Sisson, manager)

2010, Eastern, Class AA (Randy Knorr, manager)

2011, Eastern, Class AA (Tony Beasley, manager)

Manager Rick Sofield goes for a ride after winning the 1997 EL title on City Island

In 1994, Moises Alou (above) and Carlos Garcia became the first modern-era Senators named to the All-Star Game; Alou drove in the winning run for the National League

All-Stars Through the Years

Four years after they were last together on City Island, Moises Alou and Carlos Garcia were teammates again for the National League at the 1994 All-Star Game in Pittsburgh.

Garcia went 1-for-2 with a single off Randy Johnson, while Alou – after replacing Barry Bonds – doubled in his only at-bat. That 10th-inning double to left-center off Jason Bere scored Tony Gwynn from first base with the winning run in the NL's 8-7 victory at Three Rivers Stadium. Since then, Senators alumni have not missed an All-Star Game.

HARRISBURG'S MAJOR LEAGUE ALL-STARS

1937 – Gene Moore (Class of 1932), outfielder, National League, Boston Braves

1940 – Lou Finney (1931), outfielder, American League, Boston Red Sox

1943 – * Elbie Fletcher (1943), first baseman, NL, Pittsburgh

1944 – Ray Mueller (1932-1934), catcher, NL, Cincinnati

1956 – Brooks Lawrence, pitcher, NL, Cincinnati

1960 – Jim Lemon (1949), outfielder, AL, Washington

1994 – Moises Alou (1989-90), outfielder, NL, Montreal
        Carlos Garcia (1989-90), second baseman, NL, Pittsburgh

1995 – Carlos Perez (1994), pitcher, NL, Montreal
1996 – Mark Grudzielanek (1994), shortstop, NL, Montreal
1997 – Moises Alou (1989-90), outfielder, NL, Florida
1998 – Rick Reed (1988), pitcher, NL, New York Mets
    Moises Alou (1989-90), outfielder, NL, Houston
    Ugueth Urbina (1993-94), pitcher, NL, Montreal
1999 – Vladimir Guerrero (1996), outfielder, NL, Montreal
2000 – Jose Vidro (1995-96), second baseman, NL, Montreal
    * Vladimir Guerrero (1996), outfielder, NL, Montreal
2001 – Rick Reed (1988), pitcher, NL, New York Mets
    Moises Alou (1989-90), outfielder, NL Houston
    Cliff Floyd (1993), outfielder, NL, Florida
    Vladimir Guerrero (1996), outfielder, NL, Montreal
2002 – Ugueth Urbina (1993-94), pitcher, AL, Boston
    * Vladimir Guerrero (1996), outfielder, NL, Montreal
    * Jose Vidro (1995-96), second baseman, NL, Montreal
2003 – Rondell White (1992-93, 2006), outfielder, NL, San Diego
    * Jose Vidro (1995-96), second baseman, NL, Montreal
2004 – Moises Alou (1989-90), outfielder, NL, Chicago Cubs
    * Vladimir Guerrero (1996), outfielder, AL, Anaheim
    Javier Vazquez (1997), pitcher, AL, New York Yankees
    Jake Westbrook (1999), pitcher, AL, Cleveland
2005 – Moises Alou (1989-90), outfielder, NL, San Francisco
    * Vladimir Guerrero (1996), outfielder, AL, Anaheim
2006 – * Vladimir Guerrero (1996), outfielder, AL, Anaheim
2007 – * Vladimir Guerrero (1996), outfielder, AL, Anaheim
    Chris Young (2003), pitcher, NL, San Diego
2008 – * Milton Bradley (1999), designated hitter, AL, Texas
    * Cliff Lee (2002), pitcher, AL, Cleveland
2009 – Ryan Zimmerman (2005), third baseman, NL, Washington
2010 – * Vladimir Guerrero (1996), DH, AL, Texas
    Brandon Phillips (2001-02), second baseman, NL, Cincinnati
    Cliff Lee (2002), pitcher, AL, Texas
2011 – Brandon Phillips (2001-02), second baseman, NL, Cincinnati
    Cliff Lee (2002), pitcher, NL, Philadelphia

  * -- denotes starter

No former Senator has appeared in more All-Star Games than Vladimir Guerrero, who was named to the game nine times and started in seven.

No former Senator has represented more teams in All-Star Games than Moises Alou, who played in the Game for Montreal, Florida, Houston, Chicago Cubs and San Francisco.

In 2003, Jose Vidro became the last Senator to represent the Expos at the All-Star Game

The worst performance by a former Senator at the All-Star Game belonged to pitcher Ugueth Urbina in 1998 at Denver's Coors Field. In a disastrous 36-pitch sixth inning, Urbina allowed three runs on hits by Roberto Alomar, Ken Griffey Jr. and Ivan Rodriguez – all singles – a walk to Jim Thome, three stolen bases by Alomar, Griffey and Rodriguez and a wild pitch as the American League rallied for an 8-6 lead in a game it eventually won 13-8.

For his efforts, Urbina received both a blown save and the loss.

The best performance by a former Senator came 10 years later at Yankee Stadium, where in 2008 Cliff Lee was the starting pitcher for the American League. Lee worked the first two innings, striking out three batters – Hanley Ramirez, Chase Utley and Ryan Braun – while allowing only a groundball single to center field by Chipper Jones.

Lee returned to the All-Star Game two years later at Anaheim and worked a perfect fourth inning, sandwiching a three-pitch strikeout of Albert Pujols between groundouts by Martin Prado and Ryan Howard.

The Original Mr. October

When he was helping win three straight World Series titles for the Oakland Athletics in the early 1970s, Reggie Jackson went by two nicknames. "Jax" and "Buck."

The whole "Mr. October" schtick didn't come about until Jackson led the New York Yankees over the Los Angeles Dodgers in the 1977 World Series.

JIMMY SEBRING

The first "Mr. October" was not Jackson, but one-time Senators outfielder Jimmy Sebring. Five years before summering on the island in 1908, Sebring was Pittsburgh's right fielder in the 1903 Series – the first Fall Classic – against Boston.

While Jackson homered on three straight pitches from three different pitchers at Yankee Stadium to clinch the 1977 Series, Sebring hit one 74 years earlier in the seventh inning of Game 1 in Boston.

His was the first homer ever hit in a Series game.

For his historic homer, Sebring teed up Cy Young – yes, *that* Cy Young – with an inside-the-park drive to straightaway center field at Boston's Huntington Avenue Baseball Grounds. The homer was one of Sebring's six hits in 16 at-bats off Young in the Series.

Buck Freeman and Harry Smith – two others who followed Sebring to Harrisburg – also played in that first World Series with Freeman the right fielder for Boston and Smith the backup catcher for Pittsburgh. Freeman played first base on the island in 1910; Smith managed the 1915 team that split its season between Harrisburg and Newark, New Jersey.

By the time Freeman and Smith reached the island, though, Sebring was dead – a victim of kidney disease just before Christmas 1909. He was just 27.

Since pro baseball returned to the island in 1987, Harrisburg has been well-represented in the Series. In the first 25 seasons of their modern era, 19 players appeared in the World Series after spending time on the island.

PARTAKING IN SERIES PAST

1903 – Jimmy Sebring (Class of 1908), right fielder, Pittsburgh Pirates
         Buck Freeman (1910), right fielder, Boston Americans
         Harry Smith (1915, manager), catcher, Pittsburgh Pirates

1907 – Hughie Jennings (1890, catcher), manager, Detroit Tigers

1908 – Hughie Jennings (1890, catcher), manager, Detroit Tigers

1909 – Hughie Jennings (1890, catcher), manager, Detroit Tigers
         Vic Willis (1895), pitcher, Pittsburgh Pirates

1911 – Chief Meyers (1906), catcher, New York Giants

1912 – Chief Meyers (1906), catcher, New York Giants
         Steve Yerkes (1924, manager), second baseman, Boston Red Sox

1913 – Chief Meyers (1906), catcher, New York Giants

1914 – Bob Shawkey (1911), pitcher, Philadelphia Athletics
         Les Mann (1934, manager), outfielder, Boston Braves

1916 – Chief Meyers (1906), catcher, Brooklyn Dodgers

1917 – Jim Thorpe (1915), outfielder, New York Giants

1918 – Les Mann (1934, manager), outfielder, Chicago Cubs

1921 – Bob Shawkey (1911), pitcher, New York Yankees

1922 – Bob Shawkey (1911), pitcher, New York Yankees

1923 – Bob Shawkey (1911), pitcher, New York Yankees
         Hinkey Haines, (1933), outfielder, New York Giants

1926 – Bob Shawkey (1911), pitcher, New York Yankees
         Les Bell (1933-1941, 1946-1951), third baseman, St. Louis Cardinals

1929 – Joe Boley (1917), shortstop, Philadelphia Athletics

1930 – Joe Boley (1917), shortstop, Philadelphia Athletics

1931 – Joe Boley (1917), shortstop, Philadelphia Athletics

1936 – Jake Powell (1933), outfielder, New York Yankees

1937 – Jake Powell (1933), outfielder, New York Yankees

1938 – Jake Powell (1933), outfielder, New York Yankees

1944 – Gene Moore (1932), outfielder, St. Louis Browns

1948 – Joe Tipton (1946), catcher, Cleveland Indians

1949 – Billy Cox (1940-1941), third baseman, Brooklyn Dodgers

1952 – Billy Cox (1940-1941), third baseman, Brooklyn Dodgers

1953 – Billy Cox (1940-1941), third baseman, Brooklyn Dodgers

1977 – Tommy John (2002, pitching coach), pitcher, Los Angeles Dodgers

1977 – Tommy John (2002, pitching coach), pitcher, Los Angeles Dodgers

1980 – Onix Concepcion (1987), shortstop, Kansas City Royals

1981 – Jerry Reuss (2000, pitching coach), pitcher, Los Angeles Dodgers
         Tommy John (2002, pitching coach), pitcher, New York Yankees

1991 – Rafael Belliard (1987), shortstop, Atlanta Braves
         Tommy Gregg (1987), outfielder, Atlanta Braves

1992 – Rafael Belliard (1987), shortstop, Atlanta Braves

1993 – Wes Chamberlain (1989), outfielder, Philadelphia Phillies
         Randy Knorr (2010, manager), catcher, Toronto Blue Jays

Kirk Rueter was 5-0 for the 1993 Senators; he pitched for the Giants in the 2002 Series

1995 – Rafael Belliard (1987), shortstop, Atlanta Braves
                 Charlie O'Brien (2000), catcher, Atlanta Braves
1996 – Rafael Belliard (1987), shortstop, Atlanta Braves
                 Tim Raines (2007, hitting coach), outfielder, New York Yankees
1997 – Moises Alou (1989-1990), outfielder, Florida Marlins
                 Cliff Floyd (1993), outfielder, Florida Marlins
1999 – Orlando Hernandez (2010), pitcher, New York Yankees
2000 – Rick Reed (1988), pitcher, New York Mets
                 Orlando Hernandez (2010), pitcher, New York Yankees
2001 – Miguel Batista (1993-1994), pitcher, Arizona Diamondbacks
                 Orlando Hernandez (2010), pitcher, New York Yankees
2002 – Kirk Rueter (1993), pitcher, San Francisco Giants
                 Brad Fullmer (1996-1997), designated hitter, Anaheim Angels
2003 – Ugueth Urbina (1993-1994), pitcher, Florida Marlins
2004 – Al Reyes (1994), pitcher, St. Louis Cardinals
                 Orlando Cabrera (1997), shortstop, Boston Red Sox
2005 – Geoff Blum (1996, 1998), infielder, Chicago White Sox
                 Orlando Hernandez (2010), pitcher, Chicago White Sox
2007 – Jamey Carroll (1998-2000, 2002), infielder, Colorado Rockies
2008 – Matt Stairs (1991), infielder-outfielder, Philadelphia Phillies
                 Cliff Floyd (1993), designated hitter, Tampa Bay Rays
2009 – Matt Stairs (1991), infielder-outfielder, Philadelphia Phillies
                 Cliff Lee (2002), pitcher, Philadelphia Phillies
2010 – Vladimir Guerrero (1996), designated hitter, Texas Rangers
                 Guillermo Mota (1998), pitcher, San Francisco Giants
                 Cliff Lee (2002), pitcher, Texas Rangers
2011 – Jake Westbrook (1999), pitcher, St. Louis Cardinals

Same Place, Different Generation

Bob Berresford left Harrisburg in 1952, taking with him a little bit of history he had created and a lot of memories.

City Island was a place in his past, a stepping stone to what he had hoped would be a long career pitching in the majors.

Berresford had made a good enough impression on June 5, 1952. The right-hander punctuated his first season in pro ball by no-hitting the Wilmington Blue Rocks 1-0 that night on the island.

The gem was the last thrown by a Senator before the team dropped out of the Class B Interstate League following the 1952 season.

With no team, there was no reason for Berresford to return to the island from his home in upstate Pennsylvania, where he had attended West Mahanoy Township High School before turning pro.

Besides, Berresford was busy traveling in 1953 between Savannah in the Class A South Atlantic League and St. Hyacinthe in the Class C Provincial League in Canada. His career, though, stopped there. He finished that season 2-7 with a 6.67 earned-run average. The year before he had been 6-18 with a 4.89 ERA in 34 appearances for a last-place Harrisburg team that went 46-94 before disappearing.

The 6-foot-1, 200-pound Berresford would not see another game on City Island until Opening Day 1987, when he joined a crowd of 4,083 to witness Harrisburg's return to pro baseball in the Class AA Eastern League.

"It's the same field, but what a difference," Berresford, then 55, said when he looked over the island for the first time in 35 years.

"It feels good to be here again," Berresford told Larry O'Rourke of Shenandoah's *Evening Herald*. "I just hope they have better luck than we did or they'll be out of business."

Slinging Arrows

Nick Horvath Jr., then the pot-stirring sports editor at *The Patriot-News*, thought the 1987 cartoon was funny. Dave Trembley did not.

That was understandable.

Really, would you like to wake up in the morning after a nightmarish, nine-game road trip and open the local newspaper to find yourself ridiculed in a cartoon?

Actually Trembley felt more harpooned than lampooned when he saw a caricature of himself tied to a stake with a vulture looming above him and arrows representing seven Eastern League opponents running through him.

The arrow representing the Pittsfield Cubs was lodged dangerously close to his … well, let's just say had that particular arrow been real, Trembley would have become a soprano.

The cartoon was Horvath's way of trying to inspire Trembley, the manager of Harrisburg's first team back on the island in 1987. At the time, Trembley was trying to figure out how to snap the Senators' 11-game losing streak.

The cartoon ran in 100,000 or so editions on May 13, 1987. So did the screaming headline in the next day's paper, the one imploring the Senators and Trembley to "Beat Somebody."

And the Senators did that night, defeating hot-hitting Williamsport 7-2 on the island to end the 11-game slide, which entering the 2012 season remained the worst skid in modern-franchise history.

"The big thing I learned over the years is not to take things so personally," Trembley said a couple of decades later. "You don't win a lot of games as the manager and you don't lose a lot of games as the manager. You do all of your work before 7 o'clock and then you just let them play."

3rd Inning

The Forgotten Ones

"It's no disgrace to be black, but it's often very inconvenient."
--- James Weldon Johnson, 1912

To some, Paul Robeson was an artist.

To others, he was a writer, a singer, an All-American football player or an actor. To many, he was a champion of civil rights for blacks.

To those who worshipped conspiracy-loving Senator Joe McCarthy, Robeson was nothing more than a Communist, which was not such a good thing to be during McCarthy's witch hunts in the mid-1950s.

But people listened to what Robeson had to say, so when he offered his list of the four best black athletes of the 20th century, people – black and white – nodded in understanding.

Jack Johnson, the boxer. Everyone knew about him.

Jesse Owens, the sprinter. No athlete was better known or admired after he dominated Hitler's Olympics of 1936.

Joe Louis, another boxer. Many considered him to be the best until Muhammad Ali came along in the 1960s.

Robeson reserved his fourth pick for a baseball player named Spottswood Poles.

This was generally where those bobbing heads stopped.

Who, they wondered, was Spottswood Poles?

Well, let's put it this way, had Spottswood Poles been born white, he would have played in the major leagues and would quite possibly have made also-rans of Ty Cobb and Tris Speaker when historians talked of the game's greatest center fielders in the first quarter of the 20th century.

As it was, Poles was known as "the black Ty Cobb," although among black players Cobb was known as "the white Spottswood Poles."

63

The 1908 Harrisburg Giants with Spottswood Poles (bottom row, second from right)

Had Poles been born white, his exploits in World War I – five battle stars and a Purple Heart – would have been lionized by Hollywood. Instead, his deeds were mostly known only to his all-black regiment in the United States' segregated military.

John McGraw, the New York Giants Hall of Fame manager from 1902 to 1932, once said he wanted Poles to play center field in the vastness of the Polo Grounds.

There was one problem for Poles: he was black and baseball, at least Major League Baseball, was not, and wouldn't be until Jackie Robinson came along in 1947. By then, Poles was approaching his 60th birthday. The astounding .594 average he reportedly had compiled a generation earlier in exhibition games against all-white players from the majors, which went largely unnoticed at the time, were distant memories shared by few.

Today there are precious few reminders of how dominant Poles was in the game during the early years of the 20th century.

The three-story brick row home at 406 Cumberland Street near Pennsylvania's state Capitol in Harrisburg – the place where Poles and his wife, Bertha, once lived – is long gone, bulldozed in the name of urban renewal.

The shade tree out front went, too. As did the 20-by-30 foot manicured lot, though the demise of the grass there was caused more by their dog, Blackie, than by the wrecking crew.

Until his death in 1962, Poles could be found at home talking about his newest Studebaker – he bought one every couple of years – or about the war he fought in Europe against the Kaiser, the taxi service he operated in Harrisburg after the war or the baseball career he enjoyed well before the Germans sank the Lusitania in 1915.

Of course, there always was time for the horses and their races, and Spots and Bertha did love to play the ponies. Vacations were spent at tracks from Atlantic City to Churchill Downs. Their road map was the *Daily Racing Form.*

Even when he was alive, few knew of Spottswood Poles.

In death, he was all but forgotten.

His obituary in Harrisburg's *Evening News* in 1962 consisted of six paragraphs, three of which were devoted to details for his viewing and burial. There were also brief mentions of his beloved Bertha and a sister from Baltimore, and that Poles served in World War I before retiring from the old Olmstead Air Force Base in Middletown.

There was no mention of Poles' career in baseball or the medals he earned in World War I while serving with the 369th Infantry, better known as the "Harlem Hell Fighters."

Baseball's Hall of Fame had a chance to immortalize Poles in February 2006 during its special election to induct former Negro League players and other turn-of-the-century black players. The committee charged with the selection of those players was forced to rely on statistical records that were incomplete, as well as folklore from generations past.

Poles was one of 39 candidates on the ballot.

He missed joining 17 others who were elected, including two players who starred on City Island – infielder Frank Grant from the 1890 Ponies and first baseman Ben Taylor of the 1925 Giants.

Poles reportedly missed by a single vote.

"Even if all 39 (were) voted in, blacks will still be underrepresented in the Hall," said Fred Brillhart, a Negro League researcher from suburban Harrisburg and longtime advocate of Poles' induction. "It's not like blacks started playing baseball when Jackie Robinson arrived in 1947."

Among Poles' supporters was Dick Clark of Ypsilanti, Michigan, who was one of the jury of 12 Negro League experts who voted on the final ballot of 39. Prior to the vote, Clark said he believed Poles had a "reasonable chance" for election, along with five others who once played on City Island – infielder John Beckwith, outfielders Rap Dixon and Fats Jenkins and, of course, Grant and Taylor.

Grant and Taylor were chosen, getting at least the requisite nine votes from the 12 committee members.

Beckwith, Dixon, Jenkins and Poles were not.

Of the six, Poles may have been the best. But he played in the era that preceded the 1920 formation of the more organized Negro National League and, with it, the advent of what commonly became known as the Negro Leagues.

Poles' era was devoid of reliable statistics, an era in which newspaper sports sections gave preference to carrying boxscores from the all-white majors over the all-black leagues in which Poles starred.

Grant had little problem with publicity; he was considered one of the premier players – black or white – in the 19th century

Beckwith, Dixon, Jenkins and Taylor also were known by the company they kept, joining future Hall of Famer Oscar Charleston in the mid-1920s to form a nucleus that made the Harrisburg Giants one of the most formidable teams in the Eastern Colored League.

Poles had no such acclaim. There were just stories of an excellence that was on display from Cuba to City Island. The squat, muscular, bow-legged switch-hitter consistently batted well above .300 and, so went the stories, sometimes higher than .400.

Most of his hits came off black pitchers who over time were also forgotten.

The more memorable hits were off white pitchers.

Poles drilled future Hall of Famer Grover Cleveland Alexander of the Phillies for three straight hits in a 1913 exhibition game.

He picked up a hit off another Hall of Famer, Chief Bender of the Athletics, then scored the game-winning run in an exhibition game the next season.

Poles and Bender both played on City Island in 1902, but for different teams. Bender, only a couple of months removed from his graduation from the Carlisle Indian School, pitched for the Harrisburg Athletic Club; Poles, then 14, played for Harrisburg's Springdale Athletic Club.

In addition to being one of the game's best hitters, Poles also was considered one of the fastest people on the planet. Just for fun during a break from winter ball in Palm Beach, Florida, Poles – then in his mid-20s – entered a track meet and flew through the 100-yard dash in under 10 seconds.

Some considered Poles to have been faster than Cool Papa Bell, which was saying something considering Bell was said to have once scored from first base on a fly ball off Bob Lemon, another future Hall of Fame pitcher, during an exhibition game against an all-white team from the majors.

No one knows exactly how many bases the 5-foot-7, 165-pound Poles stole in his career. Accurate records simply did not exist, nor have they been adequately replicated. Depending on the database providing the information, Poles batted between .320 and .332 during his career.

Alas, those records are based only on the boxscores that were recovered, and not many were for his games from 1910 to 1922. The sampling size: 190 games from the time

SPOTTSWOOD POLES

Poles made his pro debut in 1906 as an 18-year-old outfielder with the Harrisburg Colored Giants to his final season of organized ball in 1923.

That's it, 190 games. That's all the historians could find for Poles leading up to the Hall's special election in 2006. It's likely Poles played in 190 games, or close to it, in any one year of his career. His regular-season games were accompanied by who-knows-how-many exhibition games before, during and after the summer. There also was winter ball, where Poles augmented his income by playing in Florida, Cuba or Mexico while Harrisburg and the rest of the northeast froze from December through February.

Wherever Poles played, he ran, regardless of who he was facing. It didn't matter how old he was, either. If there was a base 90 feet away, Spottswood Poles was looking to get there.

Sam Streeter first faced Poles near the start of his own career in the early 1920s.

Streeter had heard of Poles' ability to run the bases long before he ever pitched against him. Streeter quickly learned that what he had heard was true when Poles sharply grounded a ball back to the mound and easily beat the throw to first.

"He hit that ball on one hop right back to me," Streeter was once quoted as saying. "I turned to throw to first, and he crossed first before the ball got there. ... If Poles hit to third base or shortstop, there was no question about it, he was going to be on there safe."

At the time, Poles was in his mid-30s and was ready to get out of the game, come home to Harrisburg, settle down with Bertha and move on to another career.

"I was still batting above .300 when I quit (in 1923)," Poles said. "The only thing was that I got tired of all the train travel and carrying those bags around all the time. So, I got out of baseball and bought myself five taxi cabs."

Of the 18 Negro League players selected for the Hall of Fame from 1971 to 2001, only shortstop Pop Lloyd and pitcher Smokey Joe Williams were contemporaries of Poles who played the substantive parts of their careers prior to 1920, when statistics were irregularly kept.

Dick Clark, the Negro League historian, said the Hall of Fame used 1920 as the line of statistical demarcation for evaluating candidates for the 2006 election. Going back further to track down boxscores and stats would have exceeded the $250,000 grant Major League Baseball had allotted to Clark and his 11 colleagues for their five-year study on the game's lost greats.

"I would have loved to have seen a complete record to show Poles' excellence," Clark said. "Not that I mind the anecdotal stuff, but that's really not the way you want to do it."

Ted Knorr, a Harrisburg-based Negro League expert, bristled at the thought of Poles' career being evaluated on hearsay rather than complete statistics used to gauge most of the other candidates for the Hall of Fame.

"The stats they have on Poles after 1920 have him hitting .280," Knorr said. "They're missing Spots' heyday."

John McGraw, the manager and embodiment of everything that was New York Giants baseball for the first third of the 20th century, wanted Poles on his team, along with other black stars like shortstop Pop Lloyd, and pitchers Cannonball Redding and Smokey Joe Williams.

McGraw had good reason to covet Poles. According to Negro League historian and author James Riley, Poles finished in 1923 with a career batting average of over .400 against any and all competition. In exhibition games against major leaguers, Poles was credited by Riley with a .594 batting average. Another historian, John Holway, had Poles batting .394 against the barnstorming major leaguers.

Either way, not bad for a kid from Winchester, Virginia, who learned how to play baseball in the early 1890s by hitting rubber balls with a broomstick. The lessons eventually led him to Harrisburg, where Poles played three seasons for the Giants from 1906 to 1908 before spending the next nine years with teams from Philadelphia to New York.

From 1911 through 1914, the switch-hitter with Popeye forearms reportedly batted .440, .398, .414 and .487 for the Lincoln Giants. Poles stayed in New York for another three seasons before switching teams, as he often did during his career.

This time, Poles signed on with the U.S. Army, which made him a sergeant and sent him off to Europe so he could use his accurate right arm to lob grenades at the Germans.

Even as a war hero, Poles mostly went unnoticed.

While the press in 1917 made quite the story of Boston Braves catcher Hank Gowdy becoming the first major leaguer to enlist in World War I, little – if anything – was told of the enlistment of Poles, who by then was nearing his 30th birthday.

Poles was assigned to the all-black 369th Infantry, which the Army promptly attached to the French military. Poles was awarded five battle stars in a year, as well as the Purple Heart. He could heave grenades as well as anybody, but when he returned home in 1919 the war hero was told he still couldn't throw – or hit – baseballs in the whites-only major leagues.

When Gowdy died in 1966, he was remembered for his modest 17-year career in the majors, as well as for being the first active big leaguer to enlist in the armed forces for World War I. Like Poles, Gowdy was a sergeant in the Great War who spent much of his time overseas in France. When he died, Gowdy was buried, amid much fanfare and tributes to his heroism and patriotism, in his hometown of Columbus, Ohio.

Four years earlier, Poles was buried in relative anonymity at Arlington National Cemetery.

In the last dozen years of his life, Poles mentored young players.

In 1951, he worked with Brooks Lawrence, a promising right-handed pitcher and future major league All-Star. Lawrence and outfielder Joe Caffie were the first blacks to play for Harrisburg on City Island since infielder Frank Grant and catcher Clarence Williams in 1890.

A year later, Poles – at the age of 64 – picked up his last hit for the Harrisburg Giants, who by then were an integrated semipro team that he was coaching.

Tired of watching his team flail at pitches in a road game, Poles grabbed a bat and put himself in the lineup as a pinch-hitter. Age be damned, doubters be stilled.

"I really thought it was going to be embarrassing," said Reid Poles, an outfielder on that Giants team and great-nephew of the great Spottswood. "He would hit fungos to the fellas, but I never saw him take batting practice with us."

As he did four decades earlier against Hall of Famer Grover Cleveland Alexander, Uncle Spot picked out a pitch he liked and ripped it through the right side of the infield for a single.

"He got down there to first base, and he was so pumped up," Reid Poles said. "I thought, 'Did he have that kind of drive when he played?' He had to, I thought, he just had to."

The drive, yes. The recognition, no.

The Magnificent Seven

Players or managers who summered on City Island en route to the Hall of Fame in Cooperstown, New York, where the Susquehanna River begins at Lake Otsego on its way south toward Harrisburg:

Hughie Jennings, 1890, elected 1945 by Veterans Committee.
Chief Bender, 1902, elected 1953, Veterans Committee.
Billy Hamilton, 1905-06, elected 1961,Veterans Committee.
Oscar Charleston, 1924-27, elected 1976, Negro League Committee.
Vic Willis, 1895, elected 1995, Veterans Committee.
Frank Grant, 1890, elected 2006 Negro League Committee
Ben Taylor, 1925, elected 2006, Negro League Committee.

Hughie Jennings

A teenage boy growing up in the coal region of northeastern Pennsylvania during the late 1880s had few options.

He could learn to work in the mines, just like his dad. He could learn to drink at a young age, just like his dad. Or he could learn to play baseball, just like his dad – only better, so he could stay out of the mines.

In the summer of 1889, Hughie Jennings worked at the local mine, driving mules and gathering coal. He was 20 and going nowhere, except when he played ball a couple of times each week. Jennings became the best catcher in Pittston, Pa. He was the Craig Biggio of his day, standing only 5-foot-8, weighing 165 pounds and destined to star at another position.

Within a year, Jennings turned pro and was batting .320 in 13 games for Allentown of the Eastern Interstate League when the team folded. Undeterred, Jennings stayed in the league and signed with the Harrisburg Ponies for $50 a month. He finished the season batting .338 and stealing 13 bases in 69 games for the Ponies, whose star was versatile infielder Frank Grant, a future Hall of Famer.

Jennings reached the majors in 1891 and played mostly shortstop for all or parts of 18 seasons, finishing with a .312 lifetime batting average. Jennings' managerial career began in 1907, when he led the Detroit Tigers to the first of three straight appearances – all losses – in the World Series. Those were the only pennants won by Jennings, who managed his last game in 1925 with the New York Giants. He left behind a career record of 1,184-995 and .543 winning percentage.

His greatest achievement, though, may have been finding a way to co-exist with the sometimes maniacal and always edgy Ty Cobb for most of the 14 seasons Jennings managed the Tigers.

Less than 30 months after leaving the Giants, Jennings died of meningitis in Scranton. He was 58. Seventeen years later, Jennings became the first to have played on City Island to reach the Hall of Fame when he was inducted by the Old Timers Committee into Cooperstown's Class of 1945.

Chief Bender

When Chief Bender began his career in 1902, he went by the name Charles Albert – his first and middle names – and played semipro ball with the Harrisburg Athletic Club.

He was just 18 years old and a recent graduate of the Carlisle Indian School. The HAC paid him $150 each month to pitch.

"It looked like a fortune," Bender said, "and I grabbed it."

Bender had been with the team for only 10 days when he started against the Chicago Cubs, then known as the Orphans, on June 17 in an exhibition game on City Island, then known as Hargast Island.

Among those watching that day was Connie Mack, the manager of the Philadelphia Athletics of the fledgling American League.

There were conflicting reports on how the 6-foot-2, 185-pound Bender fared against Chicago, but he clearly showed enough to pique Mack's interest.

Bender played on the island for the rest of the summer before he joined the Athletics and Mack, who paid HAC manager Cal Snoddy $100 to make sure his prized right-hander signed with Philadelphia and no one else.

"That was one of the greatest bargains in baseball," Mack told author Fred Lieb in the early 1940s.

Bender also thought the deal was a bargain – for himself.

"I was so excited," he later told biographers. "I didn't even ask the terms. I just signed. Later, I read the figures -- $300 a month – and thought I had taken my first step to becoming a millionaire."

In Philadelphia, Bender teamed with Gettysburg native Eddie Plank and Rube Waddell to combine for 299 of the Athletics' 414 victories from 1903 to 1907. All three reached the Hall of Fame with Plank and Waddell being inducted in 1946 and Bender following in 1953. Bender died less than a year later in Philadelphia at the age of 70.

Bender's Hall of Fame credentials included a 212-127 record from 1903 to 1917, a no-hitter in 1910 against Cleveland and a 5-2 record in the World Series for the A's from 1910 to 1913. Bender's most unusual moment may have come on May 8, 1906, when he subbed for left fielder Topsy Hartsel and hit two inside-the-park homers off Boston's Jesse Tannehill.

Chief Bender signed with the Philadelphia A's after pitching on the island in 1902

Billy Hamilton

Billy Hamilton had been out of the major leagues for three seasons when he arrived on City Island in 1905 as the Senators' player-manager. Hamilton, one of the majors' greatest players, brought to Harrisburg a resume highlighted by a .344 batting average in 14 seasons.

More than a century after he retired from the majors, Hamilton's 914 stolen bases still represented the third-highest total in history, trailing only fellow Hall of Famers Rickey Henderson (1,406) and Lou Brock (938).

> *At the age of 39, Billy Hamilton batted .342 in 110 games as a player-manager for the Senators in 1905.*

In 1905, the 39-year-old Hamilton excelled in the independent Tri-State League. The left handed-hitting outfielder batted .342 in 110 games for the Senators with 15 doubles, eight triples and two homers.

His 76-51 record as manager wasn't too bad, either, as the Senators finished only 3.5 games out of first place. Turning 40 was not as kind to Hamilton, however. He returned to the Senators as their player-manager in 1906, but batted only .277 in 43 games while the team staggered to a 52-74 finish. He left the Senators to spend four seasons as a player-manager for Haverhill and Lynn in the Class B New England League.

The 5-foot-6, 165-pound Hamilton remains the only player in major league history with four seasons of 100 or more stolen bases. His 1.06 runs-per-game average also ranks No. 1 all-time. In 1892 – 13 years before joining the Senators – Hamilton became the first of five players in major league history to start a game with a home run and end the same game with a walk-off homer. The other four: Vic Power (1957), Darin Erstad (2000), Reed Johnson (2003) and Ian Kinsler (2009).

Hamilton was named to the Hall of Fame by the Veterans Committee in 1961 – 21 years after his death at age 74 in Worcester, Massachusetts.

Oscar Charleston

Bill James ranked Oscar Charleston fourth all-time among baseball's greatest players, placing him behind only Babe Ruth, Honus Wagner and Willie Mays and immediately ahead of Ty Cobb, Mickey Mantle and Ted Williams.

Go to any ballpark in the country and it's likely you will find plenty of fans who have heard of Ruth, Wagner, Mays, Cobb, Mantle and Williams.

Charleston? Not so much, and that's too bad.

Old-time purists who know every bit of minutiae in the game's history probably know of Oscar Charleston, as will the younger disciples of Bill James who have dog-eared every one of his publications that break down a player's worth based, in part, on a statistic James calls "Win Shares," which calculates a player's total contribution to his team's success based on a formula that is seemingly as complex as the NFL's quarterback rating system.

For his list of the 100 greatest players in history, James relied on other lists already compiled by The Sporting News, the Society of American Baseball Research and Total Baseball, as well other lists put together by noted writers Maury Allen, Donald Honig and Lawrence Ritter.

Then after all the numbers were crunched, Oscar Charleston – the player-manager of the all-black Harrisburg Giants of the mid-1920s – was ranked fourth overall.

All-time.

White ball.

Black ball.

Any ball.

Didn't matter.

As James noted in his Historical Baseball Abstract, Joe DiMaggio – the "great DiMaggio" in Hemingway's "The Old Man and the Sea" – appeared on hundreds, perhaps thousands, of magazine covers during his life.

Charleston?

Who knows? Not many, if any.

James put DiMaggio nine slots *behind* Charleston at No. 13.

As for left-handed hitters, James put only Babe Ruth ahead of Charleston.

Of those who played on City Island, Charleston likely was the best – arguably better than Vladimir Guerrero, who in 1996 dominated the Class AA Eastern League before starting a Hall of Fame-caliber career in the majors.

When Babe Ruth homered into the second row of trees beyond the island's right-field fence in a 1928 exhibition game against the Senators, the towering drive was only good enough for the second-longest homer ever on the island. Oscar Charleston previously hit one into the third row.

Like Ruth, Charleston – who was listed at 6-feet and a generously light 190 pounds – had legs that appeared too lean to hold up the beer barrel that was his chest.

Charleston spent four seasons on the island playing center field and managing the Giants.

His first team in 1924 finished 26-28 and fifth in the eight-team Eastern Colored League. The 1925 Giants went 37-18 and came in second behind defending league champion Hilldale. Another second-place finish came in 1926 at 25-17. The 1927 team went 16-12 before the ECL folded, leaving Harrisburg without a Negro League team until 1943.

All Charleston did in his time on the island was hit a reported .380, .451, .302 and .357. In three of those seasons – 1924, '25 and '27 – he led the league in homers, and no one topped his .451 batting average in 1925.

Charleston already was a star in the bigger Negro Leagues before arriving in Harrisburg, and continued to be among the best in the Negro Leagues after leaving the island. His ties to Harrisburg were bound by his marriage to Janie Blalock, the daughter of a local Methodist minister.

Charleston surely would have kept playing on the island for the Giants had they not folded after the 1927 season. His stay in the game lasted 40 seasons from 1915 to 54, either as a player, a player-manager or manager.

Charleston's managed the barnstorming Indianapolis Clowns through the summer of 1954 before dying that fall after a stroke and a fall down a flight of steps in Philadelphia. His death came nine days shy of his 58th birthday and 22 years prior to his overdue induction into the Hall of Fame.

"He was like Ty Cobb, Babe Ruth and Tris Speaker rolled into one," Negro League player and manager Buck O'Neil once said of Charleston.

Just like Spottswood Poles, the Harrisburg Giants' center fielder from 1906 to 1908, Charleston was tagged with the nickname of "the black Ty Cobb."

Oscar Charleston starred on the island for the Harrisburg Giants from 1924 to 1927

In reality, that was quite the compliment for Cobb, considering Charleston had more power at the plate than Cobb and was considered by many to be defensively superior to the Detroit Tigers' center fielder.

The fragmented records that were common in the Negro Leagues credited Charleston with a .342 career batting average against black competition, a .326 average against white major leaguers in exhibition games and a .361 average over nine seasons in the Cuban winter leagues.

"Charleston could hit that ball a mile," said Hall of Famer Dizzy Dean, one of the All-Star pitchers from the all-white majors who faced Charleston in exhibition games. "He didn't have a weakness. When he came up, we just threw it and hoped like hell he wouldn't get a hold of one and send it out of the park."

Vic Willis

Vic Willis pitched in only 73 games in the minors before embarking on a Hall of Fame career in the majors, but 11 of those games came with Harrisburg in 1895. Those appearances came quickly, too, as the Senators played just 35 games in the Class B Pennsylvania State League before folding in mid-June.

During his time in Harrisburg, Willis – all of 19 years old – went 4-4 with a 3.76 earned-run average in eight starts and three relief appearances.

> *Vic Willis won 20 or more games and pitched at least 300 innings in eight of his 13 seasons in the major leagues.*

In the majors, the right-hander won 20 or more games eight times in 13 seasons. He also worked 300-plus innings eight times before retiring in 1910 with a career record of 249-205.

Conversely, Willis' 29 losses in 1905 for the Boston Beaneaters – the forerunners of today's Atlanta Braves – remain the most by any pitcher in a single season since the turn of the 20th century.

The 6-foot-2, 185-pound Willis also pitched in two games for the Pittsburgh Pirates in the 1909 World Series with mixed results.

Working in relief of starter Howie Camnitz during the third inning of Game 2, Willis allowed a run to score before he recorded an out as Ty Cobb stole home against him at Forbes Field. Willis also started and lost Game 6 of the 1909 Series, although the Pirates recovered to win both Game 7 and the Series.

Willis was inducted into the Hall of Fame by the Veterans Committee in 1995 – 48 years after he died in Elkton, Maryland, at the age of 71.

Frank Grant

Fans lined up by the new People's Bridge – known today as the Walnut Street Bridge – for the arrival of the great Frank Grant. One of baseball's premier players had pulled into town moments earlier on the 3:20 train.

That Monday – May 5, 1890 – Grant was treated like royalty, traveling by horse and carriage from the train station to the island.

Grant had left the Trenton Cuban Giants to sign with the Harrisburg Ponies of the Eastern Interstate League. He joined the Ponies to play third base for a team in its first season playing in a new ballpark on the island.

"Everybody was anxious to see him come and there was a general stretch of necks towards the new bridge," reported the Harrisburg *Patriot*, "... all being eager to get a sight at the most famous colored ball player in the business."

Grant's talents not only made him an icon in Toronto, where he had an International League-best batting average of .366 in 1887, but in every town he visited that season.

> *"In hitting, (Grant) ranked with the best, and his fielding bordered on the impossible."*
>
> *Sol White*

The overflow crowd that greeted Grant three years later in Harrisburg alternatingly cheered for and gawked at the 24-year-old infielder, who responded simply by doffing his cap in appreciation.

Grant batted .333 in 59 games for Harrisburg, stealing 22 bases and hitting a league-high five home runs before the Eastern Interstate League folded and the Ponies jumped to the American Association.

One of Grant's teammates in Harrisburg that summer was a part-time catcher named Hughie Jennings. The pair eventually became the first black-and-white teammates to be elected to baseball's Hall of Fame, although Grant's overdue election came more than 100 years after he spent his one season in Harrisburg.

While Harrisburg's fans embraced the 5-foot-7, 155-pound Grant, the league did not – and decided to ban black players beginning in 1891. That

79

decision left Grant and Ponies catcher Clarence Williams looking for work in more open-minded, integrated environs. Of no concern to the owners was that Williams was a natural gate attraction for the Ponies, since he had been born 22 years earlier in Harrisburg and had started playing in the city as a teenager.

Alas, bigotry always dogged the light-skinned Grant, who was referred to as a "Spaniard" by the *Buffalo Express* during the 1887 season in the hope of keeping Grant from being ostracized by racially narrow-minded fans in the International League. Grant stayed in Buffalo through 1888 before moving on to Trenton in 1889 and then Harrisburg the following season.

Grant played only six seasons in integrated baseball before the team owners in so-called organized baseball quietly and unconscionably reached an ungentlemanly agreement to ban blacks from their leagues.

"(Grant) probably was the best of the black players in organized baseball during the 19th century before the color line was drawn," said Sol White, a turn-of-the-20th-century player and historian. "In hitting, he ranked with the best, and his fielding bordered on the impossible."

Grant was the last great black player in non-segregated leagues until 1946, when Jackie Robinson joined the Brooklyn Dodgers' International League affiliate in Montreal. A year later, Robinson arrived in Brooklyn to break the majors' color barrier and start leveling the playing field for all.

When he was banned from organized leagues – the all-white leagues – Grant was forced to play for touring black teams until he retired in 1903 at the age of 38. He lived out the rest of his life waiting on tables in New York City restaurants. Penniless and without family when he died of arteriosclerosis in 1937, Grant was buried in an unmarked grave in a remote section of the 80-acre East Ridgelawn Cemetery in Clifton, New Jersey.

The best black player of the late 19th century was forced to wait until the early 21st century to be honored by the Hall of Fame. Grant and 16 others were inducted in the Hall in 2006 as part of a special, long-overdue Negro Leagues election. Five years later, Grant – dead for more than 70 years – finally received a marble headstone on his grave with an epitaph that recognized his career and, more important, the man himself.

Ben Taylor

While he was not nearly as recognizable as others who dominated the Negro Leagues, Ben Taylor's life in the game really was the template for all of them.

He spent all or parts of five decades in the game, beginning in 1908 as a 20-year-old pitcher for the Birmingham Giants and finishing in 1941 with the Edgewater Giants. In between, the left-hander played for more than 20 teams, including the 1925 Harrisburg Giants.

Taylor, then 37, batted .328 for the Giants, who went 37-18 in 1925 and finished second in the seven-team Eastern Colored League.

The 6-foot-1, 190-pound Taylor was considered the best first baseman in the Negro Leagues prior to Buck Leonard's arrival in 1933.

Some historians said Taylor was to black baseball what Lou Gehrig was to white baseball. Only Taylor lasted longer. His career started 15 years before Gehrig's debut with the Yankees in 1923 and ended two years after the terminally ill Gehrig retired in 1939. By the time he was done, Taylor had amassed a .334 lifetime average.

Some believe Taylor was to black baseball what Gehrig was to white baseball. Only Taylor lasted longer. His career started 15 years before Gehrig's debut with the Yankees in 1923 and ended two years after Gehrig was forced to retire in 1939.

Only 12 years after his final game and a few years after having his once powerful left arm amputated following a fall, Taylor died of pneumonia in Baltimore. He was 64. Fifty-three years after his death, Taylor was named to the Hall of Fame in 2006 as part of the special election to recognize previously overlooked black players, managers and executives from the 19th and 20th centuries.

Doing Time With Chick Meade

Chick Meade knew how to run, especially from the police.

Meade was a schmoozer, a scammer and a thief. He also was a decent infielder, which was why he kept finding employment with all-black baseball teams during the early part of the 20th century.

Meade mostly played third base. He also habitually moved from one town to another, usually just before the local authorities caught up with him.

In a seven-year span starting in 1914, Meade played for – and subsequently fled from – teams between New York and Indianapolis and between Atlantic City and Baltimore before turning up on City Island in 1922.

In Harrisburg, the 31-year-old infielder played third and batted third for the Harrisburg Giants, an independent team that was still two years away from formally joining the Eastern Colored League.

Three years after he stopped playing in 1922, Meade became the Giants' business manager.

Apparently along the way none of the teams that had employed Meade bothered to take a close look at his résumé. Had they bothered to inquire, they might have learned what police discovered in 1931.

After he was picked up in Baltimore for writing a bogus $705 check, police learned that Meade often supplemented his income as a player by forging money orders and passing bad checks. The Baltimore police arrested him for writing a check from an account that belonged to Harrisburg physician Leslie Marshall.

The police also learned something else about Meade: He was not black, but instead a swarthy white man who passed himself off as a light-skinned black player so he could hide in the Negro Leagues.

The Guys Playing Next to "Charlie"

One had the reputation for drinking too much and being too hard to handle; the other enjoyed playing the piano, singing and saving a little money on the side.

Herbert Dixon's lifestyle led him to an early grave at the age of 41, while Clarence Jenkins' relatively calm demeanor led to a successful post-baseball business career and a much longer life.

In their youth, both were outstanding ballplayers who were better known by the nicknames of Rap and Fats, respectively.

FATS JENKINS

For four seasons from 1924 to1927, they flanked Oscar Charleston, arguably was the Negro Leagues' greatest player, if not the best known. The three shared the outfield for the Harrisburg Giants at Island Park, known today as City Island. Together, Rap, Fats and Charlie formed what some historians believed to be one of the greatest outfields – regardless of color – in the history of the game. One of them – Charleston – posthumously entered the Hall of Fame in 1976, while Dixon and Jenkins were on the final ballot for the Hall's special Negro Leagues election in 2006.

Neither, though, was among the 17 inductees.

With Charleston between them, Dixon and Jenkins played together for four seasons. And that, according to Negro League historian Ted Knorr, gave the Harrisburg Giants the distinction of having only one of nine outfields in history to play together for four or more seasons with at least one Hall of Famer in the group.

RAP DIXON

Dixon and Jenkins came within a few votes in 2006 of giving the Giants a trio of Hall of Fame outfielders to match the Philadelphia Phillies' 1891-1895 threesome of Ed Delahanty, Billy Hamilton and Sam Thompson as the game's only all-Hall outfield.

Of Harrisburg's fabulous three, Dixon spent the most time on the island and in the region after first playing semipro ball while living in Steelton in 1916. When his playing days ended in 1936, Dixon returned to Steelton and worked at Bethlehem Steel, just as his father had done 20 years earlier. The hard-living Dixon died of a heart attack in 1944 – six weeks shy of his 42nd birthday.

Personal demons aside, the 6-foot-1, 183-pound Dixon seemed to do something astounding every time he played. He was credited with:

--- Hitting the longest home run in Japan during a 1927 goodwill tour of the Orient, which ended with Dixon receiving a loving cup from Emperor Hirohito for his play.

--- Collecting a record 14 straight hits for the Baltimore Black Sox in 1929 in a pair of series against the Homestead Grays and Philadelphia's Hilldale Giants.

--- Being the first Negro Leaguer to homer at Yankee Stadium in 1930, when the right-hander drilled three of them in Baltimore's doubleheader against the New York Lincoln Giants.

--- Hitting .317 lifetime against Negro League competition and .362 in exhibition games against barnstorming teams from the majors.

Old Fats wasn't bad, either.

Like Dixon, the 5-foot-7, 165-pound Jenkins moved around from team to team during a 21-year career that lasted until 1940. The left handed-hitting Jenkins was the Giants' right fielder during his four seasons on the island, batting .322, .313, .315 and .366 before Harrisburg dropped out of the Eastern Colored League in 1927. His lifetime batting average of .321 against black competition was nearly identical to that of Dixon.

Dixon and Jenkins later joined Charleston at the Negro League's inaugural East-West All-Star Game in 1933 at Chicago's Comiskey Park.

In his offseasons, Jenkins was the captain for more than a decade of New York's Renaissance basketball team, which won 88 straight games in the early 1930s. The Rens were inducted en masse in 1963 to the National Basketball Hall of Fame in Springfield, Massachusetts – five years before Jenkins passed away in Philadelphia at age 70.

One of Jenkins' teammates with the Rens was George Fiall, a shortstop who also played for the Giants during the 1920s. He and Jenkins were called the "Heavenly Twins" for their prowess in two sports. Unfortunately for Fiall, he never hit much for average. He did not have a long life, either, dying of pneumonia on April 12, 1936 in New York City. He was 35.

Jackie Comes to Town ... Almost

Jackie Robinson had just made history in late August 1945, becoming the first black player signed by a major league team in the 20th century. He was about to accomplish another first in the spring of 1947, becoming the major league's first black player since Toledo catcher Fleet Walker in 1884.

Between his two historic moments, Robinson wanted to make a little

extra money for his family. He was earning $600 per month playing in 1946 for Brooklyn's Class AAA International League team in Montreal and his wife, Rachel, was pregnant with their first child.

Robinson had seen the money being made by Dizzy Dean, Bob Feller and Satchel Paige when they assembled barnstorming teams to play each other in previous offseasons.

Some promoted the exhibition games as gestures of goodwill between races, but Feller,

Satchel Paige barnstormed City Island in the 1950s

Dean and Paige were more pragmatic.

They saw dollar signs.

According to writer Bob Luke, Feller and Paige pulled in $80,000 to $100,000 for a couple of months' work.

So Robinson assembled an all-black team to tour in the fall of 1946. His scheduled stops included New York, Pittsburgh, Chicago, Cleveland, St. Louis and, yes, Harrisburg's City Island.

Robinson, though, never reached the island. In early October, baseball commissioner Happy Chandler curtailed barnstorming tours that might involve players participating in the World Series. Chandler worried that some less than honorable players might be tempted to get through the Series as quickly as possible – and, ahem, tank the games – to get out on the road ASAP. Chandler knew the barnstormers could make more money playing exhibition games in a month than they did for the entire season, let alone from the World Series.

Robinson then rescheduled games for after the Series, but dropped Harrisburg from his tour.

The Grays and the Beards

The island came alive on the Monday night of Aug. 31, 1931, when two of baseball's premier barnstorming teams met for an exhibition game.

The field, used during the day by the Senators of the Class B New York-Penn League, was bathed by light that night. The players from the famous House of David team brought their beards, Samson-like long hair and – most importantly – their portable flood lights for their game against the Homestead Grays.

The eight sets of lights, each attached to two poles affixed to the back of trucks, rose 40 to 50 feet above the field.

The game featured not only the rarely beaten House of David team from Benton Harbor, Michigan, but also a Homestead team that routinely was among the best in the Negro Leagues. The Grays played that season as an independent and were credited with as many as 163 victories in 186 games.

The score of this game was lost to history.

The Grays' gaudy record should come as no surprise. Their roster included Josh Gibson, then a 19-year-old rookie catcher on his way to becoming one of the greatest power hitters in history, as well as four other future Hall of Famers – pitchers Smokey Joe Williams and Willie Foster; infielder Jud Wilson and Oscar Charleston, the center fielder who starred for the Harrisburg Giants from 1924 to 1927.

4th Inning

Living the Life

Their apartment leases had expired a couple of weeks earlier on Labor Day.

Now their savings had dwindled, as had their options.

They had no place to go, at least not one they could afford on the meager salary paid most players in the minors.

So in the days leading up to what at that point would be their greatest moment in pro baseball, a handful of the Harrisburg Senators' best players decided to hunker down together for a few nights.

Right in the clubhouse on City Island.

Two of them – Andy Tracy, the team's third baseman and Eastern League most valuable player, and Jamey Carroll, the second baseman who arguably was the team's MVP – curled up for the night on the two padded but well-worn tables in the trainer's room.

Two more – relief pitchers Brandon Agamennone and Jeremy Salyers – slept on air mattresses laid on the clubhouse floor, where the carpet was thin and the germs were thick.

Another reliever, Christian Parker, squeezed into a plastic-and-metal lounge chair.

Welcome to Chez RiverSide. For a few nights in September 1999 the stadium's woefully undersized clubhouse doubled as a bed-and-breakfast for five of the Senators' best players during Harrisburg's dramatic run to the Eastern League title.

"It was like camping out," Salyers said. "We played cards. We played video games. We rented some movies. It was fun for us."

Necessary, too, after the remnants of Hurricane Floyd brought both rainouts and scheduling changes for the EL playoffs.

While their teammates found rooms in downtown hotels or with local families, the RiverSide Five relied on clubhouse attendant Mike Diehl to keep the door unlocked and their arrangement a secret, or at least as covert as possible inside a baseball clubhouse.

"I knew they were there," outfielder Brad Wilkerson said 12 years later, "but I ended up staying at the hotel with some other guys."

Wilkerson had clean sheets, fresh towels and a decent mattress. He also had his video games, just like his five teammates who stayed behind in the clubhouse.

"We played 'Mario Kart' all the time at the hotel," Wilkerson said.

"We'd stay up until 3 o'clock in the morning playing that game. We were addicted to it."

Wilkerson could easily afford the downtown hotel, given that just a year earlier he received a $1 million bonus to sign with the Montreal Expos out of the University of Florida.

BRAD WILKERSON

Carroll, Tracy, Agamennone, Salyers and Parker could have combined their salaries, as well as their initial signing bonuses, and not come close to matching Wilkerson's signing bonus. While Parker was a fourth-round draft choice out of Notre Dame in 1996, the other four were mid-round picks in drafts held from 1996 to 1998. Each had received a bonus that might have included a grand or two for spending money and a new pair of spikes, but little else. They also received airfare to the Expos' short-season, Class A affiliate in Burlington, Vermont, or, in Salyers' case, to the netherworld of the neophyte-level Gulf Coast League.

"We couldn't afford to stay in the hotel at $50 a night," Agamennone said. "You have to do what you have to do and, besides, it makes for a good story now."

Carroll, Tracy and Co. had been living on $1,500 a month – but only during the regular season.

Conversely, the minimum salary in the major leagues that year was $200,000.

By 2012, the major league minimum had increased to $480,000, yet first-year Class AA players who were not on their major league team's protected 40-man roster or had been brought into the organization as free agents were still collecting $1,500 a month.

Winning a championship – as the Senators did here in 1987 – can make players forget, at least momentarily, about the meager salaries they receive in the minor leagues

"If you could make money in the minors, you really wouldn't worry about making it to the big leagues," said Ron Calloway, an outfielder for the Senators in 2001. "That's where everything is, up there … That's the big payoff."

Calloway's "big payoff" was $600,00 for his two seasons in the majors with the Expos in 2003 and 2004. He spent another three seasons in the minors with three different organizations, none of which brought him back to the majors. Calloway's pro career ended before his 31st birthday.

Parker, too, reached the majors – for one game with the New York Yankees in 2001. He received a prorated portion of the then-major league minimum of $200,000. He promptly gave up seven runs on eight hits in three innings of a 13-4 loss to the Toronto Blue Jays in the fourth game of the season at Yankee Stadium. Afterward he was sent back to the minors, never to return.

At least Parker reached the majors; Agamennone and Salyers, despite the promise each had showed in the minors, never did.

Tracy was more fortunate; he spent parts of five seasons from 2000 to 2009 with the Expos, Colorado Rockies and Philadelphia Phillies. He spent time in four other organizations over 16 seasons before retiring in the fall of 2011 to become a minor league manager for the Phillies.

His top salary came in 2001 with the Expos, who paid him a prorated portion of the major league minimum of $200,000 as they shuttled him back and forth from Montreal to Class AAA Ottawa.

The most successful of the group was Carroll, an unlikely candidate for a lengthy major league career given the Expos' onetime disinterest in him. Carroll reached the majors at age 28 as much by happenstance as skill late in the 2002 season and – with the exception of a three-game injury re-hab assignment in 2009 – has never returned to the minors.

Carroll's career earnings were $11.8 million before he signed a two-year, $6.5 million contract with the Minnesota Twins as a free agent fol-lowing the 2011 season.

Stories such as Carroll's, though, are the exception.

While some players become instant millionaires because of their draft status, most are more like Tracy and Agamennone.

Sign here kid for a couple of grand and a new pair of shoes. Now go take your chances against hundreds of others just like you for the few spots that may open in the majors.

Agamennone took that deal in 1998 after the Expos had selected him out of the University of Maryland in the 20th round of the draft. As a mid-dle-round pick with no college eligibility remaining, Agamennone's bar-gaining position was non-existent, so he grabbed the Expos' offer of a $1,000, a new glove and spikes, and a monthly salary of $850 to play at Class A Vermont, four levels away from the majors and only one bad out-ing removed from getting airfare back home.

Within a year of signing Agamennone was saving games for the Sena-tors.

Within 20 months, he joined the Montreal Expos as a late-inning, on-ly-if-needed, mop-up reliever for a spring training game against Houston. The team bus he took that day from Jupiter, Florida, to Kissimmee was loaded the some of the best and brightest of his Harrisburg teammates from 1999 – Tracy, catcher Brian Schneider, pitcher Tony Armas and outfielder Milton Bradley.

For one day, trying to live on a Class AA salary was not a major concern for Agamennone.

"The money's OK then, because you know you're that close to the majors," he said.

"I guess if I hadn't been there in Harrisburg in '99 and seen Tracy and Armas and Schneider and Milton ... to play with those guys and then be a key member of that staff ... Then I see those same guys (on the team bus) and know they were the ones who would go, 'We have a win today because Aggie's pitching.' That gives you a lot of confidence."

But it doesn't guarantee you a job in the majors.

Parker learned that after his only game with the Yankees.

Agamennone learned it after eight mostly successful seasons in pro ball, where he was 40-12 with a 3.70 ERA in 229 appearances. Some of his best work came during his four seasons on City Island from 1999 to 2002, but that merely earned him a shot at Class AAA, nothing more.

The only real money in the minors – not counting what is squirreled away by the high-round draft choices – goes to six-year free agents, the journeymen who know how to play the game but are no longer being fast-tracked to the majors.

For some of these players, much larger paychecks await, but only if they agree to accept a different kind of role.

Longtime minor league hitters can take on the role of stable pony for a rising prospect, as onetime Senators outfielder Tyrone Horne did for the Reading Phillies in 1999.

"I never imagined in my wildest dreams that I would back there," Horne said of joining Reading in the same Class AA Eastern League where he first played seven years earlier in Harrisburg.

Horne was in Reading primarily to bat behind Pat Burrell and keep Eastern League teams from pitching around the first overall pick of the 1998 amateur draft.

Horne did not enjoy the role, especially after being signed a year earlier by St. Louis and dispatched to Arkansas to do the same thing for wunderkind J.D. Drew in the Class AA Texas League.

"I've been through the ringer a lot of times," a frustrated Horne said then of being a 28-year-old journeyman known best for being a hired bat. "I want my own recognition. I don't want to be the guy who always protects the prospects. I want to be known for being Tyrone Horne."

He would be – but never in the majors. Horne drifted through seven major league organizations, two independent leagues and the Korean Baseball Organization in 13 seasons. He was only 30 when his playing career ended in 2001. His resume included a .288 lifetime average over 1,286 games in the minors and zero days in the majors.

Longtime minor league pitchers can become surrogate coaches for young pitchers in Class AA, as former Senators starter Tommy Phelps did in 2001 at Erie.

Phelps spent four seasons on City Island from 1996 to 1999 before signing as a minor-league free agent with the Detroit Tigers in 2000. Their plan in 2001 was to send the left-hander back for a fifth season in the Class AA Eastern League so he could help mentor a staff that would eventually graduate seven pitchers – including Phelps – to the majors.

"The guys would rag me because it's my sixth year in Double-A," Phelps said, "but I showed them how to get to the field and where to eat."

Phelps was a well-paid tour guide, earning $6,000 a month with Erie in 2001 – four times the $1,500 he made after first joining Harrisburg for the final few weeks of the 1996 season.

"If I wasn't getting paid free-agent money I couldn't afford to play," said Phelps, whose wife Cassie was back home in Florida at that time finishing college and tending to their infant son, Jacob.

"Without that money, I'd have to stop."

For players without family commitments there is no stopping. The money, such as it is in the minors, is not a factor. So what if they live four to an apartment, drive hand-me-down cars lent to them by fans and dine at any place with an all-you-can-eat buffet?

They all dream, as Calloway put it, for the "big payoff."

Teams in the major leagues take advantage of that dream, too.

Whenever possible in spring training, teams will have their minor leaguers dress in a separate clubhouse near – but not too close – to another one used by the major leaguers. At any time, a minor leaguer can look down the corridor and see a major leaguer who can afford to tip a waiter more money after a meal than a Class AA player can make in a week.

"You always see that in front of you," said Noah Hall, an outfielder with the Senators in 2000 and 2003, "and when you see those players close up, you want to stick with it."

Hall, the Expos' 27th-round draft choice in 1995, stuck with it longer than most. The 2011 season was his 16th in professional baseball, although the last two seasons were spent in the independent Atlantic League. Being in his mid-30s and kicking around independent ball is a bad combination for trying to get back to Class AA, let alone the majors.

"I know that if I go up to the major leagues for just one week I will make more there than I do all year in the minors," Hall said.

In the minors, three or four players will cram themselves into a two-bedroom, unfurnished apartment.

Calloway did that in 2001 with first baseman Terrmel Sledge and outfielder Tootie Myers. The eggshell-colored walls of their suburban Harrisburg apartment were bare. The living room décor consisted of a green sofa, a matching chair and a circular table with four more chairs. The warranty and safety labels still dangled from the furniture. The light on the VCR underneath the small TV perpetually flashed "12:00."

An iron sat on the floor, which doubled as the trio's ironing board.

"Ironing boards are overrated," Myers said.

There also was a propane-fueled fireplace, but none of the three knew how to use it.

"It's OK," Myers said. "We'd probably blow ourselves up."

The three split the $930 monthly rent for their suburban Harrisburg apartment. Calloway and Myers claimed the bedrooms, while Sledge was stuck sleeping on the rented sofa in the living room.

Two of Sledge's most valuable possessions – a Bible and a baseball bat – were on the floor at the foot of sofa.

Some of their teammates lived in the same apartment complex, mostly because of its proximity to the ballpark. Their leases ran from the first of April through Labor Day, the traditional final day of the Eastern League's regular season.

"You try to get the rent to between $200 and $400 apiece," said Scott Sandusky, a catcher with the Senators from 2000 to 2003. "It's a good learning experience. It teaches you how to budget. If you can live on that kind of salary, then you can handle your finances."

Salyers and Agamennone decorated their Harrisburg apartment in Early Poverty. Scattered about their summer home were inflatable chairs, plastic lawn furniture and the same air mattresses they would later use while camping out in the clubhouse at RiverSide Stadium.

Their refrigerator was filled with pasta, chicken and anything that was microwaveable in three minutes or less.

No ballplayer's monthly expenses were complete without factoring in utility costs. Everyone needed electricity, but no one wanted to be held accountable for it.

"You hate putting that stuff in your name," said Phelps, who has pitched or coached in the minors since 1993, "because if you get moved in the organization, you have to deal with someone else shutting it off.

"And," Phelps said with a sigh, "you always lose your deposit."

Major leaguers do not have these problems. They have agents who have secretaries who take care of petty annoyances like bill-paying.

But the public perception is that all pro baseball players are wealthy.

Calloway encountered that early in the 2001 season on the Senators' road trip to Portland, Maine. He was chatting up the desk clerk and impressing upon her that he indeed was a professional ballplayer, just not a well-paid one.

"That lady at the front desk thought I was rich," said Calloway, who convinced her otherwise by pulling from his pocket the stub from the paycheck he had just received from the Expos. "I had to show her that before she believed me. She saw it and almost fell over."

The misconceptions often start in spring training, where minor leaguers wear the same uniforms as major leaguers, and those misconceptions continue through the season as minor leaguers perform community service in their temporary hometowns.

Outings are made to elementary schools, senior centers, autograph signings, summer camps and Little League functions. And with kids come questions, some of which can be embarrassing.

"They're always asking, 'Do you have a lot of money? Do you own a limousine? What kind of house do you have?' " Phelps said. "There is a misconception that minor leaguers make a lot of money. There is a small percent who do make a lot of money, but those are the guys who sign for a million dollars out of school."

Or for $15.1 million, as onetime Senators pitcher Stephen Strasburg did after the Washington Nationals selected him with the first overall pick in the 2009 draft.

Or the $9.9 million that outfielder Bryce Harper received after the Nationals took him with the top pick in 2010.

Bryce Harper was the most sought after signature for Senators fans in 2011; the one he signed on his first pro contract in 2010 cost the Nationals $9.9 million

Signing bonuses often are reflected in the type of ride a player chooses to get to and from the ballpark.

The 18-year-old Harper came to City Island driving a customized black 2011 Toyota Tundra with tinted windows and a jacked-up cab.

"I got a Ford Explorer," Agamennone said, shaking his head, knowing he spent too much. "I should have gotten a Ford Escort instead."

Journeymen minor leaguers – the overwhelming majority of guys not named Strasburg or Harper – have always needed to find offseason jobs to get through the winter.

Some scramble for the few available roster spots in winter ball. Those fortunate enough to find work playing in the baseball-crazed Caribbean and Latin America often can double or triple their $1,500 monthly pay from Class AA.

The transition to playing year-round can be difficult, especially in a country where you don't speak the language.

"It's a culture shock," outfielder Chris Stowers said. "They're a little behind on little things like transportation and nobody speaks English … Do

"If you could make money in the minors, you really wouldn't worry about making it to the big leagues. ... That's the big payoff."

Outfielder Ron Calloway

you know how hard it is to order a pizza in the Dominican?"

Minor leaguers who stay home often take offseason jobs in construction, as Calloway once did near his home in Los Banos, California, or waiting on tables, as Phelps did in West Palm Beach, Florida.

Players such as Agamennone and Chuck Crumpton, another former Senators pitcher, were substitute teachers during the offseason near their old homes in Crofton, Maryland, and Mesquite, Texas, respectively.

"It's near my hometown, so everybody knew what I did," Agamennone said. "Kids would say to me, 'My sister says you play pro ball. What are you doing subbing? Don't you make like a million dollars?'

"I'm like, 'Yeah, kid, that's why I'm here subbing.' "

Agamennone often wondered whether the seasons of living in abject poverty while playing in the minors were worth pursuing a goal that would never come true for most, including him.

Fulltime jobs passed him by, and thoughts of marriage and parenthood went unfulfilled during his playing career. Who could take care of a family, he thought, on $1,500 a month?

"You give up so much," Agamennone said. "It's just difficult."

Agamennone was done with pro ball in 2005. He was 29. Today he is president of Pro Source Athletics, a faith-based youth baseball academy, which he founded, in suburban Dallas. He finally became engaged prior to the 2012 season.

Back when he was playing, Agamennone found himself thinking more and more about holding down a steady job like the one he eventually created for himself. But in those moments of professional second-guessing, Agamennone would turn on the TV and flip to the same sports channel.

"All it takes," he said, "is watching one highlight on ESPN and you're like, 'What am I doing (thinking of a 9-to-5 job)? I'm going to take my 10 grand and play baseball."

Matt Stairs batted .333 during his MVP summer on City Island in 1991

Have Bat, Will Travel

During the baseball season, a player spends half of the summer living on the road. Some players spend half of their careers changing teams.

The most well-traveled position player in the history of the major leagues was Matt Stairs, an infielder with the Senators in 1991 and the Eastern League's MVP that season.

In 19 seasons in the majors, the onetime hockey player from New Brunswick, Canada, played with 13 teams in the majors – 12 franchises when you consider the Montreal Expos eventually became the Washington Nationals.

His travels before and after leaving City Island included 10 other minor league whistle stops and a 1993 stay with the Chunichi Dragons of the Japan's Central League. Stairs' career began at Class A Jamestown, N.Y., in 1989 and continued at Class A Rockford (1989), Class A West Palm Beach (1989-1990), Class AA Jacksonville (1990), Class AA Harrisburg (1991), Class AAA Indianapolis (1992), Montreal Expos (1992-1993), Class AAA Ottawa (1993), Japan's Chunichi Dragons (1993), Class AA New Britain (1994), Class AAA Pawtucket (1995), Boston Red Sox (1995), Class AAA Edmonton (1996), Oakland Athletics (1996-2000),

Chicago Cubs (2001), Milwaukee Brewers (2002), Class AAA Nashville (2003), Pittsburgh Pirates (2003), Kansas City Royals (2004-2006), Texas Rangers (2006), Detroit Tigers (2006), Toronto Blue Jays (2007-2008), Philadelphia Phillies (2008-2009), San Diego Padres (2010) and Washington Nationals (2011).

Joining Stairs atop the Rand McNally All-Stars with 13 teams in the majors was pitcher Octavio Dotel (1999-2012). Next at 12 each were pitchers Ron Villone (1995-2009) and Mike Morgan (1978-2002).

Other former Senator players near the top of the list include pitcher Miguel Batista (Harrisburg Classes of 1993-1994), 11 teams from 1992 to 2012; shortstop Orlando Cabrera (1997), nine teams, 1997-2011; outfielder Milton Bradley (1999), eight teams, 2000-2011; and catcher Charlie O'Brien (2000), eight teams, 1985-2000.

In a Pinch

For years, pundits said Matt Stairs could hit only a fastball and that he was all-or-nothing as a pinch-hitter. Yeah, OK, so what's the point?

Stairs, the onetime Senator who was named the Eastern League's MVP in 1991 even though he had no natural position on the field, finished his 19-year-career in the majors in 2011 with 105 pinch hits.

Twenty-three of those 105 pinch-hits were home runs, the most ever by a pinch-hitter.

Stairs' best season for homers off the bench came with Philadelphia in 2009, when he hit five during the regular season to tie the Phillies' franchise record set by Gene Freese in 1959. He had three for the Phillies in 2008, including one in Los Angeles off hard-throwing Jonathan Broxton to beat the Dodgers in Game 4 of the 2008 National League Championship Series.

"My whole career, even back in the early days, my approach was try to hit the ball out of the ballpark. And it's something I enjoy doing," said the 5-foot-9, left handed-hitting Stairs, whose weight was listed conservatively at 200 pounds during his final seasons.

"In batting practice, I try to hit every ball out of the ballpark. I'm not going to lie, it's fun. I try to hit home runs and that's it. I'm not going to hit a single and steal second base, so I think the biggest thing is to get up there, swing hard and elevate."

Years before landing in jail, Ugueth Urbina was among baseball's best prospects

The Rise and Fall of an All-Star

Few on the Senators' outstanding pitching staffs in 1993 and '94 threw a baseball better than Ugueth Urbina, and absolutely no one came close to matching his stare.

Stare downs by pitchers have always been part of the game. Batters once thought Hall of Famer Bob Gibson was staring them down, only to find out years later the reason he peered toward the plate was because he couldn't always see the signs from catcher Tim McCarver. Randy Johnson and Roger Clemens both cultivated pseudo-menacing stares, as well.

Ugueth Urbina – better known to teammates as "Oogie" – could stare down anybody. Showmanship, though, had little to do with his perpetual scowl. That scowl was understandable, considering his life growing up in Venezuela.

Urbina was only 19 years old when he arrived on City Island midway through the 1993 season.

> *"They say that it was me, so they can get money, you understand? These are people that live simply ... so by them saying it was me, they could somehow gain and take money from all of this."*
>
> *Ugueth Urbina*

He already was considered one of Montreal's top pitching prospects and helped the Senators win 100 games and the Eastern League title that season.

He returned to Harrisburg to start 1994, but left after only a few weeks when his father was killed during a robbery at the family home in Caracas,

UGUETH URBINA

Venezuela. A decade later, Urbina's mother was kidnapped, and eventually freed, in Venezuela. The ransom demand reportedly was $6 million – nearly one-fourth of what Urbina earned during his career.

Headlines of firing guns and barroom scuffles attached themselves to Urbina during his 11 seasons in the majors from 1995 to 2005. He was done in the game before his 32nd birthday, despite amassing 237 career saves for six teams, making two All-Star appearances and earning a World Series ring with the 2003 Florida Marlins. Who knows how much more he might have accomplished if not for his troubled background?

The tragic bookend to Urbina's successful start in baseball was the 14-year prison sentence he received in 2007 for attacking five workers on his Venezuelan ranch with a machete and gasoline. He claimed the workers were trying to extort money from him.

"They say that it was me, so they can get money, you understand?" Urbina told ESPN after his arrest. "These are people that live simply ... so by them saying it was me, they could somehow gain and take money from all of this."

Dear Diary

Baseball and the Internet were just getting together in the mid-1990s, when relief pitcher Shayne Bennett was approached by one of the myriad dot-coms to write a diary for his upcoming season with the 1997 Senators.

The right-hander from Australia was a good choice, given his candidness, offbeat sense of humor and his don't-give-a-Dingo's-derriere attitude of what others thought of him.

"Read me, critique me," Bennett cheerfully invited the media in spring training. "Let me know what you think."

Among Bennett's early observations for his *Roo Report*:

--- Manager Rick Sofield gave an introductory "lecture, not speech" when the Senators arrived on City Island from West Palm Beach, Florida.

--- Carry lots of money, because Sofield's fine system seemed pricey, especially for those living on a modest Class AA income.

--- And, in what no doubt gained points with his fiery manager, Bennett predicted there would be "major clashes with (Sofield's) personality before the end of the season."

Sofield's reaction: He was not pleased with his budding writer.

Bennett's reaction to Sofield's reaction: He announced he no longer was speaking to the media.

"I can't believe you wrote about that," said an uncharacteristically terse Bennett. "You know, Sofield saw that shit."

Apparently, Bennett never realized his blog could be seen by anybody with access to the Internet, including his manager.

Bennett was not the only Senator to fill cyberspace.

Third baseman Andy Tracy was an on-line contributor in 2000. So was infielder Jamey Carroll, who that year chronicled his daily pursuit of meeting Garth Brooks during the country singer's spring training "tryout" with the New York Mets.

Web surfers also had a chance to get to know Senators relief pitcher Brandon Agamennone with an on-line, Q&A session in which Agamennone revealed that if he could not play baseball then his chosen career would have been "freelance assassin."

"I don't have many other options," he said. "It's a lot of money for – what? – a couple of weeks of work."

Fashion Statements That Catch On

Hard to find a catcher today who does not wear one of those cage-style masks first made popular by hockey goalies.

The style was first introduced to the major leagues in 1997; two years later, Chris Snusz became the first Harrisburg catcher to wear the mask on the island during a 6-5 victory over Reading on July 21, 1999.

Ironically, the next Harrisburg catcher to wear the trendy cage was the same catcher who first wore it in the majors. Three years after making his fashion statement with the Toronto Blue Jays, Charlie O'Brien joined the Senators for five games early in the 2000 season. By then 40 years old and nearing the end of his career, O'Brien returned to the majors after his brief time in Harrisburg and played nine more games for the Expos that season.

He retired after 15 seasons in the majors with one World Series ring, $5 million in career earnings and the distinction of helping catchers in the 21st century protect their faces.

The Most Valuable

All six Eastern League MVPs in the Senators' modern era played during an 11-season span that reflected the greatest run in franchise history. From 1989-99, the Senators went to the EL finals nine times, won five titles and reached three other finals. Here is how the six fared in their MVP seasons:

1989, Wes Chamberlain, right fielder
Batted .306 with 21 homers and *87 RBIs

1991: Matt Stairs, infielder
*.333-13-78

1993: Cliff Floyd, first baseman
.329-*26-*101

1994: Mark Grudzielanek, shortstop
.322-11-66

1996: Vladimir Guerrero, right fielder
*.360-19-78

1999: Andy Tracy, first baseman
.274-37-*128

* -- League leader

WES CHAMBERLAIN

Bobbing for Bucks

By 2001, the popularity of bobblehead doll giveaways at ballparks seemingly had reached its zenith.

Really, just how many bobbleheads could one fan collect? Besides, the bobbles began to look alike. Same height. Same pose. Same facial structure. Scott Rolen's bobblehead in Reading looked just like Cal Ripken's bobblehead in Baltimore.

Then the Philadelphia Phillies tweaked the traditional bobblehead when they gave away one of their beloved Phanatic mascot with an oversized belly that bobbled. Just like that bobbles were cool again.

Of course, any good promotional idea by one baseball team is quickly stolen by others.

Enter the Class AAA Charlotte Knights, who in the spring of 2002 gave away 1,500 bobbles of Tommy John, their one-time broadcaster who that season was Harrisburg's pitching coach.

The upgrade the Knights made was to have the figurine's left arm bobble – a tribute to the left-hander who in 1974 underwent a then-revolutionary elbow operation that became the best-known surgery in sports history.

Tommy John Bobble, complete with scar

In a nice touch, the Knights also made sure the manufacturer added a surgical scar to every bobble arm.

"The last thing we did was add the scar on the elbow," said Knights spokesperson Shannon Motley. "It was absolutely too funny."

Funny to everyone but Tommy John.

John, a 288-game winner in 26 seasons in the majors, was miffed. First, he had a poor relationship with the Charlotte-based orthopedic surgeons who were sponsoring the giveaway. Second, and perhaps more important to him, John did not get a cut of the proceeds. To this day, John grumbles that he deserves a royalty check every time someone uses the term "Tommy John surgery."

When the bobbles began sprouting up on eBay – with one seller pulling in $314.96 for four bobbles – John announced he would not autograph any sent to him by fans.

"I'm going to come out with my own bobble," John said one afternoon while stewing on City Island. "I'm going to make 1,000 and those are going to be the official ones. I'll number each one – 1 to 1,000 – and they'll be the only ones I'll sign."

And the price?

"Whatever they go for on eBay," he said.

Thanks for Stopping Over

For the first 18 seasons after the Senators returned to City Island in 1987, their major league affiliates – Pittsburgh and Montreal – were hesitant to send injured players to Harrisburg for rehab assignments.

With the exception of pitcher Dorn Taylor, the Pirates stayed healthy enough from 1987 through 1990 to keep their broken players in Pittsburgh or send them to Class AAA Buffalo, where the playing, training and rehab facilities were superior to those found at the time on the island.

From 1991 through the end of their existence in 2004, the Expos sent only a few players – most notably center fielder Rondell White and infielder Wil Cordero – to the island for rehab work. Not that the Expos were totally healthy during those 14 seasons; they simply opted not to pay for airfare to Harrisburg when they could put their injured players in a car and dispatch them to Class AAA Ottawa.

Since the Expos moved to Washington in 2005, though, City Island has been a regular post-op ward for their walking wounded. Among the major leaguers to join the Senators for rehab assignments were onetime All-Star infielders Jose Vidro and Dmitri Young and – just in 2011 – pitchers Chien-Ming Wang and Stephen Strasburg, as well as future Hall of Fame catcher Ivan Rodriguez.

Chemistry Experiments Gone Bad

The Senators were not exempt from the finger-pointing in baseball's steroid era.

Using the term "steroid era" was a euphemism, since baseball players had been putting all kinds of questionable pharmaceuticals into their bodies for at least a 20-year span – from Jose Canseco's indulgences in the late 1980s to the dog-and-pony show that was the 2007 Mitchell Report, which was supposed to bring an end to such shenanigans.

Along with anabolic steroids, players used amphetamines, human growth hormone and, of course, those mysterious but magical B12 shots certain teammates later claimed they gave others in the butt.

Longtime first baseman Rafael Palmeiro defiantly pointed his finger at Congress in March 2005 and declared, "I have never used steroids. Period." Less than five months later, he was suspended for testing positive for taking steroids. Oops.

So no one was surprised two years later when Palmeiro and 85 others were named by former Senator Majority Leader George Mitchell as players who used performance-enhancing drugs.

Mitchell's list included four former Senators – infielders F.P. Santangelo (1991) and Mike Lansing (1992); catcher Tim Laker (1991-1992) and outfielder Rondell White (1992-1993, 1996). Mitchell said the four were customers of former New York Mets batboy-turned-muscleman-turned-dealer Kirk Radomski, and they had given Radomski more than $21,000 for anabolic steroids and/or HGH during their careers.

Never mind that during most of these players' careers, Major League Baseball never seriously addressed the abuse of steroids and HGH. That changed after the Mitchell report came out in December 2007 – two months after White, the last of the Harrisburg quartet still playing, retired after 15 seasons in the majors.

Previous to the findings of the Mitchell Report, two other former Senators – outfielder Terrmel Sledge (2001-2002) and relief pitcher Guillermo Mota (1998) – were punished for using banned substances.

In the winter of 2004, Sledge received a two-year ban from international competition for testing positive for trace amounts of a steroid

"I have no one to blame but myself."
Guillermo Mota

related to androstenedione, the performance-enhancing drug made infamous by Mark McGwire. While andro at the time was still legal to use in Major League Baseball, the drug had already been outlawed by the International Olympic Committee and the United States Anti-Doping Agency, which prohibited Sledge from playing in the 2004 Olympics.

"I was real surprised to get that call," Sledge said. "The USA trials are a precise test. There are no excuses on my part. I shouldn't have had anything in my system."

Sledge did just fine for himself, though. He spent the 2004 season playing nearly every day in the majors for Montreal and was doing the same again in 2005 for Washington before a hamstring injury sidelined him for the rest of the season. He began the 2012 season playing in Japan, his fifth year there.

Mota – then a New York Met – served a 50-game suspension to start the 2007 season after testing positive for a performance-enhancing drug, although exactly which drug was not announced.

"I have no one to blame but myself," Mota said. "I used extremely poor judgment."

While still in the minor leagues, five other Senators were suspended for their parts in using or distributing illegal pharmaceuticals – infielders Ramon Castro and Josh Labandeira in 2005, and outfielder Edgardo Baez and infielder Ofilio Castro in 2009. Those cases involved amphetamines.

Ofilio Castro and Baez each received a 50-game suspension, while Ramon Castro was banned a record 105 games for intent to deliver. Labandeira was suspended 15 games for having his name on the package of amphetamines that Castro sent to the Expos' Class AAA affiliate in New Orleans.

"I got caught in the middle," Labandeira said. "Some guys know the tests are random, so they'll roll the dice. They know the payoff is a lot bigger than the risk, so they do it."

And some get caught, as did longtime Senators relief pitcher Zechry Zinicola, who was suspended for the first 50 games of the 2012 season after testing positive for using synthetic marijuana.

At the Height of the Matter

In the waning days of spring training 2004, the Expos plucked starting pitcher Chris Young and infielder-turned-catcher Josh McKinley off Harrisburg's roster and shipped them to the Texas Rangers for journeyman catcher Einar Diaz and minor league pitcher Justin Echols.

At the time, some of Montreal's top talent evaluators believed the Princeton-educated Young wasn't tough enough to pitch in the majors. They also were not thrilled the right-hander's best fastball topped out in the high 80s.

As with most of his other moves, the trade of Young to the Rangers was destined to be another disaster for Montreal general manager Omar Minaya. With Texas, Young emerged as a front-line starter in the majors before becoming an All-Star in 2007 with San Diego.

TALLEST PITCHERS SINCE 1987
6-foot-10: Chris Young, pitcher (2003)
6-8: Chris Johnson, pitcher (1991-1993)
6-8: Derrick DePriest, pitcher (2000)
6-8: Jesse Estrada, pitcher (2009)

TALLEST POSITION PLAYERS
6-7: Desi Wilson, first baseman (2002)
6-7: Cristian Guerrero, outfielder (2005-2007)
6-6: Val Pascucci, outfielder (2001-2001)

SHORTEST PLAYERS SINCE 1987
5-6: Rafael Belliard, shortstop (1987)
5-6: Onix Concepcion, shortstop (1987)
5-6: Richie Lewis, pitcher (1991)
5-7: Todd Mayo, outfielder (1991-1992)
5-7: Josh Labandeira (2003-2005)
5-8: Albert Molina, shortstop (1988)
5-8: Damon Pollard, pitcher (1994-1995)
5-8: Jimmy Serrano, pitcher (2000)
5-8: Derek Urquhart, outfielder (2003)
5-8: Clark Parker, infielder (2005)
5-8: Charlie Fermaint, outfielder (2009)
5-8: Archie Gilbert, outfielder (2011)

Alas, the trade turned out to be a missed photo opportunity on City Island, where Young was to begin the 2004 season. Just imagine the between-pitch conferences on the mound with hyperactive shortstop Josh Labandeira, all 5-foot-7 of him, talking directly into the belly button of the 6-foot-10 Young.

> *"I asked the players what he would want.*
> *They all said that he would love to coach."*
>
> Senators manager Doug Sisson

When Flowers Just Won't Do

By the 2000 season Art Mattingly had spent more than four years schlepping the Senators from here to there and back again with nary a complaint. And he never forgot a player's birthday, showing up for the game whether at home or on the road with a cake in hand.

He was more uncle and confidant than driver to the players, which was why manager Doug Sisson wanted to reward the team's venerable bus driver for his 69th birthday.

ART MATTINGLY

Candy was out since Mattingly already kept a never-ending stash of sweets on his bus.

An exotic sports car would have been nice, but Sisson and his players hardly could afford that on their Besides, Mattingly already owned a Jaguar.

So, Sisson went with something truly unique for Mattingly's birthday on Aug. 7: He made him the Senators' first base coach for an inning.

"I didn't think we could have pooled enough money together to buy him something," Sisson said, "so I asked the players what he would want. They all said that he would love to coach."

The gift turned into an annual tradition as the eight managers who followed Sisson to City Island through the 2011 season continued to give Mattingly the same gift for his birthday.

Complete with uniform. No. 8, thank you.

Even after the Senators switched bus companies in 2010, Mattingly still made his annual appearance in the first base coach's box.

As for errant foul balls coming his way while coaching first base, Mattingly said, "Don't worry ... I can jump."

Clubhouse Confidential

During his eight seasons as the Senators' bat boy from 2002 through 2009, Jeremy Fagelman endured a lot of childish humor in the clubhouse.

He was, after all, dealing with ballplayers.

Fagelman, though, was not your stereotypical gosh-gee-caught-up-in-the-moment kind of bat boy like the fictional Bobby Savoy in "The Natural."

During his time picking up bats, passing out towels and running errands, Fagelman was working on a 4.0 grade-point average at Red Land High School. He eventually graduated cum laude with a 3.31 GPA from Gettysburg College in 2009.

"I saw bat boys when I was 8 years old and told my parents that is what I wanted to do when I got older," said Fagelman, who became the Senators' bat boy when he was 15.

As for some of the weird and wacky moments that greeted him on the island, Fagelman was:

--- Initiated on his first day on the job by being told to "get the keys to the batter's box."

--- The recipient of a big brother moment in 2002, when the players pooled their money to treat for Fagelman's postgame date. "They also gave me a condom to ensure that I would be smart on my first official baseball date," Fagelman said. "I ended up getting stood up."

--- Asked by a mother for a towel to keep her teenage daughter's thong-covered backside from roasting on one of those hard, plastic seats in the old grandstand.

--- Covered around his forehead with a black stripe after a fun-loving player discretely placed eye black on the inside of Fagelman's batting helmet. Fagelman returned the favor by having the same player's walk-up song before his at-bats changed from his customary rap music to Shania Twain's "I Feel Like a Woman."

--- Asked by a player for the name and number of a young lady who at the time was dating someone else. That someone else was Fagelman.

The All-Name Team

More than 1,600 players have summered on City Island since 1890.

Naturally, there have been some great names to go with some of those players. Getting on this 25-man all-name roster required no special talent, just the possession of an outstanding nickname, surname or, in the case of Valentino Pascucci, a name that simply sounded so cool that you wanted to take it as your own.

FIRST BASEMAN: Piggy Ward (1893).

SECOND BASEMAN: Doggie Miller (1893)

THIRD BASEMAN: Izzy Alcantara (1995-1997).

SHORTSTOP: Henry Easterday (1892).

CATCHER: Bunny Hearn (1930).

OUTFIELDERS: Spottswood Poles (1906-1908); Fats Jenkins (1924-1927) and Milton Bradley (1999).

DESIGNATED HITTER: Valentino Pascucci (2001-2002).

VALENTINO PASCUCCI

OFF THE BENCH: Catcher Chris Snusz (1999); infielders Purdy Perdy (1901) and Heinie Heltzel (1935); and outfielders Steamer Flanagan (1913), Rap Dixon (1922-1927) and Bud Weiser (1925).

STARTING ROTATION: Prince Gaskell (1910), Rip Vowinkel (1912), Sugar Cain (1931), Buck Rogers (1935) and Seung Song (2002-2003).

BULLPEN: Lefty Hefflefinger (1929, 1931-1935), King Lehr (1931); Cookie Cuccurullo (1942), Mouse Adams (1988-1990) and Ugueth Urbina (1993-1994).

DISABLED LIST: Albert Coma, pitcher (1950)

MANAGER: Les Mann (1934).

PITCHING COACH: Spin Williams (1987-1988, 1990).

HITTING COACH: Frank Cacciatore (2002, 2005)

ATHLETIC TRAINER: Atsushi Torida (2009).

Easier Said Than Done

Free parking, free tickets, an unimpeded view of the game every day. What a great deal. All you have to do is talk into a microphone. Sounds easy enough, right?

Well, go trade jobs for a day with Chris Andree, the Senators' public address announcer since the mid-1990s, and see how that works out. Especially when someone like Atahaulpa Severino comes into pitch.

"Whenever you have a name with so many vowels or even consonants in it, and you're looking at it for the first time, there is a certain fear factor that kicks in," Andree said. "It can be intimidating."

Not that Andree's predecessors, Gregg Cook and Bob Morgan, had it any easier as they did their jobs in the cramped, heat-containing, spider-riddled, mayfly-infested tin can of a trailer disguised as the press box that sat atop old RiverSide Stadium. Among the favorite tongue twisters:

Ed Yacopino, outfielder, 1988-1990
Jim Czajkowski, pitcher, 1990
Archi Cianfrocco, first baseman, 1991
Carl Keliipuleole, pitcher, 1991
F.P. Santangelo, infielder, 1991
Ugueth Urbina, pitcher, 1993-1994
Mark Grudzielanek, shortstop, 1994
Chris Hmielewski, pitcher, 1996
Rob Lukachyk, first baseman, 1996-1997
Hiram Bocachica, infielder-outfielder, 1997-1998
Trace Coquillette, second baseman, 1997-1998
Fernando Seguignol, first baseman, 1998
Chris Snusz, catcher, 1999
Brandon Agamennone, pitcher, 1999-2002
Edward Quezada, pitcher, 1999-2000
Ron Chiavacci, pitcher, 2001-2003
Gerardo Casadiego, pitcher, 2002-2004
Josh Labandeira, shortstop, 2003-2005
Ignacio Puello, pitcher, 2003-2004
Enmanuel Ulloa, pitcher, 2003

CARL KELIIPULEOLE

HIRAM BOCACHICA

Derick Urquhart, outfielder, 2003
Vince Rooi, third baseman, 2004-2005
Matt Skrmetta, pitcher, 2004
Jacobo Sequea, pitcher, 2005
Zechry Zinicola, pitcher, 2006-2011
Jonathon Albaladejo, pitcher, 2007
John Suomi, catcher, 2007
Francisco Plasencia, pitcher, 2009
Atahaulpa Severino, pitcher, 2009
Joe Bisenius, pitcher, 2010

Through Thick and Thin

HEFTIEST PLAYERS ON THE ISLAND SINCE 1987:
>   255 pounds: Fernando Seguignol, first baseman, 1998
>   255: Valentino Pascucci, outfielder, 2001-2002
>   255: Chris Young, pitcher, 2003
>   255: Mata, Gustavo, pitcher, 2003-2004
>   255: Jonathan Albaladejo, pitcher, 2007
>   255: Luis Antonio Jimenez, first baseman, 2008
>   255: Jesse Estrada, pitcher, 2009
>   255: Erik Arnesen, pitcher, 2009-2011
>   250: Willie Smith, pitcher, 1989

LIGHTEST PLAYERS ON THE ISLAND SINCE 1987:
>   150 pounds: Pedro Perez, pitcher, 1988-1990
>   150: Greg Edge, shortstop, 1990
>   150: Jesus Campos, outfielder, 1996-1998
>   155: Ender Chavez, outfielder, 2006
>   156: Omar Munoz, infielder, 1991

The list does not include major league players sent to Harrisburg on an injury rehab assignment.

No former Senators pitcher has made more money in the majors than Javier Vazquez

Show Me the Money

If nothing else, City Island has been a good place to stop on the way to the ATM.

Here are the top 30 former Senators who became multi-millionaires after reaching the major leagues.

Career earnings do not reflect signing bonuses, such as the $7.5 million bonus then-college pitcher Stephen Strasburg received in 2009 as part of his $15.1 million deal with the Washington Nationals. The list also does not include major leaguers sent to Harrisburg on injury rehab assignments.

GUERRERO	WESTBROOK	BATISTA	WHITE
$125 MILLION	$62 MILLION	$47 MILLION	$35 MILLION

113

Player	Career earnings through 2012
* Vladimir Guerrero, outfielder-DH	$125.5 million (1996-2011)
* Javier Vazquez, pitcher	$ 99.4 million (1998-2011)
Moises Alou, outfielder	$ 86.0 million (1990-2008)
Jake Westbrook, pitcher	$ 62.2 million (2000-2012)
Cliff Lee, pitcher	$ 55.9 million (2002-2012)
Cliff Floyd, outfielder-first baseman	$ 53.1 million (1993-2009)
Orlando Cabrera, shortstop	$ 51.7 million (1997-2011)
Jose Vidro, infielder	$ 49.9 million (1997-2008)
Milton Bradley, outfielder	$ 48.2 million (2000-2011)
Miguel Batista, pitcher	$ 47.6 million (1992-2012)
Brandon Phillips, infielder	$ 39.2 million (2002-2012)
Kirk Rueter, pitcher	$ 38.3 million (1993-2005)
Mark Grudzielanek, infielder	$ 36.8 million (1995-2010)
Rondell White, outfielder	$ 35.1 million (1993-2007)
Ryan Zimmerman, third baseman	$ 31.5 million (2005-2012)
Rick Reed, pitcher	$ 29.5 million (1988-2003)
Mike Lansing, infielder	$ 25.8 million (1993-2001)
Ugueth Urbina, pitcher	$ 25.8 million (1995-2005)
Brian Schneider, catcher	$ 22.4 million (2000-2012)
Michael Barrett, catcher	$ 22.2 million (1998-2009)
Matt Stairs, outfielder	$ 19.6 million (1992-2011)
Jeff King, third baseman	$ 19.0 million (1989-1999)
Guillermo Mota, pitcher	$ 18.2 million (1999-2012)
Carlos Perez, pitcher	$ 17.5 million (1995-2000)
Chris Young, pitcher	$ 16.2 million (2004-2011)
Brad Wilkerson, outfielder	$ 15.2 million (2001-2008)
Jamey Carroll, infielder	$ 14.6 million (2002-2012)
Orlando Merced, first baseman-OF	$ 13.9 million (1990-2003)
Geoff Blum, infielder	$ 12.7 million (1999-2012)
Tony Armas Jr., pitcher	$ 12.3 million (1999-2008)

* Active through the 2011 season, but had not signed with a team as of Opening Day 2012.

The Washington Nationals made Bryce Harper a millionaire before his 18th birthday

Who Wants to be a Multi-Millionaire?

Since they returned to the island in 1987, the Senators have had three players who were selected with the first pick of baseball's amateur draft.

But that has been a mixed blessing for their major league affiliate.

JEFF KING

Since the draft began in 1965, there have been two certainties that come with having the first pick:

--- The major league affiliate played so poorly the year before in compiling the worst record in the game that it was rewarded for its incompetence with the first choice in the draft.

--- The major league affiliate is going to pay an exorbitant sum of money just to sign the top pick.

In 1986, the Pittsburgh Pirates drafted University of Arkansas third baseman Jeff King with the first overall pick, paid him a then-record $180,000 to sign and sent him to City Island in 1987.

Two other former No. 1s – pitcher Stephen Strasburg and outfielder Bryce Harper – arrived on the island in their first pro seasons. Strasburg, the top pick in 2009 from San Diego State, opened the 2010 season with the Senators. Bryce Harper, drafted No. 1 out of the College of Southern Nevada as a 17 year old in 2010, joined them during the 2011 season.

The Washington Nationals spent more than $20 million in bonuses and other guaranteed money to sign those two players. Strasburg received $15.1 million, while Harper signed a contract worth, if all the incentives are reached, $9.9 million.

5th Inning

"Like a Skunk at a Picnic"

Eleanor Engle has lived in the same house since the early 1950s, a handsome two-story brick abode with white shutters located right off the main drag in the Harrisburg suburb of Shiremanstown.

Outside, the grass is always trimmed precisely to the length of the other lawns in the neighborhood.

Inside, the home she shares with her husband George is immaculate. The furniture is clean, the rugs spotless. Family pictures adorn the walls, shelves and table tops.

Hidden inside the house – Engle is reluctant to say where – are pieces of her past, remnants of a brief moment in her life that she rarely has discussed with friends, associates or strangers, let alone nosey reporters.

Eleanor Engle had successfully fended off reporters for nearly a half-century. Writers from newspapers large and small and from wire services had called at some time or another since 1952. They all wanted a piece of Engle's time, a chance to take a peek into her past.

You want stories? she would ask. *Oh, I have stories; just not the ones you want.*

"You know, I used to be a model, and I still am," Engle said proudly as she touched her brunette hair, as dark in her mid-80s as it had been when she was in her 20s.

"And I do a lot of work for my church, too. We just had another big fundraiser."

All well and good, but not what the reporters wanted.

They were far more interested in her past – a long ago past when, on an early summer day in 1952, Eleanor Engle was, at least on paper, a professional baseball player for the Harrisburg Senators.

116

They wanted to know about the contract she had signed on June 22, 1952 – a standard player's contract that would be declared null and void

the next day by National Association president George Trautman, the de facto commissioner of the minor leagues.

For one day, though, Engle was the only woman with a contract to play baseball for a professional team, even if that team was the publicity-seeking, dying-at-the-gate Harrisburg Senators of 1952.

Only rarely and grudgingly would Engle talk about that day from 1952, her 15 minutes of fame that inspired decades of curiosity from strangers.

"Oh, I don't like to talk about what happened then," Engle said. "I just don't want to talk about it."

Eleanor Engle at her 1952 workout

Yet she still has her trophies from that moment.

Tucked away in her home is the 1952 uniform with "Senators" stitched on the front and the number 11 embroidered on the back. Also tucked away is her player's contract, the one voided by Trautman, as well as a congratulatory telegram from comedian and then part-time baseball owner Bob Hope, who wrote, "Good luck, Eleanor. I bought into the Cleveland Indians because I thought the team had a squaw on it."

Engle's desire for privacy has not stopped the telephone from ringing. It's been that way ever since that long-ago late June day.

"Makes me cringe every time," Engle said. "Reporters are always calling here, and I've always told them the same thing."

That would be *no, no, no, now go away*.

Then the exceedingly polite Eleanor Engle would say thanks for calling and hang up. Another interview avoided, another writer frustrated.

Engle successfully dodged reporters for nearly 50 years before briefly relenting as the golden anniversary of her fleeting moment in baseball history approached in 2002. Only then did she consent to do an interview with the Harrisburg *Patriot-News*, which in 1952 overhyped Engle's one-day career with the Senators, then forgot about her for the next half-century.

My initial request for an audience with Engle came in 2002 and was met with an immediate rejection. Then, after two days of telephone negotiations, more hesitancy and some more negotiations, the ever-elusive Eleanor gave her approval, albeit reluctantly. There would be, she said, time for a 15-minute interview and, oh, there was a caveat.

"Baseball," Engle firmly said. "I won't talk about baseball."

OK then. Fifteen minutes for an interview. For a reporter, 15 minutes can be an eternity.

Only in 2006 – after the Hall of Fame announced its plans to include her in its redesigned exhibit on women in baseball – did Engle agree to another interview request. This one also came from *The Patriot-News*. She specified that she would only talk with me, as she did in 2002. And, just like before, there were negotiations and conditions. Another 15 minutes for an interview, she said, and no questions on baseball.

As those 15 minutes morphed into 30, Engle suddenly stopped talking about her careers as a model and stenographer, her church fundraisers, her heart surgery and her grandson, with whom she still played catch in the backyard. A smile quickly emerged on Engle's face as she repositioned herself in her favorite sitting chair, the one closest to the front window in her living room.

For one question, Engle became the interviewer rather than the interviewee.

"So," she coyly asked, "what do you want to know about the baseball part of my life?"

Oh, let's see ... how about everything?

Back in the early 1950s, while Engle was playing softball, the Senators were fielding an awful team, the worst in the Class B Interstate League. Attendance was always an issue; Harrisburg was the worst draw in the eight-team league. Constantly hemorrhaging money, the Senators were a dying team in a dying league.

Weekday games began at 8 p.m. with Sunday starts at 2 p.m. A wooden sign, painted green with yellow letters, hung outside Island Park and implored fans to *"Boost the Senators ... Let's Go!"*

The Senators were going, all right.

Right out of business.

They were on their way to 94 losses in 140 games that summer, which remains the worst finish of any team on City Island since the place opened for baseball in 1890.

Signing Engle may not have resulted in any more victories, but her presence on the team surely would have helped fill plenty of seats.

So on June 22, 1952, with the Senators going absolutely nowhere in the standings, Eleanor Engle – all 5-foot-6 and 128 pounds of her – began taking grounders at shortstop as the Senators prepared for their game against Lancaster on the island later that day.

While the 26-year-old Engle received the all of the attention, the best player on the field for the Senators was onetime Negro League shortstop Elbert Isreal, who in his first season in the minors was on his way to leading the league in batting with a .318 average.

Despite a .301 average compiled over five seasons in the "organized" minors, the gifted Isreal was ignored by major league teams. Outside of Ebbets Field, the Polo Grounds and Cleveland, the game suffered from racial myopia. Teams such as the Philadelphia Phillies and Boston Red Sox remained years away from signing black players.

If teams in the majors were so short-sighted that they would not consider adding a player such as Isreal to their nearly all-white dominions, then imagine how flustered they were by the thought of a woman playing alongside the boys.

That, however, was no deterrent to Dr. Jay Smith, the Senators' president, and Howard Gordon, their general manager. They knew of Eleanor Engle's athletic prowess as a softball and basketball player. They also knew their home crowds averaged just 440 fans, barely enough to make any noise in the stands, let alone turn a profit at the box office.

On Saturday, June 21, they offered a contract to Engle, then a stenographer with the Public Utilities Commission.

On Sunday, the 22nd, with her contract signed, they invited Engle to work out with the team.

"She can hit the ball a lot better than some of the fellows on the club," Smith told the assembled media.

Engle never had a chance to hit, though. On Monday, she was told to go back to the steno pool. Trautman had voided Engle's contract. Just to make sure there was no ambiguity, Major League Baseball commissioner Ford Frick, who like Trautman could be seen as a joyless administrator,

Eleanor Engle poses with would-be teammates Ron Esrang, left, and Joe Tuminelli

quickly announced that no team in the majors or minors could sign a woman to play without facing "severe disciplinary action."

Even before Trautman and Frick ruled on Engle, Senators manager Buck Etchison had summarily rejected the idea of playing her. Even though he let her practice before the game against Lancaster, Etchison would not list Engle on his lineup card for that day's game. She would not play, he said. Period. End of discussion. Don't ask again.

Of course, someone asked again, leaving Etchison to briefly reconsider. Yes, he declared, Eleanor Engle could play for his team but only "when Hell freezes over."

The more open-minded – and profit-minded – Gordon said he was prepared to pay Engle a monthly salary of $250 to $300. To the doubting public, he insisted, "There is no truth that this was a gimmick or a gag. Actually, we were seeking to test an unwritten law for once and for all."

The Negro Leagues tried that, too. From their flickering existence in the late 1940s to their waning days of the early '50s, the Negro Leagues signed three women – Toni Stone, Mamie "Peanuts" Johnson and Connie

Morgan. While the majors had no problem poaching players from the Negro Leagues, starting with Jackie Robinson in 1946, they never recognized the Negro Leagues' brand of baseball as equivalent to their own. They never recognized the Negro Leagues as part of "organized ball," which is how the arrogant major league owners referred to their all-white teams and minor league affiliates.

The controversy over Engle's signing came nearly two years to the day the Class B Interstate League's color barrier had been broken when a 19-year-old center fielder from Alabama – a kid named Willie Mays – made his debut with the Trenton Giants on June 24, 1950.

While Mays ultimately became one of the game's greatest players, Engle became one of its footnotes.

And that was fine with her.

Engle simply wanted to be left alone. She never returned to City Island after her moment there in June 1952.

"The publicity to me back then was horrible," Engle said. "I used to have reporters waiting for me outside of church. I felt like I was being tailed all the time. I would get on the bus to go to town and they'd say, 'Why, she doesn't have baseball player legs!' I thought, 'How cruel.' "

Engle laughed at that memory, for that's all it is now – a memory. For years, though, she kept quiet about her past. If co-workers and friends did not already know of Eleanor Engle the ballplayer, then Eleanor Engle the stenographer was not about to tell them.

"I'm very proud of how I kept that a secret," she said.

Her secret, though, was slowly revealed, done in by technology.

Thanks to the Internet, autograph hounds found her address. Some sent her baseballs and bats to be signed. Most sent the one and only baseball card printed of Engle. It was produced in 1991 by Topps as part of its 337-card Archives edition for its 1953 set. More than 50 of the cards from the 1991 set featured major leaguers Topps left out of the original set. That Engle never played in a minor league game, let alone one in the majors, did not stop the baseball card giant from putting her picture on a card.

The Archives set became popular with collectors, who would send the cards to long-retired players to be signed. Engle autographed every card sent to her, carefully making sure each letter of her signature was legible.

"I was surprised when people started sending cards to me from all over the country," Engle said. "I had to go to the computer to find out how these people were finding out about me."

Not difficult, really. All she had to do was Google herself. As the 50th anniversary of her signing approached in 2002, the Internet search engine carried 174 references to her brief moment with the Senators.

By the time the Hall of Fame included her in an exhibit in 2006, Engle was listed on more than 700 sites accessed through Google. The total topped 2,000 in late April 2012 as the 86-year-old Engle neared the 60th anniversary of her brief moment with the Senators.

Some of the cards signed by Engle regularly show up on eBay, the behemoth online auction house, regularly listed for $14.95 and up.

While she was flattered to be pictured on a baseball card, Engle was less than pleased with the photo used by Topps, which showed her sitting alone at one end of the dugout with five other Senators seated at the other.

"Look at that photo," Engle said. "I'm like a skunk at a picnic. I just went in and sat down, and somebody took that picture. Just the way they captured it was comical."

The closest player to Engle in the photo was Ron Esrang, a 20-year-old second baseman from Mauch Chunk in Pennsylvania's coal-cracking Carbon County. Esrang was an everyday player on a team that was getting worse by the day. Engle's signing was merely a blip in a season in which the Senators would finish 46-94 and quietly fold.

Esrang's only memories of Engle – his teammate for a day; more specifically for a pregame workout – were positive. Nothing, he said, like seeing Engle as "a skunk at a picnic."

"She was a very nice person to get along with," Esrang said. "There were no problems with the guys. When we went on the road and one of us booted a ball, the fans would yell, 'Put Eleanor in there!' But she didn't travel with us."

Esrang never saw Engle again after that summer's day in 1952, although he tried contacting her in 2006 to congratulate her for her inclusion in the Hall of Fame's "Diamond Dreams" exhibit on women in the game.

Engle turned down an invitation from the Hall of Fame to attend the

After Senators manager Buck Etchison refused to play her, Eleanor Engle was forced to watch from the old Island Park press box with Patriot-News writer Saul Kohler

exhibit's opening, which included a photograph of her sitting in the field-level press box on City Island. From that vantage point, dressed in uniform, Engle watched her would-be teammates play without her.

"It's an integral part of the story, but the fact of the matter is Eleanor was good enough to play," said Julie Croteau, who in the late 1980s became the first woman to play college baseball.

"Eleanor Engle was good enough to at least be on the field," Croteau said, "and that's an accomplishment, especially in those days."

But those days to Engle are just days from long ago.

Fame, let alone the Hall of Fame, was of no interest to her, especially when she was invited to come to Cooperstown, New York, on a mid-May weekend for the exhibit's opening.

"Don't they know that it's Mother's Day weekend?" an incredulous Engle said then. "I wouldn't want to be away from my family on that day."

> *"I used to have reporters waiting for me outside of church. I felt like I was being tailed all the time. I would get on the bus to go to town and they'd say, 'Why, she doesn't have baseball player legs!' I thought, 'How cruel.' "*
>
> *Eleanor Engle*

Her husband, daughter and grandson have been the top priorities in Engle's life.

Baseball and the history she made on City Island?

Not a priority.

Not even close.

Baseball was never more important to Engle than her work with the state's Public Utilities Commission, and later with IBM. Or than her successful modeling ventures, her direction of the church choir and her role as a volunteer advocate for patients' rights. She found helping senior citizens navigate the mind-numbing paperwork of the Social Security system far more rewarding than retelling tales of scooping up ground balls on a dusty infield in 1952.

"What you can do for the church and the Lord, you get back double," she said. "The baseball part is history and I know I can't run away from it, but baseball is way down the list. ... I deal with what is. That's how I am."

She does on occasion, though, indulge herself in remembering that one moment at an old ballpark in the middle of the Susquehanna River.

"I like to tell people that Ford Frick threw me a curveball and I struck out," Eleanor Engle said with a smile. "But I don't regret that I didn't have the chance to play, because so many other wonderful things have happened to me."

Say That Guy Looks Familiar

While there have been more than 1,600 men – and almost a woman – to play on the island since 1890, some achieved fame unrelated to how they played baseball.

HIZZONER: He was a backup third baseman and outfielder for the Harrisburg Ponies during the 1890 and 1894 seasons. He batted .227 in 1890 with 15 hits in 66 at-bats for the first pro team to play on the island. But his underwhelming stay in the game did not keep George Hoverter from getting the best seats in the finest downtown eateries, because he later became Harrisburg's mayor.

FUNNY MAN: He was a slender right-handed pitcher, standing 5-foot-11 and weighing 142 pounds. He went 13-13 in 1915 as Harrisburg shared a franchise that season with Newark, New Jersey. He eventually reached the majors, going 8-4 in a season-plus with Washington before he and another right-hander were slowed by sore arms in 1920. The other right-hander was Walter Johnson, who ended up making a making a nice recovery to pitch seven more seasons on his way to the Hall of Fame. The onetime Harrisburg Senator with the other sore arm was Al Schacht, who lasted one more season in the majors before embarking on a second career as the game's first "Clown Prince of Baseball."

THE GOLDEN BOY: Three years before playing baseball on City Island, he was an international sensation for winning gold medals at the 1912 Olympics in Stockholm. He later was stripped of those medals after he was deemed to have been a professional competing against amateurs. Before the Olympics – so goes the legend – he would run 22 miles or so from his home at the Carlisle Indian School to the island for track meets. Jim Thorpe would return to the island in 1915, playing in the outfield and batting .303 in 96 games for Harrisburg. Five years later, he was among the first players in the American Professional Football Association, better known today as the National Football League.

PASSING FANCY: He batted .308 over three seasons as the Senators' second baseman in the mid-1920s and was a lifetime .294 hitter in 10 years in the minors. Although the Harrisburg native never reached the majors, the 5-foot-9, 167-pound Glenn Killinger was already known nationwide as an All-American college quarterback from Penn State. He was later inducted into the College Football Hall of Fame.

> *"I went through four years of the war, and came out whole, so I guess I am lucky."*
>
> Billy Cox

Baseball's Real Draft

Some big news in 1965 came on June 8, when the Kansas City Athletics made Arizona State University outfielder Rick Monday the first overall pick of a new world order that Major League Baseball called its amateur draft.

Twenty-five years earlier – on September 16, 1940 – a more significant draft was held. In this one, the United States held its first peacetime draft to select men who in 15 months would fight in World War II.

Two months after that selection process was implemented, baseball had its first player taken on November 25, 1940.

This player was neither a Greenberg, Feller, Williams nor any other future Hall of Famer who later enlisted and would be lauded for his selflessness.

The first ballplayer drafted was 26-year-old Bill Embick, a little-known, singles-hitting outfielder who in 1940 batted .222 in 103 games for the Senators.

Embick missed out on Harrisburg's magnificent 1941 season, when it rebounded from a 60-62 finish in 1940 to go 81-43 and win the Class B Interstate League championship behind a shortstop from Newport, Pa., named Billy Cox.

Cox, then 21, topped the Interstate League with a .363 batting average, which led to his 10-game audition with the Pittsburgh Pirates at the end of the 1941 season.

Cox spent the next four seasons in the Army, which briefly allowed him to play baseball for the 1301st Service Unit out of New Cumberland. Cox was allowed to join the Pirates for their 14-5 victory over the Senators in a May 1942 exhibition game on City Island. The Army then sent him overseas with the 814th Signal Corps to lay communications lines from North Africa to Germany.

"I lost a good part of my career, but I'm not kicking myself," Cox told *The Sporting News* in May 1946. "I went through four years of the war, and came out whole, so I guess I am lucky. ... I do want to make up for lost time, and get in all the baseball I can in the next 10 years."

Billy Cox during his final season in 1955

While Embick never returned to pro ball after the war ended in 1945, Cox spent the next 10 seasons in the majors with Pittsburgh, Brooklyn and Baltimore.

At least Embick and Cox returned; one of their teammates on the 1940 Senators – catcher Harry O'Neill – was not as fortunate.

O'Neill, who batted .238 in 16 games for the Senators after appearing in one game for the Philadelphia A's in 1939, was one of two major leaguers killed in World War II.

O'Neill was a three-sport athlete at Gettysburg College before joining the Senators. O'Neill was a first lieutenant with the 4th Marine Division when he was killed on March 6, 1945 on Iwo Jima. He was 27.

Less than 10 months earlier former Washington Senators outfielder Elmer Gedeon died when the B-26 bomber he was piloting was shot down over France on April 20, 1944.

The Making of a Clown

He had always been a bit of a goof, going back to his days at West Philadelphia High School in the late 1930s. There was something a little odd about Max Patkin. He was more mashugana than mensch. Except when he pitched and, for a while there, Patkin could really throw a baseball.

Patkin, who spent most of his life as the "Clown Prince of Baseball," started out as a real player with a real dream of pitching in the major leagues. Patkin was only 21 years old in 1941, when he went 10-8 for Wisconsin Rapids, the Class D team of the Chicago White Sox. Patkin returned in 1942, only to hurt his right arm covering home plate after a wild pitch. He had a few of those at Wisconsin Rapids; his 13 wild pitches led the league in 1941.

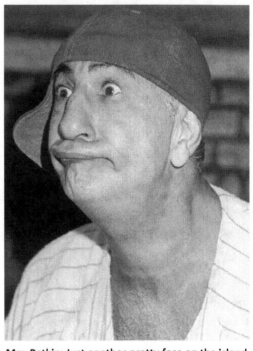

Patkin's arm recovered well enough for his next team – the U.S. Navy. For three years, the Navy wisely allowed Patkin to pitch for its service teams rather than have him do something re-

Max Patkin: Just another pretty face on the island

sponsible, like man a gun turret on one its valuable battleships.

Playing for service teams worked out well for some ballplayers who waited out the war. For every major leaguer who saw serious combat, such as Bob Feller, Warren Spahn and Eddie Waitkus, there were those such as Joe DiMaggio, Joe Gordon and Mike McCormick who bided their time playing ball until the war ended.

For a dead-armed minor leaguer like Max Patkin, pitching in the Navy started him toward a second – and more lasting – career as a clown.

Being the class clown was something Patkin knew well. He informally started his schtick by aping Joe DiMaggio's home run trot after the great one homered off Patkin during a service game in Hawaii. Unbeknownst to DiMaggio as he glided around the bases, Patkin was right behind him, stride for stride. Patkin's antics brought a roar of approval from everyone other than the stoic DiMaggio.

After the war, Patkin signed a minor league contract with the Cleveland Indians, who in 1946 sent him to Wilkes-Barre in the Eastern League. Patkin struggled in five games, and that was enough for the Indians to realize that Patkin was a far better clown than he was a pitcher.

And they told him so, suggesting that he give up playing for clowning. That was good advice, given that Al Schacht, the "Clown Prince of Baseball" was nearing his 54th birthday and the end of his second career in the game. Schacht also had been a pitcher and played for the Harrisburg Senators in 1915. Like Patkin, Schacht also had a sore arm, an injury that kept him off the mound but on the field as the game's resident comic.

With some prodding from Wilkes-Barre general manager Mike McNally, Patkin went to City Island in May 1946 for the Philadelphia Athletics' exhibition game against the Senators, the Cleveland Indians' Class B team. McNally offered up the 26-year-old Patkin to Les Bell, telling the Senators' manager that Patkin could help entertain the crowd in the event his team started getting whacked by the A's.

Bell did indeed need the help. So Patkin took the field with his still-raw, but promising, routine. He was a hit. Among those laughing the loudest was Philadelphia manager Connie Mack, who for decades was thought by many to have no sense of humor at all.

"For years and years," Patkin said, "Earle Mack, Connie's son, would pull me over to his father and say 'Dad, this is the guy who made you laugh in Harrisburg.' "

That gig led to another on the island for Patkin. This time he was paid $100 to perform during the Senators' exhibition game against their parent affiliate from Cleveland before a crowd of 3,333 on July 9, 1946.

"I go down there and do the same show," Patkin said. "It goes over terrific, except that I tear a ligament in my knee. I was coaching first and I threw my leg up in the air. Threw it up so high it ripped my knee."

No worries. A short time after the injury, Patkin received a call from Indians owner Bill Veeck with an offer to perform at Cleveland's

Max Patkin had a captive audience of Senators in 1988; OK, maybe not Jeff King (right)

Municipal Stadium. One campy bit led to another. Before long Veeck offered Patkin $650 a month to be a part-time coach and full-time clown for the Indians. Patkin received $1 to coach and $649 to clown.

By then, the 6-foot-2, 165-pound Patkin began turning his cap sideways, dancing around the field as if he had squirrels in his pants – being double-jointed had its advantages – and mocking batters, pitchers, umpires and anything else he happened to see.

"He looks like he was put together by somebody who forgot to read the instructions," Veeck said of Patkin, who surely was a long-necked goose in a previous life.

Over the next 50 years, from the time he made his comic debut on the island in 1946 until he retired in 1996, Patkin perfected the same routine with his baggy pants, dirt-encrusted jersey, oversized glove and a geyser bit that few could figure out.

Patkin returned to the island 42 years after getting his start there and was again embraced by the Senators. Well, most of them. Some, like third baseman Jeff King, avoided him.

Not that Patkin minded players like King who wore their game faces 24/7, because old Max was just glad to be in the ballpark and getting paid for, well, making a fool of himself.

"You see, I work under a great handicap," he said. "I have no talent."

Patkin was nearing 70 then. He was, though, just starting to find renewed interest in his act, thanks to the 1988 release of "Bull Durham." The film, in which Patkin played himself, allowed Max to continue to being Max. Same schtick, different venue, no pretenses.

"It's hard to be funny every night … I don't think Bob Hope is funny every night," Patkin said then. "Certain nights, I do go stale."

Some loved Patkin and his goofiness; others loathed him and an act that never changed. Rarely was there an in-between on how fans felt about him. His consecutive games streak around the majors and minors dwarfed that of Cal Ripken Jr. before ending at 47 years and 4,000-plus straight games. The travels took Patkin more than 7 million miles. From Harrisburg to Havana, Salt Lake to Savannah and Walla Walla to Wherever.

The streak was stopped by a sprained left ankle Patkin suffered when slipping in the dugout at Fenway Park on Aug. 18, 1993. The injury, coupled with an aging, aching body and the rise of kid-oriented furry mascots, slowed Patkin. He finally retired in 1996 and died three years later of a heart aneurysm. He was 79.

Say Hey, He's Here

Hoping to generate a crowd of more than family and friends for a game in late August 1950, the Senators promoted "Ladies Night" as part of three doubleheaders in three days against Trenton.

They would have been better off hyping Trenton's promising center fielder. Alas, the Senators' management knew little if anything about the 19-year-old rookie from Birmingham, Alabama. The kid? Willie Mays.

A crowd of just 1,168 – knowing just as little about Mays – ventured to Island Park on Aug. 27, 1950 to see two teams chasing the Wilmington Blue Rocks for the Class B Interstate League championship.

They saw Mays hit one of only four homers he would total in 81 games that summer for Trenton. Within a year, Mays reached the majors with the New York Giants and hit the first of his 660 career homers. When he retired after the 1973 World Series, Mays was arguably the greatest all-around player in history.

While Mays' career blossomed shortly after the few games he played on the island, history was not as kind to the Senators. After finishing 77-62 in 1950, the Senators fell to 55-84 in 1951 and 46-94 in 1952, after which the franchise folded. By the time pro baseball returned to Harrisburg in 1987, Mays had been in the Hall of Fame for eight years.

Talking a Good Game

As the Senators careened toward oblivion in the early 1950s, they had a couple of final, shining summers on the island in 1949 and 1950.

They had a former major league third baseman for a manager in Les Bell. They had a future major league all-star outfielder in Jim Lemon. They had a pair of a playoff teams.

They also had another future major leaguer, although no one could have predicted that at the time since this skinny kid with a flat-top haircut hardly was a prospect. Nonetheless, the kid not only ended up reaching the majors but also staying there longer than anyone else who ever wore a Senators uniform.

He did it by talking a good ballgame. Literally. Andy Musser, the wisp of a kid from just over the bridge in Lemoyne, went from being a bat boy for the Senators during their last great run to becoming a broadcaster with the Philadelphia Phillies for 26 seasons.

Musser actually worked his first Phillies game as an 18-year-old student, calling part of a Phillies' 1956 home game alongside the team's legendary announcers, Gene Kelly and By Saam.

Musser's first break with the Phillies came when he was selected as one of nine winners from a pool of 400 youngsters who entered a junior sportscaster contest.

Musser's second break came 20 years later, when he replaced Saam in the Phillies' booth and joined the team's next legendary broadcast team of Hall of Famers Harry Kalas and Richie Ashburn.

The trio stayed together until Ashburn's death in 1997.

"I couldn't have envisioned this," Musser said of parlaying that 1956 contest into a five-decade broadcasting career that included regional work with the NFL's Philadelphia Eagles, the NBA's 76ers and Villanova University, as well as national gigs covering the World Series, Super Bowl and the Masters golf tournament.

"I still pinch myself, because I've been so fortunate," Musser said before his death in January 2012. "The only one more fortunate than me was Richie Ashburn. He never worked a day in his life. He went from the playing field to the radio booth to the pine box."

Wonderboy

In the final moments of "The Natural" Robert Redford's character of Roy Hobbs fouls off a pitch and – gasp – breaks his prized "Wonderboy" bat.

Hobbs then tells batboy Bobby Savoy to "pick me out a winner" for a replacement. With another bat, Hobbs promptly crushes a three-run homer, shattering the light standards atop the stadium's right-field roof and winning the National League pennant for the New York Knights.

CHRIS POLLACK

At least that's the way the movie plays out. In real life, though, "Wonderboy" did not split in two.

Even before the movie was released in 1984, the bat – still in one piece – had already found a good home as Redford gave one of Hollywood's best known props to the son of longtime friend Bernie Pollack.

Pollack was the movie's costume designer and brother of Academy Award-winning director Sydney Pollack, who had worked with Redford on seven other films.

Seems Bernie's son used to hang around the set of "The Natural" during filming. Had the teenager been a few years older, he easily could have been cast as one of the ballplayers in the movie. As it was, the kid threw batting practice for Redford to help the actor prepare for his role as Hobbs.

In gratitude, Redford gave "Wonderboy" to the kid and playfully signed it, *To Chris, this bat is impervious to your pitching – Robert Redford/Roy Hobbs."*

As for the kid, Chris Pollack grew up to become a professional pitcher who would win 17 games for the Class AA Senators over the 1991 and '92 seasons.

But not even "Wonderboy" could help Pollack as the left-hander totaled only two singles and a double while striking out seven times in 26 trips to the plate during his two seasons on City Island.

M*A*S*H

Fifty-three years after Eleanor Engle nearly became the first woman to play for the Senators, Beth Jarrett became the team's first female athletic trainer.

Jarrett, believed to be the only female athletic trainer in pro baseball during the 2005 season, found herself working in a ridiculously cramped clubhouse at aging RiverSide Stadium.

Her work space was tucked away in a room adjacent to the showers and toilets, and included two well-worn treatment tables, an outdated whirlpool and a hand-me-down desk from the 1970s.

She barely had enough room to tape an ankle, let alone fit anyone over 6-foot-3 comfortably on one of those tables. Have we mentioned those midnight bus rides to such exotic Eastern League ports of call as Erie, Norwich and Trenton?

RiverSide's amenities, or lack thereof, were only a small obstacle for Jarrett, who simply was grateful for the opportunity to work in Class AA after toiling for eight seasons in the low minors and, even worse, independent ball.

Jarrett, who was 29 when she arrived on City Island, stayed with the Senators for four seasons before moving up to Class AAA Syracuse in 2009.

"At first, it bothered me that a female trainer was in the clubhouse," said onetime Senators shortstop Josh Labandeira, who first met Jarrett in 2002 at Class A Clinton before working with her again in 2005.

"You didn't feel like you could do your normal stuff," Labandeira said, "but after a couple of weeks, it was pretty cool. I thought if she could handle it, then I could handle it, too."

No big deal, Jarrett said.

To her, twisted ankles are not gender specific.

"My dad is an OB/GYN," Jarrett said with a shrug, "so to me this is not much of a difference."

Going, going, gone

Long before establishing himself as one of the major leagues' most durable relief pitchers, Guillermo Mota was a shortstop in the minors.

Mota was 6-foot-6 and 200 pounds, and he was – to be blunt – simply awful as a shortstop in the lower rungs of the New York Mets' farm system.

He committed 66 errors in 122 games during the 1995 season at Class A Capital City in Columbia, South Carolina. In 1996, the Mets moved him to St. Lucie in the Class A Florida State League, where the chuck-and-duck Mota had 38 errors in 81 games at shortstop and another six in 22 games at third base. While he showed sporadic power as a hitter, Mota never batted higher than .249 in four seasons in the Mets' system.

The Mets left Mota unprotected before baseball's winter meetings in 1996. To the surprise of some in the game, Mota was quickly taken by the Montreal Expos in the minor league portion of the Rule V draft.

The Expos saw something else in Mota – a pitcher.

The conversion of Mota from shortstop to pitcher began in 1997 with 23 starts for Cape Fear

GUILLERMO MOTA

in the same Class A South Atlantic League where just two years earlier his throws from shortstop had terrified fans sitting near first base.

After developing his pitches as a starter, Mota moved to the bullpen in 1998. He began that season at Jupiter of the Class A Florida State League. He finished the summer as the Eastern League's playoff MVP, helping lead the Senators to their third straight championship.

Nine months later, Mota was in the majors, where he became one of the rare players in big league history to homer in his first at-bat.

His moment came on June 9, 1999, during the Expos' 13-1 interleague rout of the Boston Red Sox. Pitching in relief of onetime Senator Mike Thurman, Mota was allowed to bat with two outs, two on and an 8-1 lead in the eighth inning. He promptly drove Mark Guthrie's 1-1 pitch over the left-field wall for a three-run homer.

"I swung and look what happened," Mota said after the game. "I wasn't looking to hit a homer. Maybe I'll play shortstop tomorrow."

Um, no.

Of the 110 players to homer in their first at-bat in the majors entering the 2012 season, five others had ties to the Senators.

Brad Fullmer (Classes of 1996-97) homered as a pinch-hitter for Montreal on his first at-bat on Sept. 2, 1997, when he slammed a 2-0 pitch from two-time Cy Young Award winner Bret Saberhagen over the center-field wall at Olympic Stadium in another interleague victory over Boston 6-5.

Pitcher Tom Milone (Class of 2010) found his way into history on Sept. 3, 2011 at Nationals Park in Washington, D.C. Batting with one out and two on in the bottom of the second, Milone hammered Dillon Gee's first pitch to him down the right-field line for a three-run homer and a 5-0 lead. Alas for Milone, one of the Eastern League's premier pitchers in 2010, he lasted only four innings and was not eligible to pick up the win in the Nationals' 8-7 victory. Milone's chances of hitting another homer were diminished on Dec. 23, 2011, when the Nationals traded him to Oakland in the designated hitter-happy American League.

Three others – Dave Machemer, Esteban Yan and Elijah Dukes – entered the record books before joining the Senators or, in Yan's case, before getting the chance to play for them.

Machemer, the Senators' manager in 2003-04, became the first player to homer while leading off the top of the first inning in his major league debut, tagging Geoff Zahn on June 21, 1978 in Minnesota.

Yan, a pitcher, homered for Tampa Bay on the first pitch to him from the Mets' Bobby Jones in the second inning of the Rays' interleague game against the Mets on June 4, 2000 at Shea Stadium. Unlike Mota, Yan never pitched for the Senators, although he made the team out of training camp in 1996. Before Yan had a chance to play for the Senators he was pulled off the team bus 10 minutes prior to departing for Opening Night in Trenton and was told the Expos had just sold him to Baltimore.

Dukes, an enormously talented but equally troubled outfielder, spent two games with the Senators on an injury rehab assignment in 2009 – two years after making his debut for Tampa Bay on Opening Day 2007 and homering off Carl Pavano to center field at Yankee Stadium.

All-Meal Team

FOOD PREPARERS
Jeff Cook (outfielder, 1987-1990)
Jason Baker (pitcher, 1998-1999)
INVOCATION
Derrick DePriest (pitcher, 2000)
APERITIF
Lefty Wineapple (pitcher, 1930)
ENTREES
Piggy Ward (first baseman, 1893)
Buck Freeman (first baseman, 1910)
Possum Poles (infielder, 1924)
Hamilton Fish (outfielder, 1926)
Rabbit Whitman (outfielder, 1933)
Bob Trout (outfielder, 1949)
Bruce Chick (outfielder, 1995)
Josh Karp (pitcher, 2002-2003, 2005)
SIDE DISH
Lance Rice (catcher, 1993-1994)
GARNISH
Jim Lemon (outfielder, 1949)
CONDIMENTS
Pepper Daniels (catcher, 1924)
Sugar Cain (pitcher, 1931)
Todd Mayo (outfielder, 1991-1992)
DESSERTS
Cookie Cuccurullo (pitcher, 1942)
Rick Sweet (manager, 1998-1999)
ADULT BEVERAGES
George Stroh (catcher, 1909-1910, 1913)
Bud Weiser (outfielder, 1925)
George Hennessy (pitcher, 1935)
RUDE CUSTOMER
Jason Belcher (catcher, 2004-2005)
HIDING FROM THE DEPARTMENT OF HEALTH
Mouse Adams (pitcher, 1988-1990)
BENEDICTION
Lord (second baseman, 1924 … no first name known, but do you really need a first name for the Lord?)

JEFF COOK

SUGAR CAIN

BUD WEISER

6th Inning

The Pride of Harrisburg

The newspaper story from 1993 had been cut out, glued to a piece of slate gray construction paper and taped to the wall of John Bricker's classroom in suburban Harrisburg.

Above the story, Bricker's wife, Sue, wrote four words.

Reach for your dreams.

The story stayed on that classroom wall for 13 years until Bricker retired in the spring of 2006 from the Central Dauphin School District in Lower Paxton Township.

Bricker had taught mathematics to hundreds of kids over his 35 years in the classroom. He believed the message from the story on his wall taught kids more about life than anything he could teach them about math.

Whenever one of his students complained, *"Mr. Bricker, I can't do this,"* Bricker would turn toward the yellowed-over-time newspaper clip and point to the picture of the man in the story.

"I would tell them, 'If you want to say you can't do something, you read this first and then tell me you can't,' " Bricker said. "I told my students don't ever say you can't do something because here is a guy who had every reason to say he couldn't, and he never did."

"He" was Curtis Pride, then a backup outfielder with the vaunted 1993 Senators.

Pride had been one of those borderline players who can be found filling out the roster on any minor league baseball team. Once a prospect based on his athleticism, his status faded during seven mostly mediocre seasons in the lower ends of the New York Mets' farm system.

Pride's eighth pro season started in Class AA Harrisburg. The Expos signed Pride as a minor league free agent to be a bench player for the Senators in 1993. What they ended up getting was a budding major leaguer.

The story that Bricker kept on his wall for all of those years was about the beginning of Pride's breakthrough season with the Senators and about how he never gave up on himself, even after the Mets dismissed his chances of succeeding.

Accompanying the story was a photograph of Pride standing on third base, talking with Harrisburg manager Jim Tracy during a game early in the season.

Not visible beneath the left flap of Pride's batting helmet was his hearing aid.

Without it, Pride was lost on the field.

With it, he was trying to become the major leagues' first deaf player since outfielder Dick Sipek appeared in 82 games for the Cincinnati Reds in 1945, the last year journeymen from the minors and military 4-Fs were used to fill out rosters. Sipek was one of those players, one-armed outfielder Pete Gray was another. Prior to Sipek, the majors had not seen a deaf player since William Hoy roamed the outfield from 1888 to 1902, and Luther Taylor, George Leitner and William Deegan pitched in the early years of the 20th century.

CURTIS PRIDE

Pride never knew how Bricker used his story as an inspiration for students who doubted their own abilities. Nor did he know how many people across the country he helped motivate – whether they were struggling students like those in Bricker's classroom, others who were deaf, or simply those fading prospects who, like Pride, were trying to keep alive their dreams of reaching the majors.

"I haven't let this stop me," Pride said, pointing at his hearing aid. "I want to show people that if I can do it, they can do it, too."

For a long time no one was sure exactly what Pride could do on a baseball field.

Carmen Fusco, then a rising scout with the Mets, first heard of Curtis Pride only a few days before the 1986 amateur draft.

The draft is a combination meat market and crapshoot in which major league teams restock the minors with high school graduates and college players they hope one day will help them win a World Series.

Many factors can keep those players from developing into major leaguers, let alone All-Stars or starters for championship teams.

Money often gets in the way, as do egos. Then there is that little thing called talent, which all players have in varying degrees. The smarts to succeed, though, often are in short supply.

In the spring of 1986, Fusco knew only that Pride was a high school shortstop from Silver Spring, Maryland.

"There were no other reports on him. Nothing," Fusco said. "I just heard that I should come see this kid play."

Just prior to the draft, Fusco arrived in Silver Spring with no preconceived notions and no expectations. What he found was a player who could run faster than anybody else on the field, and a left-handed batter who could hit a baseball harder and farther than anybody else.

Fusco also found a player who was 95 percent deaf.

"In the scouting business, you can justify anything," Fusco said. "I easily could have said this guy isn't going to make it because he's deaf. But this kid had one hell of a mental makeup. You add in physical abilities and it spells prospect."

Baseball, though, was not Pride's best sport. He was an All-American soccer player at Silver Spring's John F. Kennedy High School who gravitated toward baseball because, as he put it, "there was no future in playing soccer."

On Fusco's "strong recommendation," the Mets used their 10th-round pick in the 1986 amateur draft to select Pride. Only two of the Mets' first nine picks would reach the majors – pitcher Kip Gross and Eddie Zosky. Their careers are best remembered only by immediate family members.

Pride ended up playing all or parts of 11 seasons in the majors from 1993 through 2006, hitting .250 in 421 games with six teams. His 20 career homers and 29 stolen bases may not seem like much until you consider his background.

Pride never would have reached the majors without first turning around his career in the early spring of '93 on City Island. He stumbled through the Mets' system, spending four unspectacular summers in rookie-level, short-season Class A ball. He then spent the 1990 and '91 seasons in full-season Class A, but had only sporadic success at Columbia in the South Atlantic League and St. Lucie of the Florida State League.

Pride was going nowhere in 1992, when he batted .227 in 118 games for Class AA Binghamton while striking out 110 times in 388 at-bats.

Pride left the Mets after the season.

He also thought about leaving the game, but the thought of quitting was a fleeting one as the Expos quickly offered him a new start.

Not that the Expos had any grand plans for the 24-year-old Pride.

Pride and Tyrone Woods, another spare part, were supposed to be little more than complementary puzzle pieces, sitting on the bench and watching top prospects Cliff Floyd, Rondell White and Glenn Murray play in the outfield.

Short List, Long Odds

Deaf players in the major leagues since 1900:

William Hoy, outfielder, 1900-1902
Luther Taylor, pitcher, 1900-1908
George Leitner, pitcher, 1901-1902
William Deegan, pitcher, 1901
Dick Sipek, outfielder, 1945
Curtis Pride, outfielder, 1993-2006

Jim Tracy, the Senators' manager in 1993, already knew Pride was ridiculously fast, and that his time of 6.35 seconds in the 60-yard dash was the best of any player that spring in the Expos' minor league camp.

Tracy also knew of the secondary status the Expos had assigned to Pride on their loaded Class AA affiliate. Not that Tracy cared about that. In Pride, he saw a hitter who was challenged, and immediately went to work on breaking down and rebuilding Pride's swing.

"His numbers (with the Mets) really didn't tell you a whole lot," Tracy said, "but once I saw him for a few days in spring training with the way he ran, the way he played the outfield … that's when I started asking myself, 'Hey, how can this guy only hit .210? I'm going to figure out the answer to that.' That's the fun part of my job."

While Tracy was fixing the flaws in Pride's swing, nature was working to give Pride an unexpected opportunity for real playing time. While the Senators were finishing spring training in dust-swept Lantana, Florida, parts of City Island sat under water – the results of another rapid spring thaw in upstate New York that had traveled down the Susquehanna River before spilling onto the island.

For much of April 1993, RiverSide's outfield was damp, leaving Tracy to routinely call Montreal farm director Dan Duquette for guidance as to where Cliff Floyd, the organization's top prospect, should play.

Worried Floyd might get sucked into the mire that was becoming left field, Duquette's decision was clear. Since they had more money invested in one of Floyd's hamstrings than they had in Pride's entire body, the Expos decided to save the prospect and sacrifice the roster filler. Tracy was told to move Floyd to first base, where the ground was firm and dry, buy Pride a snorkel and send him out to left field.

Given the chance to expand his role beyond that of a pinch-hitter or occasional designated hitter, the 6-foot, 195-pound Pride began hitting line drives off the outfield walls, with some of the more majestic ones easily clearing the fences. He rapidly morphed into the sort of dangerous hitter he had never become with the Mets.

With Floyd playing at first base, left field became Pride's domain. Running down balls in the alley was never a problem; no gap existed between Pride and Rondell White, another top prospect whom the Expos considered the heir apparent to All-Star Marquis Grissom in center field.

Their method of communication was simple: If Pride called for the ball, White backed off. If White wanted the ball, he used hand signals to call off Pride. Not once did the two collide.

"You don't even think about it out there," White said. "I had seen him play before, so I knew there wouldn't be any problems. And, he worked hard at it."

Pride worked hard at everything. He absorbed Tracy's lessons and began the season hitting better than the uber-prospects surrounding him in the Senators' lineup. By the end of May, Pride was hitting .347 – trailing Canton-Akron's Manny Ramirez by just six points for the Eastern League's top batting average.

"When you have a guy who has some ability and who wants to work, there's no telling what you can do," Tracy said. "Makeup and work ethic, if you have some ability, are very important. That's something that separated Curtis Pride from a lot of guys."

Batting leadoff most of the time, Pride had 10 home runs in his first 43 games as a Senator, matching the career high he had established the year before in 118 games for the Binghamton Mets. "Curtis is as strong as a bull," said Binghamton pitching coach Randy Niemann. "He's always had the power; he just hasn't always made the contact."

Ergo, the stuff that often separates prospects from wannabes. By early in the 1993 season, Curtis Pride again was a prospect. He had finally

> *"I get great satisfaction in proving other people wrong."*
>
> *Curtis Pride*

become the type of player the Mets had hoped for, but never found, in seven seasons in their system.

"I'll tell you what," said Steve Swisher, the former All-Star catcher in the majors who managed Pride in Binghamton. "I've had guys who can hear out of both ears who don't have as much desire as Curtis Pride."

Pride's lack of development in the Mets' system, especially in his first four seasons, might have been traceable to certain off-field activities that make scouts nervous. Things like pursuing higher education and earning a degree.

When Pride signed with the Mets out of high school, he told them his seasons would start late and end early because he was committed to attending college at William & Mary. Pride told them he wanted to pursue a degree in finance, as well as play basketball at the Division I school.

This naturally flummoxed scouts and minor league instructors, nearly all of whom believed Pride needed to think less about finance and basketball and more about fastballs and breaking balls.

But before he even tried to convince the scouts he could play baseball professionally, Pride had to convince his parents, John and Sallie, that he could excel in the classroom.

As a child, he had refused to learn to sign language – a skill he did not pick up until becoming the baseball coach at Gallaudet University in 2009. Nearly 30 years earlier, when he was in seventh grade, Pride pleaded with his parents for permission to leave the special education classes he had been attending so he could join the mainstream student body.

"They said I'd be the only deaf person in the whole school," Pride said, "but they let me give it a try to see how well I could perform."

He did just fine, earning a 3.8 grade-point average in high school before posting a 3.0 GPA at William & Mary.

"That 3.0 is kind of embarrassing," Pride confessed. "I could have done better."

Really? How many college kids could earn a 3.0 GPA majoring in finance at William & Mary while also playing Division I basketball in the winter and pro baseball in the summer, and doing it all without the ability to hear?

"I've had a lot of people doubt my abilities because of my deafness," said Pride, whose mother contracted rubella during her pregnancy.

"I've been trying all of my life to show people I'm an educated person. I can speak well. I can read lips well. I can communicate with other people," Pride said. "I don't want people to treat me different because I'm deaf. I want to be treated the same way as other people."

In 1993, on a team filled with high draft choices, top prospects and strong personalities, the unassuming Pride was Harrisburg's best player at the start of the season. He batted .356 in only 50 games for the Senators with a career-high 15 homers before being promoted in early June to Class AAA Ottawa. In Harrisburg, Pride's on-base percentage was .404, his slugging percentage .672.

By the end of the season, the deaf kid from the D.C. suburbs found himself in the major leagues. His maturity enabled him to handle the sights of the majors, if not its sounds. His deafness quickly became a non-issue for the Expos.

"We worried about him, how to treat him," Expos manager Felipe Alou told Pat Jordan of *Men's Journal*. "But after three days, we forgot he couldn't hear. Hell, I know a lot of players who can hear and can't play this game for shit. Curt's just a normal player."

Pride's first at-bat in the majors on Sept. 14, 1993 – four days ahead of the debut of the more ballyhooed Cliff Floyd – ended with an unremarkable flyout in the ninth inning of the Expos' 12-9 victory at St. Louis' old Busch Stadium.

His second at-bat came three days later at Montreal's Olympic Stadium. Pinch-hitting in the seventh inning for reliever Chris Nabholz, Pride lined the first pitch he saw from the Phillies' Bobby Thigpen into left-center field for a two-run double.

The crowd of 45,757 – a remarkable feat itself in Montreal – gave Pride a standing ovation that he could not hear. Finally, third-base coach Jerry Manuel called time and motioned to Pride to acknowledge the crowd.

> *"I've had guys who can hear out of both ears who don't have as much as desire as Curtis Pride."*
>
> *Binghamton manager Steve Swisher*

"He was telling me to take off my helmet and at first I thought, 'What's wrong with my helmet, is it dirty or something?' " Pride told Ross Newhan of the *Los Angeles Times*.

"Then I realized what he was getting at."

As he was being showered in applause, Pride was "reliving my whole life – being born deaf, having to fight to get the chance to play T-ball, spending eight years in the minors, almost quitting one year, battling, sticking with my dream and finally making it."

Pride recognized the irony of the moment – deafening applause being given to a deaf man – and savored it.

"I could *feel* it," Pride said.

Two batters later, Pride scored on Marquis Grissom's single to left, tying the score at 7 in a game the Expos would win 8-7 in 12 innings.

Before the end of his first 18 days with the Expos, Pride achieved the unusual distinction by completing a cycle with his first four hits in the major leagues.

Each of them came with Pride pinch-hitting; three of the four hits drove in runs.

Pride followed his double off Thigpen with a ninth-inning RBI triple to right field off Atlanta's Greg McMichael on Sept. 23 in Montreal; a tie-breaking, two-run homer to right in the ninth against Florida's Richie Lewis on Sept. 30 at Joe Robbie Stadium; and a seventh-inning single to center off Pittsburgh's Dan Miceli on Oct. 1 in Montreal.

Within a year of his extraordinary turnaround that began on City Island, Pride became a cover story for national publications from *The Sporting News* to *Reader's Digest*. The picture on the *Reader's Digest* cover showed Pride tipping his helmet to the crowd, a sign not only of courtesy in mainstream society but also of recognition and applause in the deaf community.

Pride lasted long enough in the majors to earn more than $800,000 during his career.

He retired in 2008 after kicking around one more season in the Angels' minor league system and another in the independent Atlantic League, where at the age of 39 he still managed to hit eight homers and steal eight bases in nine attempts.

"I get great satisfaction in proving other people wrong," Pride said. "When people say, 'You can't do that,' I say, 'Oh, I can prove them wrong.' "

He did. All of them.

Off and running

The Senators' 1993 season-opening outfield of Rondell White, Glenn Murray and Cliff Floyd might have excelled in another sport – track.

Before the season, in what had become an annual event during spring training, the Montreal Expos lined up their minor leaguers for the 60-yard dash.

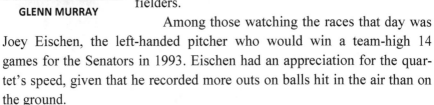

GLENN MURRAY

White was clocked at 6.4 seconds. Murray, still recovering from an offseason gunshot wound above his left knee, checked in at 6.37. Floyd, the wunderkind, was even better at 6.36.

Not a bad start to a relay team.

The anchor would have been Curtis Pride, who turned in a camp-best time of 6.35 before starting the '93 season as one of the Senators' backup outfielders.

Among those watching the races that day was Joey Eischen, the left-handed pitcher who would win a team-high 14 games for the Senators in 1993. Eischen had an appreciation for the quartet's speed, given that he recorded more outs on balls hit in the air than on the ground.

"If you put the ball in the air with this team," Eischen said, "it's either going to hit some leather or it's going over the fence."

Catching a Break

There was a certain irony that Jeff Banister's first hit in the major leagues in 1991 was an infield single – a ground ball that found a place between Atlanta third baseman Mark Lemke and shortstop Jeff Blauser. And on slick artificial turf, by a slow-footed catcher, no less.

Actually, the sight of Banister simply standing at first base after the hit was remarkable enough, although few if any in the crowd of 21,664 at Pittsburgh's Three Rivers Stadium on July 23, 1991 knew why. They would not have known of Banister's background unless they were well-versed in the subject of reading X-rays.

JEFF BANISTER

Long before he played on City Island from 1988 to 1990, Banister underwent seven surgeries on his cancerous left ankle while still in high school in Texas. Early on, doctors considered amputating the ankle. Then came a fractured neck suffered during a collision at home plate while he was playing junior college baseball in Texas.

That play left Banister with three fractured vertebrae.

"I thought I was dead," Banister told *The Patriot-News*. "I was dazed and everything seemed to go in slow motion. Even the voices around me sounded slurred."

The collision and the fractures left the 6-foot-2 Banister in traction and without feeling in his right leg. He was 10 weeks shy of his 20th birthday at the time. He spent two months in the hospital, leaving for home just before Christmas 1984. He lost more than 65 pounds during the ordeal, dropping from 205 to below 140.

"God makes us all better people in different ways," Banister said. "I don't think, 'Why me?' … I can't quit now. I have to know what I can accomplish."

Within 18 months of leaving the hospital, Banister was selected by the Pirates in the 25th round of the 1986 amateur draft.

Two years later, he was catching on City Island.

And within five years, he was making his major league debut, pinch-hitting for pitcher Doug Drabek to start the bottom of the seventh against the eventual National League champions from Atlanta. Facing onetime 19-game winner Dan Petry, Banister reached base after pulling Petry's 1-1 pitch into the hole between Lemke and Blauser.

Banister's batting average was a perfect 1.000 – and it stayed that way. Following their 12-3 rout of the Braves, the Pirates returned Banister to Class AAA Buffalo. He never played again in the majors.

Sleight of Hand

A cluster of fans from Harrisburg had made their annual pilgrimage to spring training along Florida's Atlantic Coast to watch players they thought they might see that summer on City Island.

Such journeys gave fans bragging rights over the ones still stuck in Pennsylvania's final weeks of winter.

On a mid-March day in 2003, as the fans chatted on the back fields of Vero Beach, the Senators were playing the Los Angeles Dodgers' Class AA team.

Given this was yet another mind-numbing minor league preseason game, the fans gave little notice to the thick-bodied lefty pitching in relief for Harrisburg.

None of them noticed as Chad Bentz threw a 90 mph-plus inside fastball to jam the first batter he faced. Nor did anyone pay attention as Bentz deftly maneuvered his glove as he delivered his next pitch, a nasty slider down and in.

"No one even notices, do they?" Brent Strom, the Montreal Expos' minor league pitching coordinator, asked after Bentz completed another scoreless inning.

What no one noticed, unless specifically looking at the delivery, was that Chad Bentz was missing most of his right hand, which had been gnarled since birth 22 years earlier in Juneau, Alaska.

Teammates who were unaware of Bentz's physical disability were given a quick introduction to their new teammate by Senators manager Dave Machemer early in spring training.

"The first day of camp, Mac calls me, 'Righty,' " Bentz said with a smile. "I thought, 'Oh, here we go.' "

Bentz had grown accustomed to nicknames – most of them unflatter-ing – since the Expos had selected him out of Long Beach State in the seventh round of the 2001 amateur draft. He answered to, among other things, "Sebastian," as in the crab from "The Little Mermaid," as well as "Nub."

Bentz's reaction: A shrug of the shoulders.

"I know people are just fooling around," said Bentz, who at 6-foot-2 and 215 pounds had an occasional nasty streak that makes you wonder why anybody other than a masochist would want to tease him.

"Even if they're making fun of me, it doesn't matter. ... I like proving people wrong. It gives me a boost."

The boost Bentz really needed – and received – came during his collegiate career at Long Beach State, which was where he first met Jim Abbott. Like Bentz, the left-handed Abbott had been born without full use of his right hand. Just as Abbott did during his remarkable 10-year career in the majors, Bentz cradled his glove in his truncated right hand before delivering a pitch, and then deftly slipped the glove onto the nub of a finger where his right hand should have been.

No one made fun of Bentz's performance in 2003. He saved 16 games for the Senators with a 2.55 earned-run average in 52 relief appearances. The effort was spectacular, but more importantly, his numbers were good enough to earn Bentz a spot on the Expos' Opening Day roster in 2004. Alas, he struggled that season with Montreal, compiling a 5.86 ERA in 36 appearances in the majors before going back to the minors.

"I feel that if I make my pitch where I want to make it, then I can get anybody out," Bentz said then, "and that includes Barry Bonds."

Bonds, though, was not among the 140 batters Bentz faced during his brief time in the majors, which ended after only four appearances for the Florida Marlins in 2005. There were, however, four future Hall of Famers who never touched Bentz. Jim Thome, Mike Piazza, Ken Griffey Jr. and Ichiro Suzuki were a combined 0-for-7 with four strikeouts against Bentz.

Not bad for someone who did not throw a baseball in earnest until 1989, when Bentz was 9 and Abbott – his long-distance inspiration – was beginning his career in the majors.

"When I was younger, I didn't even like baseball," Bentz said. "I'd go out there and people would say, 'What are you doing? Get off the field.' I thought, 'Screw this.' Then, I saw Abbott pitch and I thought, 'What the heck, if he's up there in the big leagues, I can at least try.' "

And Liberty For All

Baseball players curse. Now there's a revelation.

Swearing has been part of the game since, well, forever.

But the game on City Island changed in 2011.

For the first time in their modern era – perhaps for the first time since baseball was first played on the island in 1890 – the Senators had a couple of guys who just didn't curse. None of the players ostracized them for not dropping an F-bomb or two, because the couple of guys who didn't curse were manager Tony Beasley and pitching coach Randy Tomlin.

Past managers such as Mike Quade, Dave Jauss and even the laid-back Jim Tracy had been known to use colorful language. Some instructors – pitching coaches Bo McLaughlin and Dean Treanor quickly come to mind – didn't seem happy unless they were cursing.

Beasley and Tomlin? Heck, no. Cursing – even for effect in making a point to some biscuit head hitting .212 – just wasn't part of their DNA.

Beasley and Tomlin first met at Jerry Falwell's Liberty University, where they were teammates in 1988. When they were reunited on the island in 2011, the number of expletives coming out of the Senators' dugout decreased precipitously.

Beasley, Tomlin and the rest of the choir prospered that summer, as the Senators returned to the Eastern League playoffs for the first time since 2002. Their 80 victories were the most on the island since the 1997 Senators, led by manager – and Type A personality – Rick Sofield, won 86 games and their second straight EL championship.

Along the way, Beasley became the latest person to disprove Leo Durocher's decades-old bromide that "nice guys finish last."

"That's just a cliché," said Beasley, who through 2011 had never managed a professional team to a losing record.

"I just feel like you have to be who you are and stay true to yourself. Ultimately, when it's all said and done, I have to go to sleep and I have to be content with how I conducted myself."

In Beasley's case, that would be as a devout Christian, even though being a devout Christian has not always played well in a sport dominated by wonderfully gifted, supremely confident and, at times, equally narrow-minded Alpha males.

For generations, the most devout of players, coaches and managers kept their beliefs to themselves for fear of being labeled by management – or worse, teammates – as being too soft to play the game.

"He's a great man, a man of character," Tomlin said. "Tony's honest. He is who he is. He doesn't change the way he acts if he's in one place or another. He's the same guy I knew at Liberty."

At Liberty, Beasley was a middle infielder who was good enough to be selected by the Baltimore Orioles in the 19th round of the 1989 amateur draft, but not good enough to play above Class AAA. He was, though, smart enough to teach other players and help them onto a path to the majors.

Prior to working with the Nationals' Class AA prospects on the island, Beasley had managed five seasons in the Pittsburgh Pirates' system before reaching the major leagues in 2006 as the Nationals' third base coach. He had a similar role with the Pirates through the 2010 season before rejoining the Nationals in 2011 as their Class AA manager.

Never once in his time as a manager did Beasley turn over a postgame buffet table in frustration as a way to get his players' attention after a lackluster effort on the field. Hot dogs, coleslaw and nachos never felt as safe in the clubhouse as they did on Beasley's teams.

The tactics of intimidation that for generations worked for managers such as Leo Durocher are foreign concepts today for managers such as Beasley.

"I've never had to do that," Beasley said. "I can say whatever needs to be said to a player. Where someone else yells at a guy, I can sit down and look him in the eye and tell him, 'That's not good enough.' … That's much more of an attention-getter than someone who every day takes that other approach. Players nowadays will tune out that guy. The tough guy approach doesn't work."

Top of the 7th Inning

"Clemente is Alive in Harrisburg"

By 1996, Carmen Fusco had risen in the New York Mets' hierarchy. As a scout for general manager Joe McIlvaine, Fusco helped assess the talent and make the trades that turned the Mets from the National League's worst team in 1983 into the World Series winner three years later.

Like so many scouts, the 41-year-old Fusco looked older than he actually was, prematurely aged by too many hours in the sun watching prospects and too few hours sleeping, wondering if any of those prospects would ever turn into a front-line major leaguer.

He had seen and evaluated thousands of players, from amateurs competing on crab grass to major leaguers performing on the most pristine of greens. His job as a scout always had a simple objective: Separate the winners from the weeds.

On a pleasant, cloudless day in early May, he was preparing to see an already acclaimed winner: Vladimir Guerrero, the Harrisburg Senators' new right fielder and arguably the top prospect in the minor leagues.

"When you're looking at a player," Fusco said, "you always want to ask yourself, 'Can he be a starter on a first-division team?' If he can't start on a first-division team, then you don't want to waste your time with him. If he can only start on a second-division team, that's all you'll be as a team: Second division."

Fusco was not one to arrive early at the ballpark to watch batting practice, which was a ritual for the cadre of scouts who followed the minor leaguers from town to town. To him, batting practice in Harrisburg looked just like the batting practice in Reading, which looked just like BP in Binghamton, Hagerstown and Williamsport.

Fusco would change his routine on this day, arriving on City Island more than two hours before the game to watch batting practice. He took a seat in the grandstand behind home plate, 15 rows up from the backstop.

He had plenty of company.

Scouts from other teams also were there to see the same player, the one with gangly walk and a blonde-colored, Louisville Slugger C271-model bat in his right hand.

Guerrero was waiting for his turn to hit.

Fusco knew of Guerrero's reputation and what others gushingly had written about him in *Baseball America*, but Fusco had never seen the wide-bottomed but otherwise wiry-framed right fielder swing a bat.

Fusco watched first and listened second.

In batting practice, Harrisburg manager Pat Kelly served up straight, four-seam fastballs that were not all that fast. Guerrero, a refugee from the sugar fields of the Dominican Republic, obliged by rocketing those meatballs to all parts of City Island's outfield.

The scouts were taking notes but mostly gawking.

Every ball coming off Guerrero's bat looked good and sounded even better. The sound was not so much the usual, clichéd crack of the bat; more like the bark of a cannon. The noise reverberated through City Island's old metal grandstand.

"The ball just sounds different coming off his bat," Kelly said. "You can say that about very few players."

Some of the scouts quickly noticed that Guerrero did not wear batting gloves, which had become the norm throughout baseball. Of course, they noted that for their reports.

What they could not see was Guerrero unconsciously sticking out his tongue as Kelly prepared to delivery each pitch, seemingly knowing – and subsequently enjoying – what was coming his way.

In batting practice, Guerrero never missed crushing the ball, no matter where Kelly put his pitches. Guerrero would routinely lunge at – and hit – everything thrown from the ear flap of his batting helmet to the eyelets of his spikes.

No one dared suggest Guerrero do anything differently. Certainly not Kelly, whose career in the majors consisted of seven at-bats for the Toronto Blue Jays in 1980. And most definitely not Jeff Livesey, the Senators' hitting coach in 1996 whose career batting average in eight seasons in the minors was an underwhelming .217.

Vladimir Guerrero's batting practice routine: Stick out tongue, crush next pitch

A couple of hours after BP, Fusco took a seat down the first-base line, away from the pack of scouts. Fusco liked this vantage point, where he could better see the right-handed Guerrero take his swings. Like every other scout to see Guerrero that night, Fusco left the island impressed.

Very impressed.

"He's as complete of a player as I've even seen," Fusco said.

Fusco quickly graded out Guerrero as the best prospect he had seen at that point in 20 years of scouting, which was saying something considering the thousands of other prospects and suspects who had played before his eyes.

His previous No. 1 prospect was not bad, either.

"That," Fusco said, "was Barry Bonds."

Bonds had been one of baseball's premier players even before he was tied to using performance-enhancing drugs over the last third of a 22-year career that ended in 2007. He was born to privilege, the son of All-Star outfielder Bobby Bonds. His superior skills, though, often were overshadowed by churlish behavior that alienated teammates, media and fans.

In contrast, Guerrero's childhood was spent in the Dominican Republic, surrounded by poverty. He was part of a family of 11. His stepfather, Damian, drove a shuttle bus; his mother, Altagracia, ran a food stand, where young Vladimir often sold produce. He spent the rest of the time with his brothers and cousins playing baseball on sandlots with, at best, second-hand equipment.

He dropped out of school after the fifth grade and eventually signed with the Expos as an 18-year-old, non-drafted free agent in 1993. Less than a year earlier, the Los Angeles Dodgers took a look at Guerrero, the skinny kid with mismatched shoes on his feet, and summarily dismissed him as a prospect.

The cost to the Expos was $3,500 and a pair of spikes that fit.

In the spring of 2009, as the media obsessed over Bonds' perjury trial for lying to a federal grand jury about his use of performance-enhancing drugs, no one seemed to care that Guerrero admitted to lying about his age when he signed with the Expos in 1993.

That meant he really was 21 years old rather than 20 when he summered on City Island in 1996. Big deal.

By 2009, Guerrero had produced his own Hall of Fame-caliber resume, which included being named the American League's most valuable player as a member of the Anaheim Angels in 2004. The resume was even stronger through the 2011 season, which Guerrero finished as the Baltimore Orioles' designated hitter with a .318 career batting average, 2,590 hits, 449 home runs and 1,496 runs batted in.

"In all the years I have managed, and all the players I have managed who have gone on to the big leagues, I don't know if I've seen anyone with the presence he has," Kelly said.

Kelly saw that quickly as Guerrero batted .424 in his first 25 games for the Senators in 1996 with 11 doubles, three triples, seven homers and 22 RBIs. Before the end of his third full week in Harrisburg, Guerrero had been named the Eastern League's player of the week – twice.

"Obviously," Kelly added with a smile, "it's not anything he does verbally."

No, definitely nothing verbally.

Behind all of Guerrero's smiles in the summer of 1996, there were few words as Guerrero was petrified of talking to the English-speaking media without a translator. His translators in Harrisburg ranged from future All-Star second baseman Jose Vidro to backup outfielder Jesus Campos and trainer Alex Ochoa.

Kelly never gave much thought to the language barrier.

"I just tell him how great he is," Kelly said, "and pat him on the back."

Kelly would pat Guerrero a great many times that summer, which finished with the Senators beating the Portland Sea Dogs, then the Florida Marlins' Class AA affiliate, in four games of the best-of-5 Eastern League finals. Guerrero was the only member of the Senators not to return home after the title-clinching Game 4 in Portland. He stayed behind to travel the next day from Maine to Montreal, where the majors awaited.

Twenty-one other Senators from that 1996 championship team eventually graduated with Guerrero to the majors, but none radiated on the field as much that summer as Guerrero.

Guerrero finished his four-plus months in Harrisburg leading the Eastern League with a .360 batting average – the league's highest average since Tommy Gregg batted .371 for the Senators in 1987.

In only 118 games with Harrisburg, Guerrero totaled 32 doubles, eight triples, 19 homers and 78 RBIs. Fifty-nine of his 150 hits went for extra bases as he finished with a league-leading 255 total bases.

Guerrero's 13 intentional walks were a byproduct of a general consensus of fear among Eastern League pitchers. Better, they figured, to put Guerrero on base than to risk taking one of his line drives off the forehead. Sixty feet, six inches is just too close for comfort. Sounds too much like six feet under.

No batter in the Eastern League in 1996 matched Guerrero's unearthly 1.050 OPS – the combination of on-base and slugging percentages – a stat that did not come into vogue until well after Guerrero left the island.

Yet the summer's most impressive stat, given a personal strike zone that seemed to extend from the top to the bottom of his 6-foot-3 frame was Guerrero's strikeout total. In 479 plate appearances for the Senators, Guerrero struck out only 42 times.

"That's just amazing," Fusco said. "That's tremendous command of the strike zone."

That command carried over to the major leagues, where Guerrero never struck out more than 95 times in any of his first 16 seasons.

"Oh, he gets fooled sometimes," said Pat Roessler, the Expos' minor league hitting coordinator during Guerrero's time on the island. "He takes some ugly swings sometimes, but he gets three hacks. It's very rare you see Vlady take a strike. Some guys strike out not because of the last pitch they took, but because they took the first two pitches when they weren't swinging. Vlady doesn't get to that point often."

Guerrero finished the summer of '96 as the obvious choice for the Eastern League's most valuable player award, joining Wes Chamberlain (1989), Matt Stairs (1991), Cliff Floyd (1993) and Mark Grudzielanek (1994) as Senators named MVP in an eight-season span.

"Guerrero is the only guy in the league who can go 4-for-3 in one night," mused Jim Essian, the Norwich manager and former major league catcher.

Essian would have gushed more about Guerrero if he had not grown so tired of watching him wear out his pitching staff.

Refusing to gush at all was Reading Phillies manager Bill Robinson, who by early July 1996 had grown weary of the fawning attention Guerrero had been receiving throughout both the Eastern League and Minor League Baseball.

"Guerrero has some juice in that bat and he's the talk of the league right now," Robinson said, while crushing out his third straight cigarette in the visiting manager's office on City Island.

"But I don't want to get caught up talking about him," Robinson said. "You know, I have a pretty good player in my locker room, too. Why don't you ask me about him?"

That player was third baseman Scott Rolen, who like Guerrero was on his way to an outstanding career in the majors.

Rolen might have led the Eastern League in hitting that summer with a .361 average – one point higher than Guerrero – but his midseason promotion to Class AAA kept him from reaching the minimum number of plate appearances needed to qualify for the title.

Todd Helton, Torii Hunter, Richie Sexson and Luis Castillo – all future All-Stars, Gold Glove winners and multi-millionaires in the majors – also starred in the Eastern League that summer.

None, though, could match Guerrero.

"Vlady's the closest thing to a natural hitter that I've ever seen," said Rob Lukachyk, a journeyman first baseman and designated hitter whose arrival on City Island in May 1996 coincided with that of Guerrero.

The Expos brought in the 27-year-old Lukachyk to hit behind Guerrero in the lineup with the idea that he would protect their prized prospect from being pitched around.

Lukachyk benefitted, too, batting .326 for Harrisburg because opposing pitchers often found themselves in trouble after facing Guerrero one batter earlier.

Lukachyk stayed with Harrisburg for only 27 games before being promoted to Class AAA Ottawa, but that was long enough for Guerrero to adjust to a league where pitchers who succeeded usually ended up in the majors.

"It's like he was put on this Earth to play baseball," Lukachyk said. "You can make him look so bad on one pitch and, if you throw him the same pitch again, he'll hit it hard somewhere."

In only a matter of weeks on the island, Guerrero had replaced future major league All-Star outfielders Cliff Floyd and Rondell White of the 1993 Senators as the best prospect to play for the Senators since pro baseball returned to Harrisburg in 1987. And there were an inordinate number of front-line prospects to play on the island during the franchise's golden decade from 1991 to 2000 – a 10-season run during which the Senators reached the Eastern League playoffs nine times and won the championship five times.

During those 10 seasons, which coincided with the first 10 years of their affiliation with the talent-rich Expos, the Senators sent an astounding 115 players to the majors.

But none of them before, during or after Guerrero's time on the island in 1996 drew comparisons to Hall of Famers like Roberto Clemente, Willie Mays and Andre Dawson. Hundreds of stories from *Baseball America* to the Dominican's *Listin Diario* were devoted to Guerrero's play of today and his promise of tomorrow.

Cliff Floyd was the closest to match Guerrero's talents. In 1993, many scouts and pundits debated whether the 6-foot-5, 220-pound Floyd would leave Harrisburg to become the next Willie McCovey. Understandable, since Floyd was named the Eastern League's MVP after batting .329 in 101 games with 26 homers and 101 RBIs. Cliff Floyd turned out to be, well, the first Cliff Floyd, which was not all bad given he dealt with injuries for much of his 17-year career in the majors, where he batted .278 with 233 homers.

The afterglow of Floyd's magnificent 1993 season lasted less than three years on City Island, replaced by the season Guerrero put together in 1996.

Floyd's aura began dissipating during Guerrero's first night on City Island on May 1, 1996. Batting in the bottom of the sixth inning of the second game of a doubleheader against New Haven, Guerrero launched a changeup from future major leaguer John Thompson halfway to Lemoyne for a two-run homer.

"The report I sent back on Guerrero in 1996 said, 'Roberto Clemente is alive and playing right field in Harrisburg.' That's all I had to write about him," remembered Ben McLure, a longtime scout who was working for the Toronto Blue Jays when Guerrero was working over Eastern League pitchers. "I wrote him up as the best player I had seen since Ken Griffey Jr. was in high school and that was in 1987."

Every manager in the league, even Reading's Bill Robinson, made similar comparisons before Guerrero left the Eastern League.

All the accolades meant little to Guerrero during his time with the Senators. He did not understand the prose being written or the words being spoken, nor did he seem especially interested in finding out. He just saw himself as another player from the Dominican, the latest import from an island nation where the greatest export is baseball talent.

"I don't read English," Guerrero said with a shrug through Ochoa, "so whatever people are saying, the information isn't getting to me."

Despite prodding from Harrisburg teammates such as infielder Charlie Montoyo to learn English so he could better adjust to the United States, Guerrero never bothered. He would pick up on some of the language but never really change. A decade after leaving Harrisburg, Guerrero still leaned on translators.

"He's more comfortable that way," Fernando Cuza, one of Guerrero's agents and long-time translators.

There were times, of course, when Guerrero was not comfortable, period. He was forced to leave his Dominican cocoon for the United States in the summer of 1994, joining the rest of the Expos' wannabes in Florida's entry-level Gulf Coast League. His pro experience at the time had consisted of 59 games in two seasons with Montreal's affiliate in the Dominican Summer League.

When he arrived in Harrisburg, Guerrero, then 21, was only a couple of months removed from competing in the Dominican winter league, where minor leaguers have forever tried to measure themselves against the big leaguers there. While Guerrero played for the team from Estrellas, he studied the outfielders from Escogido – Moises Alou, Raul Mondesi and Sammy Sosa.

Turned out, they were watching Guerrero.

"They would tell me, 'Hey, you have the capabilities of getting to the big leagues, so watch yourself,' " Guerrero said. "They don't look at me as No. 1; they just know I have the potential."

They also gave some advice to Guerrero.

"They wanted me to be careful with the people who befriend me just because I'm a baseball player."

Guerrero followed that advice throughout his career. He would be protected – by Cuza, his agent, and by his mother, who lived with her son in Montreal and in Anaheim after Guerrero joined the Angels in 2004.

While Mother Guerrero never reached City Island in the summer of 1996, Guerrero had a built-in support group within the Senators' clubhouse.

Vladimir Guerrero was shy with teammates and media, but could be outgoing with fans

The Senators that summer had the most culturally diverse group of players in the Eastern League. This was a byproduct of the Expos' outstanding international scouting department led by Fred Ferreira, who along with Arturo DeFreites had signed Guerrero for $3,500 in 1993.

In Harrisburg, Guerrero's locker was the second from the right in a row of six that stretched along the west wall of the Senators' cramped clubhouse.

The first four lockers belonged to future major leaguers Jose Vidro, Jolbert Cabrera, Israel Alcantara and Geoff Blum. On the other side of Guerrero was backup catcher Ramsey Koeyers, who was Guerrero's roommate.

The row was its own United Nations with a Puerto Rican, a Colombian, another Dominican and a laid-back Californian surfer dude. Koeyers, the only one of the six who would not reach the majors, was from the Dutch Netherlands and was fluent in a handful of languages.

Along this row, Spanish was the tongue of choice, giving Guerrero his comfort zone.

That is, when he spoke to anybody.

"He's shy," Koeyers said of Guerrero, who is only six months younger than Koeyers. "He's good. He never drinks. He never goes out. He just stays at home and relaxes. … He's learning what to do."

He learned fast in 1996.

Batting between rising prospect Brad Fullmer and a rejuvenated Vidro in the lineup during August and September, Guerrero led the Senators' drive to the Eastern League playoffs.

Once there, the Senators pounded Trenton and future All-Star pitcher Carl Pavano in the semifinals before defeating Portland and Livan Hernandez, another future All-Star pitcher, in the finals.

"We wouldn't even pitch to him back then," Doug Harris, a former Portland pitcher, said 15 years after those Eastern League finals. "He was the one guy in that Harrisburg lineup who could really hurt you. Basically, he won the championship by himself."

Guerrero mostly celebrated that championship alone. He was not with his teammates when the Senators, in the hours after their title-clinching victory, rode home from Maine's Hadlock Field in the early morning hours of Sept. 12. Instead of returning to City Island on a charter bus fueled by gasoline, beer and cigar smoke, Guerrero stayed behind in Portland, preparing to travel north to Montreal and join the Expos for the final days of their season.

Playing at Atlanta's Turner Field a week after joining the Expos, Guerrero bounced a single up the middle off Steve Avery for his first hit in the majors.

More than 2,500 hits and nine All-Star appearances followed.

Only one other Dominican-born player – Albert Pujols – had a higher career batting average than Guerrero's .318 through the 2011 season.

Of the three after whom he once modeled his game – Alou, Mondesi and Sosa – none was close to matching Guerrero's eventual success.

Alou, the onetime Senator who was born in United States when his father, Felipe, was playing with Atlanta in 1968, finished his career with a .303 batting average. Mondesi and Sosa each ended up hitting .273 during their checkered careers.

Of the 542 Dominicans to have played in the majors through 2011, only the steroid-tainted tandem of Sosa and Manny Ramirez have more career homers and RBIs than Guerrero. Through 2011, only 21 players in the history of the game had better career slugging percentages. His .556 mark exceeded those of Hall of Famers Hank Aaron, Ralph Kiner, Hack Wilson, Chuck Klein, Duke Snider, Frank Robinson, Al Simmons, Earl Averill, Mel Ott, Willie Stargell and Mike Schmidt.

As he approached his mid-30s, back and leg injuries had slowed Guerrero, who had been forced to play on Montreal's unforgiving artificial turf from 1997 to 2003. He then escaped as a free agent to Anaheim and the American League, where he would begin the transition from playing right field every day to becoming a fulltime designated hitter at the end of his career.

Even then, Guerrero maintained that "wow" presence. He never lost his title as baseball's best bad-ball hitter since Roberto Clemente a generation before.

Guerrero added to that reputation in mid-August 2009, swinging at – and connecting on – a pitch in the dirt from Baltimore's Chris Tillman. The 1-2 curveball bounced in front of home plate before Guerrero reached out for the ball and dumped it into left-center for a single.

Three years earlier, Guerrero had struck one of his all-time best bad-ball hits off Los Angeles' Brad Penny at the All-Star Game in Pittsburgh.

The Dodgers' right-hander started the game by striking out Ichiro Suzuki, Derek Jeter and David Ortiz in the first inning before retiring Alex Rodriguez on a groundout to start the second.

With the count 1-1 to Guerrero, Penny threw a 98-mph fastball that was shoulder high and outside, a waste pitch that no batter would consider trying to hit.

Except Guerrero.

As catcher Paul Lo Duca of the New York Mets reached up and out for the pitch, Guerrero flicked his bat at the ball and lined the pitch the opposite way down the right-field line and into the stands at PNC Park.

Officially, Guerrero's homer traveled 356 feet. What it lacked in distance, it made up for in amazement since the probability of anyone hitting such a high pitch with such force down the line for an opposite-field home run was slim.

"Guerrero's just a freak," one American League scout said. "He goes against every book ever written. You can usually set a guy up with a certain pitch – a breaking ball, a backup slider – but it doesn't matter with him, because he can cover every pitch you throw at him."

Of course, Guerrero had done this for six-plus seasons in Montreal, a venue from which ESPN showed few highlights over the years. Had he played in Boston or New York, Guerrero would undoubtedly have had every one of his bad-ball hits replayed on SportsCenter.

One of the game's all-time best bad-ball hitters, Vladimir Guerrero picks up a hit off a pitch in the dirt while playing on City Island in 1996

As it was, few cameras showed up early at Montreal's Olympic Stadium, where Expos infielders feared what might happen if they found themselves in the path of one of Guerrero's cup-high, one-hoppers during BP.

"I used to worry about that all the time in Montreal with that hard turf we had there," said former Harrisburg infielder Jamey Carroll, who was Guerrero's teammate in Montreal in 2002 and 2003. "When Vlady came up to hit in BP, everybody just stopped taking ground balls and waited until he was done hitting."

Long before Carroll and the Expos' other infielders began dodging those vicious hits in batting practice, Guerrero's story had become the stuff of lore.

Those associated with the Expos already knew Guerrero's backstory, of how he went from being an 18-year-old kid whom Fred Ferreira and Arturo DeFreites signed for $3,500 to becoming a man with more than $125 million in career earnings through the 2011 season.

They knew the tale of how Ferreira in 1993 came upon an outfielder wasting away at the Dodgers' winter camp for aspiring players in the Dominican. When he saw Guerrero run the 60-yard dash, make some throws from right field and swing a bat, Ferreira – a legend in Latin America for his ability to find raw talent – signed Guerrero on the spot. He was more than willing to take a chance on the kid with the small torso and big butt from the southern region of the Dominican Republic known as Nizao Bani.

Nizao Bani is where the pre-teen Guerrero dreamed of becoming a tomato farmer. Instead, he became another find for Ferreira, who during his career discovered future All-Stars in Vidro, Orlando Cabrera, Javier Vazquez, Bernie Williams and Roberto Kelly.

"Oh, yes, the Dodgers," Guerrero said with a laugh of his career that never happened in Los Angeles. "I remember that, but I don't look back at it. I'm just glad I was able to sign with Montreal, spend those four years in the minor leagues and get up there to play."

Guerrero gladly accepted that original $3,500 signing bonus – an enormous sum to him at the time, considering $2,400 was the average annual income for an adult in the Dominican Republic.

In time, Guerrero would add an inch to his height and more than 70 pounds to a frame that was listed at 6-foot-2 and a generous 158 pounds when he first joined the Expos.

By the time he reached the majors in 1996, Guerrero had shoes that fit.

By the time he left the Expos as a free agent in 2003, Guerrero could buy anything he wanted.

No Senator had ever graduated from City Island to become more feared in the majors than Guerrero, who after he retires may well become the first former Senator elected by the Baseball Writers Association of America to the Hall of Fame.

Seven others who had played for Harrisburg on City Island – Hughie Jennings, Frank Grant, Vic Willis, Chief Bender, Billy Hamilton, Oscar Charleston and Ben Taylor – are in the Hall of Fame, but they were selected by Cooperstown's ever-morphing Veterans Committee or through one of the Hall's special elections on long-forgotten Negro League players.

Guerrero reinvested much of his $125 million-plus in career earnings into the lives of his neighbors in Don Gregorio de Nizao. There, in a coastal town of 15,000 people, Guerrero's business ventures with his three brothers included a cold storage facility for local fishermen, a cement block business for home builders, a propane distributorship to provide fuel for those homes, two butcher shops, a women's clothing store, a food market and a 24-acre farm.

If the cliché is true that it takes the village to raise a child, then the once malnourished child returned home as a wealthy man intent on raising the village. Not bad for somebody who dropped out of school after the fifth grade and shared with eight brothers and sisters a home that had dirt for a floor and a roof covered only by palm leaves.

Not that Guerrero would talk about such things. Too modest, especially around the Anglo-speaking media with whom he has rarely spoken.

"He understands some English," said Cuza, Guerrero's omnipresent agent. "He knows the generalities of the language, but he's not comfortable speaking it."

In French-speaking Montreal, where he could walk downtown without being singled out by the populace, Guerrero grew wary of the local media.

For a time in 2000, he stopped talking with most of the reporters there.

"He's like a machine," Expos manager Felipe Alou told the Montreal-based writers who had been offended by Guerrero's boycott. "Machines don't talk. They just go out and destroy."

Destroy. Now there was an apt description for Guerrero, whose .318 batting average through 2011 trailed only St. Louis' Albert Pujols, Seattle's Ichiro Suzuki, Minnesota's Joe Mauer and Colorado's Todd Helton among active players with more than 3,000 career plate appearances.

Guerrero's lifetime batting average was better than those of 10 Hall of Famers who hit between .315 to .318, including Clemente.

Not that Guerrero noticed.

"Oh, no, no, no," he insisted. "I never think about those things."

Others have thought about those things. In little more than seven seasons with the Expos, Guerrero became arguably the greatest force for a franchise that had Hall of Famers with catcher Gary Carter and outfielder Andre Dawson, a borderline Hall of Famer in left fielder Tim Raines, and All-Star outfielders in Moises Alou, Larry Walker and Rusty Staub.

"I look back now and realize just how special he is," said Carroll, the former Senators infielder who took four years to get off City Island, compared with Guerrero's four months there.

Carroll spent the last month of the 2002 season and all of 2003 in Montreal marveling at Guerrero before Guerrero left as a free agent to join the Angels in 2004. Carroll was an old rookie in 2002, making his major league debut at the age of 28. At the same age, Guerrero already had played 1,104 games in the majors for the Expos with 234 homers and 722 runs batted in.

"When you play next to him every day, you take him for granted," Carroll said. "Then he goes to the Angels, wins the MVP and shows everybody that he can play just as well wherever he plays. There's a big difference for him there between playing in Montreal and playing in Los Angeles."

In Montreal, Guerrero could lose himself in a city where many of the locals spoke French, yet another language that Guerrero neither knew nor cared to learn.

With the Expos, Guerrero was the face of a franchise that Montreal residents did not care whether it stayed or moved, especially after the 1994 strike wiped out the Expos' last, best chance to reach the World Series.

The fans' bitterness was still there in 2003, when Guerrero was earning $11.5 million. The salary was reasonable for a player of his talent, but far too high for the frugal Expos with a fleeing fan base.

With Guerrero looking for a big contract as a free agent after the season, Montreal general manager Omar Minaya let his best player walk away without so much as offering him salary arbitration, which would have ensured the Expos additional choices in the upcoming amateur draft.

"It's like losing your bank account," Expos manager Frank Robinson said after Guerrero left for Anaheim. "You put money away in it, but then it's gone. I banked on him."

Others simply studied Guerrero as if he were some kind of lab experiment. To pitchers and catchers, he was a Skinner Box rat with a bat.

How does he handle a certain type of pitch? Can he cover the outside part of the plate? What happens if you come inside, then go low and away? What if we just roll the ball up to the plate?

"Our pitchers are told, literally, to 'Just throw four pitches wherever you can and, hopefully, he will hit it at somebody,' " said Chicago White Sox catcher A.J. Pierzynski.

"You can't set him up. You can't work the count on him. You can't do anything with him," Pierzynski said. "You can throw a pitch over his head and he hits it for a home run. You can throw one in the dirt and he hits that for a double in the gap."

> *"You can't set him up. You can't work the count on him. You can't do anything with him. You can throw a pitch over his head and he hits it for a home run. You can throw one in the dirt and he hits that for a double in the gap."*
>
> *White Sox catcher A.J. Pierzynski*

Some of the game's best pitchers knew the copious notes their advance scouts made on Guerrero were largely a waste of time.

"Really, he is a guy who doesn't have a scouting report, because he can pretty much hit anything you throw at him," said left-hander Scott Kazmir, who in six-plus seasons with Tampa Bay faced Guerrero 13 times and gave up four hits and a walk.

"With a hitter like Guerrero, you start way off the plate and keep working off it," said Roy Halladay, a Cy Young Award winner in both Toronto and Philadelphia who managed to get by allowing only 10 hits and a walk in his first 39 encounters with Guerrero. "He's so rare to have that type of power, the kind that goes all the way across the plate and off it. It's tough to pitch to him when the only pitch he can't hit is a ball."

Guerrero has hit those too, as Brad Penny and Chris Tillman can attest.

Others, including onetime Baltimore and Toronto closer B.J. Ryan, just wanted to avoid Guerrero.

"I wouldn't want to see him in the first inning, let alone the ninth," said Ryan, who struck out Guerrero in two of their five late-inning match-ups but gave up two singles and a walk in the other three.

"He's a guy who makes you nervous. He's not only a guy who can hit a good pitch a long way, but he can hit a bad pitch a long way, too," Ryan said. "You have to be extremely careful with him, but when it comes down to it, you're going to walk him."

There was at least one brave soul who would pitch to Guerrero. That was the Yankees' Mariano Rivera, the greatest closer in the history of the game who preceded Guerrero to the Eastern League by two years with Albany-Colonie in 1994.

Rivera said he was careful, not fearful, of Guerrero. Of course, it's easy to have no fear when throwing a cut fastball no one can hit.

"You have to throw it everywhere against him," said Rivera, who despite his own greatness had given up six hits, two walks and a sacrifice fly in the 20 times he faced Guerrero through 2011.

"With him," Rivera said, "you throw inside, outside, up, down and, God, you just hope you find a way to get him out. The guy is the best bad-ball hitter, but he's a good hitter, too. You have to trust your stuff when you pitch to him."

Asked how he would pitch to himself, Guerrero just shrugged.

"I don't even think about it," Guerrero said. "I just go up there to see the ball, swing the bat and hit the ball."

That was as far as Guerrero went in dispensing advice: See the ball, hit the ball. Henry Aaron often offered – and followed – the same advice during his own Hall of Fame career from 1954 to 1976.

And that was the only advice Guerrero would give on hitting.

"I can't give kids advice on hitting," Guerrero said. "How can I do that? How can I tell them what pitches to swing at, when I know I swing at balls that I know I shouldn't be swinging at. How can I tell them not to do what I do?"

Trendsetters? Um, Maybe Not

Moises Alou and Vladimir Guerrero have had so much in common besides, of course, playing for the Senators on their way to outstanding careers in the majors.

Both spent most of their All-Star careers terrifying National League pitchers, a pair of right-handed hitters with lifetime batting averages on the plus side of .300. They also share roots in the Dominican Republic. Alou's father Felipe and uncles Matty and Jesus were among the first from that tiny island nation to star in the majors.

MOISES ALOU   Mo and Vlad shared another little-known habit during their playing careers: Each liked to pee on his hands before hitting, claiming that rubbing urine into the skin helped – depending on the source – to either soften or harden the hands. Great for calluses, too, Alou said.

Sounds like an endorsement deal in the making. Then again, who's going to shake on it?

Dominican Hit List

With a single off Boston's Josh Beckett on Sept. 26, 2011 at Camden Yards, Baltimore designated hitter and former Senator Vladimir Guerrero collected his 2,587[th] career hit to move past Julio Franco for the most by a Dominican-born player – 542 of whom have played in the majors since Ozzie Virgil's debut with the New York Giants in 1956.

Vladimir Guerrero	2,590 hits, 1996-2011
Julio Franco	2,586 hits, 1982-2007
Manny Ramirez	2,574 hits, 1993-2011
Sammy Sosa	2,408 hits, 1989-2007
Miguel Tejada	2,362 hits, 1997-2011
Tony Fernandez	2,276 hits, 1983-2001
Felipe Alou	2,101 hits, 1958-1974
Cesar Cedeno	2,087 hits, 1970-1986
Albert Pujols	2,073 hits, 2001-2011
Adrian Beltre	2,033 hits, 1998-2011

The Understudies Weren't Bad, Either

The players on the Senators' 1993 juggernaut knew they were better than anyone else in the Class AA Eastern League. The Montreal Expos had built Harrisburg's roster not only to win but to dominate.

For the first half of their 100-win season of '93, you couldn't move around the Senators' undersized clubhouse without bumping into prospect.

For pitchers, they had Gabe White and Joey Eischen, Kirk Rueter and Miguel Batista. For hitters, they had Cliff Floyd and Rondell White, Glenn Murray and Shane Andrews.

For the Eastern League, all of them were trouble.

The only question on Opening Night wasn't how good the Senators would be, but how many of the top prospects would still be on the team when the EL playoffs began in September? The inevitable promotions to Class AAA Ottawa and the majors figured to strip the team of its elite prospects by August, never mind September.

"We expected this," Expos general manager Dan Duquette nonchalantly said as the Senators gutted the league by the all-star break in July.

By Aug. 1, when Floyd left for Triple-A, only Batista, Andrews and Murray remained from the Opening Day core of wunderkinds. At the time of Floyd's promotion, the Senators were 70-33, a .680 winning percentage.

The replacements from Class A West Palm Beach were integrated into the team as the promotions started to Ottawa. They helped the Senators win 24 of their final 35 regular-season games, then six of nine in the playoffs from Albany-Colonie and Canton-Akron.

Their winning percentage, including the playoffs, was .682.

Most of the Class A call-ups who contributed to winning the league title played the best ball of their careers on the island in the second half of the 1993 season.

Second baseman Mike Hardge was one of those players; utility player extraordinaire Matt Rundels was another. Starting pitchers Rod Henderson and Brian Looney, and left fielder Tyrone Horne were all key players who never achieved the same level of consistency after winning in Harrisburg.

Of course, the newbies from West Palm might have been inspired – or possibly terrified – by the parting advice given to them by pitcher Joey Eischen, who was the Senators' resident tough guy before he left for AAA.

"I told them, ' Don't screw up my ring.' "

No-Hit Wonder

The wait seemed interminable.

Hit or error. Pick one. C'mon already.

So went the thinking of Senators manager Dave Machemer as he stood on the pitcher's mound in the top of the ninth inning on April 28, 2003. Machemer knew starting pitcher Seung Song was approaching his 110-pitch limit. He also knew Seung was working on a no-hitter against the Erie SeaWolves.

Machemer's antsy behavior was preceded by a play that still bewildered fans years later.

After Corey Richardson walked with one out, Erie's speedy Nook Logan put down a perfect bunt that Seung fielded along the first-base line. Seung slipped as he hurriedly picked up the ball, and his throw to first baseman Glenn Davis sailed high and off the bag. Didn't matter, though, since Logan already was past the bag when the ball arrived.

A nanosecond later, Machemer emerged from the dugout to take out his prized right-hander. In Machemer's mind, Erie finally had a hit and Seung was done for the night since there no longer was a no-hitter to pursue. The same thought went through Seung's head, too, as well as what was left of the Monday night crowd of 1,375 on the island.

But there was doubt in one mind – that of official scorer Dave Wright, who was considering whether he should give a hit to Logan or an error on Seung.

Wright pondered for a moment. Or two. Or five.

As Machemer stood on the mound next to Seung, catcher Scott Sandusky and the Senators' infield, he alternatingly glanced toward the scoreboard and then press box. He could think of six words.

Make up your #$%@& mind already.

As Machemer waited on Wright, Wright waited on Machemer.

"I wanted to see if Machemer was going to take Song out or leave him in," Wright said. "I was waiting to see what he was going to do."

For his part, Wright could think of a few words, too.

This job is not worth twenty-five bucks a game.

"The whole thing seemed like it never ended. It's like I woke up yesterday morning and it was still wasn't over," Wright said in February 2012, nearly nine years after the most controversial scoring decision on the island since the Senators returned in 1987.

"I don't know how long Machemer was standing on the mound," Wright said, "but it was longer than it should have been. I wish I had replay in the press box. The more I tried to replay it in my head … it was like sending a copy through the fax again and again. It just gets blurrier."

Finally, Wright – one of the most conscientious official scorers in the Senators' modern era – finally ended the wait and made his call.

Sacrifice bunt for Logan, error on Seung.

The ruling made little sense, especially with Erie trailing 2-0 with one out and only one runner on base.

Logan needed to reach base more as the tying run than he needed to sacrifice the second out of the inning with a bunt, especially with the

In 2003, Seung Song became the first Senator to throw a no-hitter on the island in 51 years

light-hitting Scott Tousa due up next for the SeaWolves.

"Clearly a base hit," Logan told *The Patriot-News* after the game.

"I had already passed the bag when the ball got to the bag."

Richardson later scored on Tousa's sacrifice fly before Seung struck out Noochie Varner for the final out.

"I think they were going to say hit," the 22-year-old Korean said, "but they put up error."

Equally flabbergasted, although not nearly as polite, was Erie manager Kevin Bradshaw, who vowed to send Wright a video tape of the play, although he never did.

Machemer also was stunned by the call.

"I came to take out Song, because I thought it was a hit," Machemer said. "Then, I wasn't sure. I had to wait there on the mound looking at the scoreboard until I saw a hit or an error."

Wright said that almost right away he thought he may have made the wrong call. He confirmed his gnawing suspicion the next day when he asked the umpires for their opinion and they told him the play should have been ruled a hit.

Wright said he then tried to get a tape of the play from Gregg Mace, a sportscaster with Harrisburg's ABC affiliate.

"He was in the press box a couple of days later and I asked him if he had a copy, and he said he did and would get me one," Wright said. "I'm still waiting for it. To this day, I have never seen a replay."

Seung's no-hitter was oddly similar to the previous one thrown by a Harrisburg pitcher on the island. That came in 1952, the season in which the Senators finished an inglorious 46-94 in the Class B Interstate League before dropping out of professional baseball for 35 years.

NO-HITTERS ON THE ISLAND SINCE 1987

Jason Grimsley
Reading Phillies
May 3, 1989
Final: 3-0, seven innings, first game of doubleheader

Bill Pulsipher
Binghamton Mets
Sept. 12, 1994
Final: 2-0, Game 2 of EL finals

Seung Song
Harrisburg Senators
April 28, 2003
Final: 2-1

Tyler Clippard
Trenton Thunder
Aug. 17, 2006
Final: 9-0

On June 5 of that season, and just two days before his 21st birthday, right-hander Bob Berresford no-hit Wilmington 1-0.

Only Berresford spent much of the game having no idea he was throwing a no-hitter. Like Seung, he had fielded a bunt – this one in the first inning rather than the ninth – and subsequently thrown the ball past his first baseman. And, like Seung, Berresford believed the bunt was a hit. Without a detailed scoreboard behind him to show an error, Berresford immediately dismissed any thought of pitching a no-hitter.

"I thought the bunt was a hit," Berresford said years later to Larry O'Rourke of the Shenandoah *Evening Herald*. "About the sixth inning, I started to get an idea (of having a no-hitter), because nobody would talk to me."

Everyone seemingly wanted to talk about Wright and his call. The story of Seung's pseudo no-hitter made headlines around the country. Nothing major; just some jabs at what appeared from afar to be a blatant hometown call, an admitted mistake by a man who made precious few of them in his five seasons as the Senators' official scorer.

"I don't mind making headlines," Wright said, "but I'd rather do it for saving a life instead of botching a call in a Double-A baseball game. I've never done the former, but I've done the latter."

```
                      The Automated ScoreBook
                  Erie Seawolves at Harrisburg Senators
             Apr 28, 2003 at Harrisburg, PA (Riverside Stadium)

Erie Seawolves 1 (11-11)              Harrisburg Senators 2 (13-11)

                 AB  R  H RBI                          AB  R  H RBI
LOGAN   cf        3  0  0  0      WATSON   cf            2  0  0  0
TOUSA   2b        2  0  0  1      HALL   lf              3  0  1  1
VARNER  rf        4  0  0  0      WARE   rf              3  1  1  1
MUNOZ   1b        3  0  0  0      MCKINLEY 2b            2  0  0  0
DAIGLE  dh        3  0  0  0      BAILEY   dh            3  0  0  0
HANNAHAN 3b       3  0  0  0      DAVIS  1b              2  0  0  0
ST. PIERRE  c     3  0  0  0      DIAZ  3b               3  0  2  0
BAUTISTA  ss      3  0  0  0      SANDUSKY  c            3  0  0  0
RICHARDSON lf     2  1  0  0      MACHADO  ss            3  1  2  0
LARRISON  p       0  0  0  0      SONG  p                0  0  0  0
SPIEGEL  p        0  0  0  0

Totals......     26  1  0  1      Totals......          24  2  6  2

     Score by innings:                        R  H  E
     Erie Seawolves        000 000 001   -    1  0  0
     Harrisburg Senators   101 000 00X   -    2  6  1

E - SONG. DP - Erie 1. LOB - Erie 2; Harrisburg 3. HR - WARE(3). SH -
LOGAN; WATSON. SF - TOUSA; HALL. CS - HALL(3); MACHADO(2).

                  IP   H  R ER BB SO  WP BK HP IBB   AB BF Fly Gnd
LARRISON L 1-3   7.0   6  2  2  2  2   0  1  1  0    21 26   4 11
SPIEGEL          1.0   0  0  0  0  0   0  0  0  0     3  3   2  1

SONG W 2-0       9.0   0  1  0  2  4   0  0  0  0    26 30  12 11

HBP - by LARRISON (WATSON). BK - LARRISON.

Strikeouts - TOUSA; VARNER; DAIGLE; ST. PIERRE; WARE; MCKINLEY. Walks -
TOUSA; RICHARDSON; MCKINLEY; DAVIS.

Umpires - Home:Kevin Causey  1st:Brent Persinger  3rd:Adrian Johnson
Start: 0   Time: 2:00   Attendance: 1375

Next Day's Pitchers:
Erie Sea Wolves: 31 Jeremy Johnson (2-1; 2.49)
Harrisburg Senators: 24 Gerardo Casadiego (0-1; 9.00 ERA)
Official Scorekeeper: Dave Wright
```

OFFICIAL BOX SCORE OF SEUNG SONG'S NO-HITTER, SIGNED BY SEUNG

From Here to There

One of the great beauties of baseball is that you cannot hide or, for that matter, be hidden. Somebody will find you. There once was a time when teams stashed away players in their farm systems, and no other team could touch them.

Then, over time, Major League Baseball implemented its minor league draft – commonly known as the Rule V draft – to give players stuck in the minors a chance to be selected by another big league team. For $50,000 and the promise to provide a roster spot in the majors for the next season, any team at the winter meetings could pluck a player off another team's roster, so long as that player had enough service time in the minors but had not yet been placed on his major league team's protected 40-man roster.

RICH SAUVEUR

Just save your receipt. If you don't like the player you drafted, then ship him back to his previous team for $25,000 – half of the price you paid to select him in the first place.

The major league portion of the Rule V draft is how Roberto Clemente joined the Pittsburgh Pirates rather than remain Bob Clemente stuck on the bench for the Brooklyn Dodgers' Class AAA team in Montreal during the 1954 season.

The Rule V draft also uncovered players who later became All-Stars, Gold Glove winners, MVPs and Cy Young Award winners. Among them are Shane Victorino, Dan Uggla, George Bell, Josh Hamilton and Johan Santana.

Alas, most Rule V picks are destined for brief, mediocre careers in the majors – presuming, of course, they remain there and not offered back to their original teams. For every Josh Hamilton there have been a couple of dozen players like Tony Blanco – raw talents plucked from the minors before they had a chance to fully develop.

In their first quarter-century back on City Island, the Senators produced 13 players who became Rule V picks. Some of them – outfielder Kevin Northrup and relief pitcher Zechry Zinicola – were returned by their drafting teams before the start of the next season, while others like pitchers Stan Spencer and B.J. Wallace stayed with their new organizations, but never stayed healthy enough to help them.

"To be honest, I didn't know if I'd ever pitch in the big leagues. I certainly wasn't overconfident about it," said pitcher Bill Sampen, who became a 27-year-old rookie in the majors in 1990 after being picked by Montreal in the 1989 Rule V draft. "I was moving along so slowly (in the minors) and didn't seem to be going anywhere in a hurry."

Sampen wasn't in a hurry to leave either, as he spent five seasons in the majors.

Of the 13 Senators drafted for a look-see in the majors, three were selected by the Philadelphia Phillies – Wallace, pitcher Michael Mimbs and utility player Michael Martinez.

The most successful of the Senators' Rule V picks was right-handed pitcher Al Reyes, who set an Eastern League record with 35 saves for the Senators in 1994 before being selected by Milwaukee.

In return for their 50 grand, the Brewers used Reyes in 127 games over the next four-plus seasons, over which he went 10-4 with two saves and an American League-OK 4.12 ERA.

Reyes later worked a career-high 65 games in 2005 for the World Series-winning St. Louis Cardinals in 2005. Two years later, he saved a career-high 26 games for the Tampa Bay Rays.

THE 13 WHO WERE RULED:

Rich Sauveur, pitcher, 1987 (from Pirates to Expos)
Bill Sampen, pitcher, 1989 (from Pirates to Expos)
Stan Spencer, pitcher, 1991 (from Expos to Marlins)
Billy Brewer, pitcher, 1992 (from Expos to Royals)
Al Reyes, pitcher, 1994 (from Expos to Brewers)
Michael Mimbs, pitcher, 1994 (from Expos to Phillies)
Kevin Northrup, outfielder, 1994 (from Expos to Mets)
B.J. Wallace, pitcher, 1995 (from Expos to Phillies)
Alejandro Machado, infielder, 2006 (from Nationals to Twins)
Zech Zinicola, pitcher, 2009 (from Nationals to Blue Jays)
Michael Martinez, utility player, 2010 (from Nationals to Phillies)
Brad Meyers, pitcher, 2009-2011 (from Nationals to Yankees)
Erik Komatsu, outfielder, 2011 (from Nationals to St. Louis)

Right Man, Right Place, Right Time

Jim Bowden's tenure as the Cincinnati Reds' general manager still was being measured in hours when he made his first bold move in the fall of 1992.

Bowden was the boy genius, hired by Reds owner Marge Schott to a position usually filled by someone between the age of 45 and senility. At 31, Bowden was the youngest GM in history, so naturally his every move –

JIM TRACY

and there would be hundreds in the coming decade – would be scrutinized.

Some of his moves were brilliant; others were just awful. If nothing else, Bowden was bold and loud.

One of Bowden's first moves turned out poorly for the Reds, but was ultimately a boon for the Montreal Expos and their Class AA affiliate in Harrisburg.

Bowden liked to distance himself from his predecessor's hires. Among his first moves as the Reds' GM was to fire field co-ordinator Jim Tracy, despite the fact Tracy had overseen a farm system that had just produced the best aggregate record in all of minor league baseball.

The 36-year-old Tracy was out of work for, maybe, 48 seconds.

Among those calling his home in Sarasota, Florida, were the Expos.

Say, Trace, how would you like to manage our Double-A team in Harrisburg? We're going to have our best prospects there. Nothing but Baseball America cover boys, so what do you say, Trace?

Tracy accepted, and why not? The Expos planned to stock the 1993 Senators with four former first-round picks – Cliff Floyd, Rondell White, Shane Andrews and Gabe White – and other prospects such as pitchers Miguel Batista, Reid Cornelius, Joey Eischen and Kirk Rueter, and outfielder Glenn Murray.

The result: The Senators won 100 of 147 games – going 94-44 in the regular season before beating Albany-Colonie in the Eastern League semifinals, then rallying on the road from an 0-2 hole to beat Canton-Akron in the best-of-5 finals.

Twenty-two of Tracy's 42 players in Harrisburg reached the majors, including 10 of the 11 starting pitchers he used that season.

Eight of those 22 – outfielder Curtis Pride, pitcher Ugueth Urbina, Batista, Floyd, Eischen, Rueter and both Whites – each played more than a decade in the majors. Floyd, Urbina and Rondell White became All-Stars.

Tracy and pitching coach Chuck Kniffin also reached the majors. Tracy was the Expos' bench coach in 1995 before becoming the Los Angeles Dodgers' manager in 2001, while Kniffin was the Arizona Diamondbacks' pitching coach from 2002 to 2004.

The Senators' .681 winning percentage during the 1993 regular season was the Eastern League's best since 1983 and remained so entering the 2012 season. They had the league's MVP in Floyd, who batted .329 with 26 homers and 101 RBIs in only 101 games; .the EL pitcher of the year in Eischen, who was 14-4; and, of course, the manager of the year in Tracy.

"I guess I got smart in Harrisburg," Tracy diplomatically said years later when asked of Bowden's impetuous move to fire him in 1992.

"I'm not a vindictive person. One person's opinion of me is not necessarily the general opinion of the multitude."

In May 2001, Minor League Baseball, in its summer-long promotion to celebrate its 100th season, named the 1993 Senators as the minors' 73rd best team since the start of the 20th century.

"You put the players in a position to win and then let them go out and win," Tracy said. "I did that in 1993 in Harrisburg. I didn't throw any pitches or get any hits or lay down any bunts. I was just there to point a group of guys in the right direction."

While winning was the byproduct of their enormous talent, the secret behind the success of the 1993 Senators was how Tracy handled the egos inherent in a clubhouse filled with Alpha males. Egos never ran amok on that team. Outsiders wouldn't have known if they were talking with a former No. 1 pick on his way to an All-Star career in the majors or the last man on the roster whose career was hanging by the thread of a ligament that no longer worked so well.

"It was a baseball team that made a unique name for itself," Tracy said. "The thing that was special about that group of guys is that they were unselfish. It made them all better, individually and collectively."

Calling the Shots

Nine players, managers and coaches who worked on City Island since 1890 went on to manage in the majors. Some, including Hughie Jennings and Jim Tracy, had long careers there. Others such as Jim Lemon and Joe Kerrigan, lasted one season or less.

Hughie Jennings (catcher 1890 Ponies)
    1,184 wins, 995 losses with Detroit Tigers, N.Y Giants, 1907-1925
Doggie Miller (infielder, 1893 Senators)
    56-76 with St. Louis Browns, 1894
Bob Shawkey (pitcher, 1911 Ponies)
    86-68 with New York Yankees, 1930
Earle Mack (first baseman-manager, 1917 Islanders)
    45-77 with Philadelphia Athletics, 1937 and 1939
Jim Lemon (outfielder, 1949 Senators)
    65-96 with Washington Senators, 1968
Dave Trembley (manager, 1987-89 Senators)
    187-283 with Baltimore Orioles, 2007-2010
Mike Quade (manager, 1991-92 Senators)
    95-104 with Chicago Cubs, 2010-2011
Joe Kerrigan (pitching coach, 1991 Senators)
    17-26 with Boston Red Sox, 2001
Jim Tracy (manager, 1993 Senators)
    792-782 with Los Angeles Dodgers, Pittsburgh Pirates, Colorado Rockies, 2001-active in 2012

MIKE QUADE

Thanks for Helping, Now Get Out

For all of the success he had in 1994, Senators manager Dave Jauss should have had a more relaxing summer on the island.

Instead, he had to deal with a variety of issues, beginning with the early season loss of injured starting pitcher B.J. Wallace, whose career was never the same after his once-gifted left arm was overused by Team USA at the 1992 Olympics. Then came all of those irritating questions early in the season as Jauss constantly – and, really, unfairly – was asked how his team compared to the 100-win team the Senators had just the year before.

Jauss clashed in early June with his three best hitters – Mark Grudzielanek, Kevin Northrup and Randy Wilstead. Each was hitting above .340, but none was receiving enough love from the manager.

"Yeah, right now, they're swinging the bat well," Jauss said then, "but all it takes is good pitching to stop them. I'll tell you what, if those guys hit .380 this year, I'll kiss your ass."

Ultimately there was no need for Jauss to pucker up; none of the three came close. Each, though, had a career year. Grudzielanek batted .322 on his way to being named the Eastern League's MVP. Northrup led the league in hitting with a .331 average. Wilstead, despite missing 17 games with injuries, batted .294 with 13 homers and 64 RBIs.

Overcoming an ever-changing roster created by 69 player moves, Jauss led the Senators to 88 victories in 139 games. While not quite matching the 1993 Senators' 94 regular-season wins, Jauss' team still posted the second-highest win total in franchise history.

"His club is better prepared than probably 99 percent of the clubs in Double-A baseball," Expos general manager Kevin Malone said just before the 37-year-old Jauss was named the EL's manager of the year.

A few days later – as Harrisburg lost to Binghamton in the finals – Malone told Jauss his contract would not be renewed for 1995.

The reason was not performance but economics. Jauss was among the Expos' highest-paid instructors in the minors.

"It's sad, but it's necessary," Malone told the Canadian Press after the cash-challenged Expos also fired former major leaguers Terry Kennedy and Wallace Johnson from their Class A posts. "We must do these things to ensure our survival."

Right Man, Right Place, Right Time II

For 20 seasons, Dave Trembley rode the buses along the back roads of the lower minor leagues and caught the red eye flights that were the norm in Class AAA. He won championships with a couple of teams, including the 1987 Senators, and came close to winning a couple more.

His record over two decades in the minors was 1,369 victories and 1,413 losses. However, his bosses over those decades – the Pittsburgh Pirates, San Diego Padres, Chicago Cubs and Baltimore Orioles – cared more about how their prospects played for Trembley than how many games they won for him.

He helped develop dozens of players for the majors. Some, such as Jeff Banister, had big league careers that lasted for a game while others, such as Moises Alou, Kerry Wood and Carlos Zambrano, became All-Stars. All of his players – in the majors or minors – were exposed to Trembley's fundamentals-first approach to the game.

The Orioles, once among the most fundamentally sound teams in baseball, initially hired Trembley in 2003 to manage their fundamentally flawed Class AA team in Bowie, Maryland.

Trembley was brought in to rebuild the "Oriole Way" that had been introduced decades earlier by longtime coach Cal Ripken Sr., but had seemingly been rotting away since Ripken was fired by the team in 1992.

In the fall of 2006, after four seasons of reintroducing fundamentals to the Orioles' minor leaguers, Trembley was called to Baltimore to meet with team executives Mike Flanagan and Jim Duquette.

They asked Trembley if his teaching methods could work for a major league team that had not had a winning season in 1997.

"I said, 'Do you want me to tell you the truth, or do you want me to tell you what you want to hear?' " Trembley said. "They said to give it to them straight, so I told them the way we've done it in the minor leagues would work up here."

Flanagan and Duquette quickly made Trembley their field coordinator for the major leagues – a fancy title that essentially amounted to setting up pregame workouts. At least Trembley, after 3,000 games in the minors and winter ball, was finally getting a chance to work in the majors.

Then Trembley found himself in a strange position.

As spring training approached in 2007, bullpen coach Rick Dempsey – the former Orioles catcher and local icon – told the team he would rather work in the broadcast booth than getting relievers warmed up.

Just like that Trembley became the bullpen coach.

As spring training started, Orioles bench coach Tom Trebelhorn left the team to return home to Arizona after his wife suffered an aneurysm.

Just like that Trembley became the bench coach for manager Sam Perlozzo.

At age 55, Trembley was a major league rookie – 20 years after guiding the Senators through the first season of their modern era and to the first of six Class AA Eastern League titles in a 12-year span.

"I was never obsessed with, 'I've got to get to the big leagues,' " Trembley said. "I never thought my worth was going to be measured if I got to the big leagues or not. I always thought my worth would be (gauged) in the players I developed.

"The best ally I had in getting here (to the majors) was my four years in the minor leagues with the Orioles," he said. "I came along at just the right time with getting back to doing things the 'Oriole Way.' I came here at a time when a return to fundamentals, structure and discipline were in high demand."

Then after a 29-40 start in 2007, Perlozzo was fired.

And, just like that, Trembley was the interim manager.

The Orioles played hard enough and well enough to finish the season 40-53 and have the "interim" removed from Trembley's title.

Trembley kept the job fulltime through the 2008 and '09 seasons, slipping to 68-93 before fading to 64-98. A disastrous 15-39 start in 2010 brought to Trembley the same fate – being fired – that had befallen most of the 671 other men who had managed in the majors from 1871 through 2011.

Trembley, though, was not out of work long. He was hired by the Braves prior to the 2011 season to oversee their minor league system.

"I've managed 3,000 games in the minor leagues (and winter ball), and I wouldn't trade it," Trembley said. "What we tried to do in the minor leagues is make a difference, not only with people as players but in their lives, too.

"But one day in the big leagues," Trembley said with a smile, "that makes it all worthwhile."

7th Inning Stretch

The Next Great Thing

Before the arrival of Vladimir Guerrero, the Senators never had a prospect with that definitive "it" quality, a player who always made others stop to watch when he took batting practice.

Nine seasons in the team's modern era passed before he arrived. Another nine years would pass before the arrival of the next great thing, third baseman Ryan Zimmerman.

Like Guerrero, Zimmerman arrived on City Island as a soft-spoken, gap-to-gap hitter who gave scouts reasons to drool, opposing pitchers reasons to pause and teammates reasons to stop their own pregame routines to watch the newest Senator take BP.

By the time Zimmerman showed up on the island, a farm system that had once produced the talent to send the Senators to the Eastern League playoffs 10 times in 12 seasons from 1991 to 2002 had been scuttled.

A talent pool that was once the envy of everyone in baseball had been depleted by the time the Montreal Expos morphed into the Washington Nationals after the 2004 season.

Overseeing the dismantling of Montreal's once-rich farm system was Major League Baseball in general and Omar Minaya in particular.

Minaya became Montreal's general manager in 2002 when Expos owner Jeffrey Loria abandoned the franchise to take over the Florida Marlins. Within a few months of Minaya's hiring, the organization began trading front-line talent both in the majors and minors for marginal players who would have little or no impact with the Expos.

In less than two years, Minaya virtually gave away Barrett; pitchers Carl Pavano, Chris Young and Guillermo Mota; utility player extraordinaire Geoff Blum; and Jayson Bay, a future All-Star outfielder who was then a mid-level prospect in Class A.

Then came the really, really, really bad trade – the one that set back the franchise's farm system for years and left the rest of baseball stunned by Minaya's short-sightedness.

Believing the Expos would be folded by commissioner Bud Selig after the 2002 season, Minaya traded three of the team's top 10 prospects to Cleveland for pitcher Bartolo Colon in the unlikely hope that Montreal could catch Atlanta in the National League East or chase down a wild card playoff spot.

The Expos never came close, finishing 19 games behind the East champion Braves and 12.5 games behind San Francisco for the wild card.

For that, Minaya surrendered his franchise's future. Shortstop Brandon Phillips, pitcher Cliff Lee and center fielder Grady Sizemore, then in Class A, all went to Cleveland for Colon, who would be repackaged by Minaya and traded to the Chicago White Sox after the 2002 season for three players who never made a significant contribution to the Expos.

By 2004, the Expos could not field a farm team with a winning record on any level in the minors; their affiliates finished the season an aggregate 104 games under .500. Even the Senators, once their cornerstone affiliate and the scourge of the Eastern League, lost 90 games.

Not that Minaya hung around for the end. He bolted from the Expos in the final days of the 2004 season to become the New York Mets' general manager. The results were the same there. Despite working with $731 million in payroll over the next six seasons, Minaya failed to produce a championship team before he was fired in 2010.

Before Minaya bolted for New York, Doug Sisson – the manager who in 1999 led the Senators to their last championship – was brought in as the Expos' minor league field coordinator, charged with sifting through the rubble.

"Realistically, you've got two to four bona fide guys on every level," Sisson said. "So, now if you lose eight of those guys, it's going to take some time to rebuild."

Enter Jim Bowden, the onetime wunderkind general manager of Cincinnati who in 10 years with the Reds made so many trades that the annual team photo was often outdated before it returned from the printer.

Bowden was the perfect hire as the Expos headed to Washington, where he figured to fit in nicely with the rest of the capital's movers, shakers and headline makers.

Bowden quickly overpaid in the fall of 2004 for free agent shortstop Cristian Guzman and third baseman Vinny Castillo, signing the pair for

$23 million. He wanted to impress the team's new fan base, hoping that come April 2005 they would embrace the Expos-turned-Nationals.

The real prize, Bowden knew, would come in June, when baseball held its annual amateur draft of high school seniors and eligible college players.

With the Nationals picking fourth overall, Bowden knew this would be the moment that would define his stay in D.C., no matter how long it lasted.

Pick right, you're a genius.

Pick wrong, you're a fool.

While Bowden had embraced his reputation in Cincinnati for trading away players with nearly the same rapidity with which he acquired them, he had been staggeringly weak with his first-round selections in the amateur draft.

Ryan Zimmerman drew early comparisons to Brooks Robinson and Mike Schmidt

Pat Watkins, C.J. Nitkowski, Johnny Oliver, Matt McClendeon, Brandon Larson. Austin Kearns, Ty Howington, Dustin Moseley, David Espinosa, Jeremy Sowers, Chris Gruler, Mark Schramek.

Not a front-line player in the group, let alone an All-Star.

The draft in June 2005 was Bowden's first chance to give the Nationals their face of the future, and he knew that face had to be better than the ones he had given the Reds.

Early in the scouting process, Bowden narrowed his focus to Ryan Zimmerman. The junior third baseman from the University of Virginia was an accomplished .355 batter in three seasons there who could catch and throw the ball even better than he could hit it.

Didn't matter to Bowden that Zimmerman three years earlier hadn't been drafted out of high school.

The Zimmerman of 2002 was a proficient but hardly dominant 6-foot-1, 185-pound shortstop.

The Zimmerman of 2005 had filled up and out as a 6-foot-3, 210-pound third baseman. Bowden now saw a player he compared with Brooks Robinson and Mike Schmidt, the two greatest third basemen in the history of the game.

"As far as the players I've seen, Zimmerman is the player with the highest ceiling with the least risk," one scout said after the draft. "I wish my team was in a position to take him."

The Expos once turned out high-ceiling prospects like Zimmerman on an annual basis. In the decade leading up to Minaya's disastrous tenure, Harrisburg's pipeline to Montreal included future All-Stars in Cliff Floyd, Rondell White, Mark Grudzielanek, Ugueth Urbina, Jose Vidro, Jake Westbrook and, of course, Vladimir Guerrero.

Bowden had seen the collapse of the Expos' system from afar when he was Cincinnati's GM. By the time the Expos became the Nationals in the fall of 2004, Bowden had inherited a burned out tenement that once had been a palace of elite prospects.

"The penthouse has very little value if you don't have the foundation in place," Bowden said after taking over the Nationals. "If you don't have that foundation, you're going to crash."

Bowden was not particularly impressed with the foundation that the Expos brought to Washington, a core that included Vidro, outfielder Brad Wilkerson and journeyman pitcher Livan Hernandez.

The Nationals also had Frank Robinson, their manager and Hall of Famer, who had coaxed winning seasons from the Expos in 2002 and 2003 before Minaya's earlier strip mining of the minors caught up with the major league team in 2004.

In time, Bowden would systematically rid himself of the players and coaching staff who had relocated from Montreal. He would begin rebuilding his franchise's image in the 2005 draft, and that makeover would begin with Zimmerman.

Zimmerman fell to the Nationals at No. 4 after Arizona selected Justin Upton, a high school shortstop from Virginia Beach with the first overall pick, and Kansas City and Seattle followed by taking University of Nebraska third baseman Alex Gordon and Southern Cal catcher Jeff Clement.

While teams often have protracted negotiations with their top picks, Bowden wasted little time – maybe four minutes – in signing Zimmerman for $2.975 million. He then set a timetable to send his shiny new prize to the minors for some seasoning before unveiling him to the masses in D.C.

First, Bowden would send Zimmerman to play a few games for Savannah in the Class A South Atlantic League.

Once that went well, the next stop would be Harrisburg's City Island, where the hype for Zimmerman's arrival easily surpassed that generated by the arrival of the great Guerrero nine years earlier.

That may have been due, in part, to the fact that Zimmerman's every move during his four-game stay with Savannah was chronicled by *The Patriot-News* in Harrisburg. And, in part, because Zimmerman seemed to enjoy talking with the media. He frequently called the newspaper with updates, including one on his pending promotion to Harrisburg.

Nearly everybody enjoyed knowing of Zimmerman's whereabouts, which become routine fodder in Internet chat rooms. Kind of like "Where's Waldo?" in spikes.

One exception was Senators manager Keith Bodie, who did not care to the play "Where's Zim?" The easily irritable Bodie was annoyed by the attention for a player who was not yet on his roster.

"Any moves today?" would be among the questions Bodie fielded every day for a week prior to Zimmerman's arrival on June 25.

"Anything happening yet with Zimmerman?"

Bodie's response came in the form of a bark.

"No," Bodie would say, "he hasn't called me yet. You have a number for him that I can use?"

Bodie's preconceived notion of Zimmerman was that his new third baseman – whenever he arrived – would be just another college prima donna, an instant millionaire who would come to the ballpark in a tricked-out ride, accompanied by an inflated sense of entitlement.

Bodie, who 21 years earlier had been a third-round pick of the Mets, hated prima donnas.

But Zimmerman wasn't one. He was keenly aware of others' opinions of him, especially of people who had yet to meet him. Such as Bodie.

Even with a signing bonus of nearly $3 million and the general perception that he would be a short-timer in Class AA en route to the majors, Zimmerman made sure he arrived in Harrisburg with humility.

Ryan Zimmerman was an instant fan favorite after arriving on the island in 2005

He vowed not to flaunt a Porsche 911 with quadraphonic Blaupunkt speakers the way Nuke Laloosh had in "Bull Durham." Zimmerman's ride to the island was a white 1992 Nissan Maxima with the odometer closing in on 180,000 miles.

"It wouldn't look good to show up in a $60,000 car," Zimmerman said. "That's not the best first impression I can make."

After drafting Zimmerman at No. 4 overall, the Nationals selected 47 other high school kids and college players. Ultimately, they signed 21 of them, but none received the same attention as Zimmerman. Only four of those 21 had reached the majors by the time Zimmerman appeared in his first All-Star Game in 2009. And none of those four – outfielder Justin Maxwell (fourth round) or pitchers Marco Estrada (sixth), John Lannan (11th) and Craig Stammen (12th) – was considered a franchise player like Zimmerman.

Draft choices all have talent. Even the worst player on the roster in the minors was once special, whether in high school, college, or both.

Those with enough talent reach Double-A outposts such as Harrisburg. Getting to Triple-A and the majors requires more. This is where composure and baseball IQ separate the prospects from the wannabes.

Zimmerman never was close to being a wannabe.

"His makeup is off the charts," said one scout who spent three years watching Zimmerman, even though he knew his team would never get close enough to draft him. "We give out health questionnaires for players to fill out and send back. Sometimes, I have to call a kid back six weeks later and ask, 'Where's the form?' Zimmerman? I gave him a form on a Thursday and I had it back in the mail that Saturday."

The scouts had been watching Zimmerman since his days at Floyd E. Kellam High School in Virginia Beach.

There he had played for a traveling AAU all-star team, but not well enough to play his natural positions of shortstop and third base. He was pushed over instead to second base, so the elite team could play B.J. Upton at shortstop and David Wright at third base. At the time, Zimmerman and Upton were 16, Wright was 17. The bat boy was 13-year-old Justin Upton, who less than five years later would be the first pick in the same 2005 draft in which Zimmerman went fourth.

"We were pretty good," Wright said with a smile. "We didn't lose too many games."

The team's two top stars turned pro out of high school. Wright was picked by the New York Mets with the 38th overall pick of the 2001 draft; B.J. Upton went to the Tampa Bay Rays with the second overall pick the following year. Both reached the majors in 2004, more than a full year before Zimmerman arrived directly from Harrisburg.

"Ryan hadn't filled out yet (as a 16 year old)," Wright said after both he and Zimmerman were in the majors. "I don't think he was ready physically or mentally to make the jump from high school. Going to Virginia and getting those three years of good baseball were big for him. Some guys need those three or four years of college to mature and blossom. Ryan was one of those guys."

In 2009, Wright – the Mets' starting third baseman since midway through the 2004 season – and Zimmerman were National League teammates at the All-Star Game in St. Louis.

The 2009 season also ended with Zimmerman supplanting Wright as the National League's Gold Glove winner at third base. Zimmerman became the first former Senators third baseman to win one, although Billy Cox surely would have won a few for the Brooklyn Dodgers if the award had existed during his career from 1941 to 1955.

The 2012 season started with Zimmerman receiving a six-year, $100 million contract extension designed to keep him with the Nationals through 2019.

All-Star. Gold Glove winner. Fixture at third base. The $100 million face of a franchise.

This was the type of player Bowden envisioned on draft day 2005, when he compared Zimmerman to Robinson and Schmidt. This was before Zimmerman had played a game in the minors.

"My first reaction when I heard that was, 'Wow, he must be a pretty good player,' " said Robinson, who won a record 16 straight Gold Gloves with Baltimore from 1960 to 1975.

"He has a lot to live up to, I'll tell you that," Robinson laughed.

Like Vladimir Guerrero before him, Zimmerman tried to ignore the hype that preceded him to City Island and the gushing accolades that came with his play there.

Guerrero was able to do that in 1996, in part because he neither read the newspaper stories about him nor understood the "Wow-look-at-this-guy-play" commentaries from the English-speaking writers and sportscasters. Guerrero embraced his life inside a vacuum of blissful ignorance.

Zimmerman was not as fortunate.

"It's tough to tune out," said Zimmerman, who resisted inhaling the potentially intoxicating and distracting accolades mostly because he seemed to be closer to 40 in maturity than to 20, his age when drafted.

"You actually can't tune it out. You just try to take it in stride. When people say something to you, you thank them. You appreciate it, but after they say it, you have to forget about it. If you try to be a superstar, you're not playing your game and you're going to do worse than you think."

After a week at Class A Savannah, Zimmerman made his Class AA debut in Harrisburg on June 25, 2005. He batted third and played third on a night when temperatures approached triple digits during an 8-6 victory over Akron. He had three hits in his first game, then added 73 others in his next 62 games for a .326 batting average with nine homers and 32 RBIs.

Defensively, Zimmerman made more spectacular plays in 55 games at third base for the Senators than they had received from all the others at the position from 1987 to 2004. Among Zimmerman's specialties on defense was playing back just enough to entice a hitter into thinking that a bunt down the third-base line would make for a nice, easy hit.

One of Zimmerman's best decoys came on an August night on City Island against an unsuspecting Michael Bourn, the Reading Phillies' ridiculously fast leadoff hitter who saw Zimmerman playing back at third and promptly dropped a bunt down the line.

Zimmerman threw him out by a step.

"I laugh because I know they're going to try and bunt on him," Senators infielder Dan DeMent said. "It's like he dekes them into trying to bunt."

Later in the same game, Zimmerman sprinted down the left-field line in pursuit of a foul fly off the bat of Reading's Ryan Barthelemy. Zimmerman met the ball and the fence in front of the lower box seats at the same time, and somehow made the catch. When Derek Jeter makes the same play for the Yankees – and he has – it lives forever on SportsCenter and YouTube. Zimmerman made the play in front of only 1,975 fans.

"I don't have those 'Go Go Gadget' arms like he does," DeMent said with a sigh. "You know, special players make special plays, and he's been doing that from the day he got here."

The next night against Reading, Zimmerman dove hard to his right to snare Brian Hitchcox's drive down the third-base line. No worries if you missed the play. Just dig out the old videos of Brooks Robinson in the 1970 World Series and you'll get the idea.

"Just another day for him, whether he's high-stepping it into the stands to make a catch or diving to his left or right to make a catch," said Senators relief pitcher Danny Rueckel. "He's just amazing."

Zimmerman's diving stop of Hitchcox's liner was his last great play on the island. Minutes after the game – his 67th in the minors – Zimmerman was promoted directly to the majors for the final month of the season.

"He had a cup of coffee in the minor leagues," first baseman Larry Broadway said, putting a new twist on one of baseball's oldest clichés.

As was the case in Savannah and Harrisburg, Zimmerman was unfazed by the pitching in the majors, where he hit .397 in 20 games for the Nationals. He had 10 doubles among his first 23 hits. His play impressed even the most skeptical of his new teammates.

"He's way ahead of the game," said Nationals reliever Joey Eischen. "You can see his composure out there in the field."

That composure was built not just from Zimmerman's expertise on the field but from growing up in a home where the advice of his parents, Keith and Cheryl, always superseded anything he learned in baseball. Be grounded in life or be grounded in your room.

"I try to stay as humble as I can," Zimmerman said. "My parents have always taught me that. They would tell me that things can happen at any time and put you right back in your place."

As Zimmerman learned in 1995. That's when he was told his mother, who had starred in lacrosse for Lock Haven University in the early 1980s, was diagnosed with multiple sclerosis.

Cheryl Wallace Zimmerman's athletic genes were passed on to her sons, Ryan and Shawn, who were not yet teenagers when she was stricken with MS. Humility for the Zimmerman boys came from seeing their mother watch their games from a wheelchair.

"She doesn't let any part of her situation bring me or my brother down. She's upbeat all the time," said Zimmerman, who during his first full season in the majors in 2006 established the ziMS Foundation to benefit people with the illness.

"What happened to her taught me and my brother about life, about how anything can happen. She was an athlete, played sports in college. Now, anytime we think something is going bad for us, we look over at her and see how things can really go bad."

Zimmerman carried that humility with him to college at Virginia, where before his junior season he first met Brooks Robinson.

Robinson, the guest of honor at Virginia's annual baseball banquet, spent much of the evening sitting near a large video screen that replayed highlights of Zimmerman's college career. Then the Hall of Famer met Virginia's most recent BMOC.

The past talked to the future, and the past was impressed.

"He's the nicest kid you'd ever want to meet," Robinson said.

And one of the quietest.

At first, Zimmerman studied Robinson from across the room, too shy to approach a Hall of Famer he had only known through books, videos and stories passed down from anyone old enough to remember how Robinson's defense lifted the Orioles past the Reds in the 1970 World Series.

"It's a lot different meeting someone rather than just watching him play," Zimmerman said. "To just meet him … he's one of the best to have ever played the game. It was nice just to talk to him."

Not to mention being compared to him.

And the Children Shall Lead ... to the ATM

Lest you worry that all players – future major leaguers or not – who spent time on City Island lived in abject poverty, please take comfort. There have been a select few who could afford more. Much more. They became millionaires before ever reaching Harrisburg, thanks to signing bonuses they received after being selected in the amateur draft.

THE NOUVEAU RICHE (and their signing bonuses)

$7.5 million – Stephen Strasburg, pitcher (Senators Classes of 2010-2011), San Diego State, 2009 draft, first round (1st pick overall).

$6.25 million – Bryce Harper, outfielder (2011), College of Southern Nevada, 2010 draft, first round (1st overall).

$2.975 million – Ryan Zimmerman (2005), third baseman, University of Virginia, 2005 draft, first round (4th overall).

$2.95 million – Justin Wayne, pitcher (2001-2002), Stanford University, 2000 draft, first round (5th overall).

$2.65 million – Josh Karp, pitcher (2003, 2005), UCLA, 2001 draft, first round (6th overall).

$2.5 million – Clint Everts, pitcher (2009), Cypress Falls High School, Houston, 2002 draft, first round (5th overall).

$2.15 million – Ross Detwiler, pitcher (2009-2010), Missouri State, 2007 draft, first round (6th overall).

$1.75 million – Bill Bray, pitcher, (2005), William & Mary, 2004 draft, first round (13th overall)

Strasburg signed a major league contract in 2009, bringing the guaranteed value of his deal to $15.1 million. Harper also signed a major league deal in 2010 that, including his signing bonus, was worth $9.9 million.

The one who got away was center fielder Grady Sizemore. The Expos selected Sizemore in the third round of the 2000 draft and paid him $2 million to forego a football scholarship to the University of Washington. Sizemore was on target to play on the island for the Senators in 2003, but Montreal traded him, along with Cliff Lee and Brandon Phillips, to the Indians in a disastrous 2002 midsummer trade.

Sizemore eventually reached the island in 2003 with Class AA Akron on his way to the majors and three straight All-Star Games for the Indians.

The Greatest Season Ever

At 5-feet-9, Joe Munson was not overly tall.

At 184 pounds, though, the left handed-hitting outfielder was immensely strong.

In the middle of the Roaring Twenties, as Babe Ruth was dominating the majors, Munson was lording over the Class B New York-Penn League – the forerunner of today's Eastern League.

As a Senator, Munson became the Eastern League's first – and still only – batter to hit .400 in a season. He also totaled 33 homers and 129 runs batted in, again leading everyone in both categories to become the league's first Triple Crown winner.

Munson also led the league in slugging percentage (.755), total bases (355), hits (188), runs scored (132) and triples (17). His season was the greatest by a Senator, even though the team played that summer at the West End Grounds in uptown Harrisburg.

JOE MUNSON

No player who followed Munson to Harrisburg ever came close to matching his 1925 season. Not Jim Lemon in 1949. Not Tommy Gregg in 1987. Not even Vladimir Guerrero in 1996.

But not even Munson could save the 1925 Senators, who went 61-69 and finished sixth in the eight-team league.

By the end of the season, Munson was in Chicago, sold by the Senators to the Cubs. He made his major league debut on Sept. 18 at Wrigley Field, playing right field and going 1-for-5 with a single off right-hander Virgil Barnes in an 8-3 loss to the New York Giants.

Munson played in eight more games for the Cubs that season, batting a Harrisburg-like .400 in those games with 12 hits in only 30 at-bats. He played another 33 games for the Cubs in 1926, batting .257 with three homers in 33 games before being demoted to the minors on June 4.

Munson never returned to the majors, bouncing around in the minors before retiring in 1932 at the age of 32. He left the game as a .335 career hitter in the minors with 208 homers and 2,050 hits in 1,718 games.

Had he played today, Munson's numbers in the minors would be good enough to earn a roster spot in the majors. Instead, Munson, originally from Renovo, Pa. and educated at Lehigh University, retired during the

Great Depression. He stayed in Pennsylvania and settled in Drexel Hill, where he died in 1991.

Munson never stopped thinking about his one season in Harrisburg, which he always listed among his career highlights. Nor did Munson ever stop thinking about hitting, which he believed he still could do even as he aged.

"I'm in good health," Munson wrote in a letter decades after his retirement, " … only wished I were 40 years younger to get a crack at that juiced up rabbit ball."

The Long Ball

Joe Munson held Harrisburg's single-season record for home runs for 74 years – longer than Babe Ruth held the major league record with 60 from 1927 to 1961 and longer than Roger Maris owned the record of 61 before the steroid-tainted Mark McGwire came along with 70 in 1998.

When Munson hit 33 homers in 1925, however, the Senators were playing off the island and in uptown Harrisburg at the West End Grounds.

His franchise record stood until Andy Tracy hit 37 homers in 1999.

As for those who played their home games on City Island, the following is the progression of Harrisburg's single-season home run record holders since 1890:

5: Frank Grant, 1890
 John Meister, 1893
9: Dummy Stephenson, 1894
10: Merle Whitney, 1909
11: Glenn Killinger, 1927
 Ray Flood, 1928
18: Ray Flood, 1929
 Bobby Estalella, 1935
21: Arnold Greene, 1940
24: Ed Mutryn, 1946
27: Jim Lemon, 1949
37: Andy Tracy, 1999

ANDY TRACY

The Greatest Performance Ever

Joe Munson certainly had some great games for the Senators during the 1925 season in which the outfielder became the Eastern League's first and only .400 hitter, as well as its first Triple Crown winner.

Oscar Charleston, the Hall of Famer from the all-black Harrisburg Giants of the mid-1920s, surely had his memorable games, too. Same through the years for Billy Cox, Jim Lemon, Moises Alou, Vladimir Guerrero, Ryan Zimmerman and Stephen Strasburg.

Then there was journeyman first baseman Ron Johns, who arguably had the greatest single game on City Island by anybody. Ever.

RON JOHNS

Johns played 40 games for the 1987 Senators, batting .302 with nine homers and 44 runs batted in. The first three of those homers and nine of those RBIs came on one night – June 17 – during a 26-9 rout of the Albany-Colonie Yankees.

All Johns did before a crowd of 4,197 was go 6-for-6 with five runs scored, three singles, and those three homers and nine RBIs.

Batting cleanup, the 6-foot-2, 195-pound Johns singled in each of his first three at-bats. He launched a solo homer to left field off Yankees reliever Mo Guercio in the fifth inning, a grand slam to right-center off Guercio in the sixth and a two-run homer to left off Steve George in the seventh. Each homer came with two outs.

He was playing in only his third game on the island after being acquired a few days earlier from St. Louis for Senators outfielder Ben Abner.

John's performance overshadowed career games by Tommy Gregg, and Dimas Gutierrez, who were each 5-for-6. Batting third, Gregg's single, triple, homer, single and single came in consecutive innings from the third through the seventh. Hitting sixth, Gutierrez had three singles, a homer and triple in five straight at-bats spanning the third through eighth innings.

"I was dreaming tonight," Johns told *The Patriot-News*. "I hit two home runs a couple of times, but not three, not even close to it."

Within a year, Johns was back on the island, batting just .213 for the 1988 Senators with one homer in 19 games before leaving pro baseball at the age of 25.

The Natural

Geoff Blum was a 25-year-old infielder whose career was going nowhere in the spring of 1998.

He had been a star at the University of California four years earlier, when he had been selected by the Montreal Expos in the seventh round of the 1994 amateur draft. He finished that summer batting .344 for Montreal's entry-level team in the Class A New York-Penn League.

That outstanding start as a pro was a memory by 1998.

The higher Blum climbed in the Expos' system, the more his production dropped. The .344 average from 1994 was followed by .263 for Class A West Palm Beach in 1995 and then .240 with Harrisburg in 1996 before an equally unimpressive .238 at Triple-A Ottawa in 1997. In those three seasons, the 6-foot-3, 195-pound Blum had only five homers in 1,454 at-bats, making him the largest slap-hitting middle infielder in the minors.

Unbeknownst to most, Blum's right elbow was throbbing. After a dismal 4-for-23 start for Ottawa in 2008, Blum elected to have surgery to remove bone chips from his elbow.

Initially the operation changed nothing. Even with the chips gone, Blum's skid continued. He batted just .167 in neophyte-level Gulf Coast League before hitting .276 in the Class A Florida State League.

Clearly, this was not the best path back to Triple-A, let alone the majors. So, the Expos gave Blum a choice: Return to Ottawa and sit on the bench for the rest of the 1998 season or go back to Harrisburg, play every day and provide protection in the lineup for Michael Barrett, the latest rising star in the Expos' organization.

Blum opted for Harrisburg, where he batted .309 in 39 games with 21 extra-base hits and 21 RBIs, helping the Senators win their third straight Eastern League title.

Along the way – on the night of Aug. 6, 1998 – Blum made history on City Island.

Against New Haven, the Colorado Rockies' Class AA affiliate, the body-pierced, switch-hitting infielder from Redwood City, California, accomplished arguably the rarest of all single-game feats for a batter.

He needed only four at-bats to hit for a natural cycle – a single, double, triple and home run in that order.

Blum also drove in all three of the Senators' runs in a 3-2 victory before a crowd of 6,126 at RiverSide Stadium.

Hours before the game, Senators manager Rick Sweet posted his lineup card with Blum batting fourth – a position in the order he had never occupied before with the Senators. Batting cleanup on the island often was reserved for an elite prospect like Cliff Floyd, not for perceived roster fillers like Blum.

Geoff Blum sits alone in Senators' record book

"I was giving Sweet a hard time before the game, asking him if he really was trying to win," Blum said.

Swinging left-handed in all four at-bats, Blum started his night with a bases-loaded single off the right-field wall in the bottom of the first, then broke his bat on a double to right in the third.

For his next at-bat in the sixth inning, Blum switched to a non-personalized, blonde C-271 model bat – standard issue for minor leaguers – and tripled down the right-field line, scoring Barrett to tie the score at 2.

Blum admittedly turned selfish in his final at-bat in the eighth inning.

He went for the home run.

"To be honest with you," he said, "… yeah, I was trying to hit one."

When reliever Heath Bost, a 24-year-old righty in the midst of a 10-year career in the minors, fell behind in the count 2-1, he did the predictable thing in the eighth inning of a tied game: He threw a fastball.

Blum elevated his swing. The result: A homer to right-center.

"I was thinking he didn't want to fall behind 3-1," Blum said. "I was thinking he would want to throw a fastball for a strike. I got lucky and guessed right."

The Worst Trade Ever?

To this day, older Cincinnati fans rue the day after the 1965 season when Reds president Bill DeWitt figuratively cut open Frank Robinson's leg, counted the rings as if he were a tree and declared his best player to be "an old 30."

DeWitt shipped Robinson to Baltimore for middle-of-the-rotation pitcher Milt Pappas, declining reliever Jack Baldschun and journeyman outfielder Dick Simpson.

The trade probably had less to do with Robinson's age and more to do with the raise the All-Star right fielder believed he deserved on top of the $57,000 he earned from the Reds in 1965. In his first season in Baltimore, Robinson won the Triple Crown and American League's Most Valuable Player award while leading the Orioles to their first World Series title.

Early in the 1966 season, Robinson – careening toward his 31st birthday and, in DeWitt's mind, certain implosion – became the only player to hit a ball completely out of Baltimore's Memorial Stadium when he drove Luis Tiant's 1-2 pitch 451 feet to left field. After clearing the bleachers, the ball rolled another 90 feet before stopping more than a city block from home plate.

By this time, of course, Reds' fans already knew their team had made one of the worst trades in history. The rest of baseball soon agreed, putting the Robinson-for-spare-parts deal right up there with the 1964 trade that sent 25-year-old outfielder Lou Brock from the Cubs to the Cardinals for two fading pitchers – Ernie Broglio and Bobby Shantz – and light-hitting outfielder Doug Clemens.

Like Robinson, Brock ended up in the Hall of Fame.

Then there was the 1971 deal that sent the hard-throwing, then-erratic, future Hall of Fame pitcher Nolan Ryan and three prospects from the New York Mets to the California Angels for aging infielder Jim Fregosi. Twenty-years later, Baltimore dealt three future All-Stars – pitchers Curt Schilling and Pete Harnisch, and outfielder Steve Finley – to Houston for power-hitting first baseman Glenn Davis. Davis did little for the Orioles, totaling 24 homers in three seasons after averaging 24 homers over seven seasons with the Astros.

Brandon Phillips was the Expos' top prospect in 2002 when he was traded to Cleveland

Take your pick as to which falls first under the heading of "Worst Trade Ever" during the 20th century.

The start of the 21st century, though, brought a trade that quickly joined the list of all-time giveaways.

This one came on June 27, 2002, when the Montreal Expos shipped three of their top prospects, along with journeyman first baseman Lee Stevens, to Cleveland for sporadically brilliant pitcher Bartolo Colon and reliever Tim Drew.

The three prospects were shortstop Brandon Phillips and pitcher Cliff Lee, who were already starring in Harrisburg, and Grady Sizemore, an emerging center fielder in Class A scheduled to reach City Island by 2003.

The scuttling of Montreal's once-flourishing farm system – Phillips, Lee and Sizemore were among the Expos' top 10 prospects – was made by neophyte general manager Omar Minaya.

In the confusion and BS that was commissioner Bud Selig's talk of folding two teams – the Expos being one of them – Minaya assumed the role of fantasy league owner.

With little, if any, forethought, Minaya dealt away premier prospects from a franchise he believed had no future in return for Colon in the desperate hope the right-hander could revive the Expos' playoff chances.

At the time of the trade, the Expos were in second place in the National League East, seven games behind the Atlanta Braves with 86 games remaining in the season.

When the summer ended, the Expos were still second, but 19 games behind Atlanta. No fault of Colon's, though; he went 10-4 in 17 starts for Montreal.

But then Minaya turned around in the offseason and inexplicably traded Colon, who still had a year left on his contract, to the Chicago White Sox for pitchers Orlando Hernandez and Rocky Biddle, and first baseman Jeff Liefer.

Both Biddle and Liefer struggled for the Expos while Hernandez, a onetime World Series star with the Yankees, never pitched an inning for Montreal.

As for Phillips, Lee and Sizemore – the centerpieces in the trade from Cleveland's perspective – they turned into All-Stars, and more, in the major leagues.

Lee was 83-48 in seven-plus seasons for the Indians – including going 22-3 and winning the American League's Cy Young Award in 2008. Cleveland then flipped him to the Philadelphia Phillies in 2009 for four prospects.

Sizemore became one of the American League's premier center fielders, representing Cleveland in three straight All-Star Games from 2006 to 2008 before injuries slowed his career.

After clashing with the Indians' management, Phillips was traded to Cincinnati, where he switched positions with the Reds and became one of the National League's most productive second basemen.

Entering the 2012 season, Lee, Sizemore and Phillips had combined for eight All-Star appearances, six Top 25 finishes in the MVP voting, five Gold Gloves, two Silver Sluggers and a Cy Young Award.

Colon, too, was still hanging around in 2012 at age 39, having exchanged uniforms six times since he was an Expo with his latest stop coming in Oakland.

Sill, you can't help but wonder how Lee, Sizemore and Phillips would have turned out for the Expos and, later, the Washington Nationals.

One of a Kind Beats Four of a Kind

From the first World Series in 1903 through the 2008 Fall Classic, only four pitchers struck out 10 or more batters in a postseason game while walking absolutely no one.

Only four times in 1,229 postseason games. The odds of any pitcher accomplishing this feat are staggeringly slim.

Pittsburgh right-hander Deacon Phillippe was the first to do so, and he did so rather quickly, striking out 10 Boston batters and walking none in the first World Series game played on Oct. 1, 1903.

Cliff Lee as a Senator early in the 2002 season

Don Newcombe of the Brooklyn Dodgers was next, striking out 11 without allowing a walk on Oct. 5, 1949 at Yankee Stadium. Like Phillippe, Newcombe was a right-hander.

Unlike Phillippe, though, Newcombe lost his game when Tommy Henrich led off the bottom of the ninth with a solo homer to right that gave New York a 1-0 victory in Game 1 of that Series.

Tom Seaver was even better than Newcombe, although he suffered the same outcome. The New York Mets' right-hander struck out 13 in Game 1 of the 1973 National League Championship Series on Oct. 6 at Riverfront Stadium. Seaver, though, lost the game 2-1 on Johnny Bench's solo homer with one out in the bottom of the ninth.

Fifteen years later, Padres left-hander Sterling Hitchcock struck out 13 batters and walked none in only six innings of a 6-1 victory over Houston in the deciding game of the 1998 NLCS on Oct. 4 in San Diego.

Of course, no one knows what might have happened if the 1904 and 1994 postseasons had been played.

Then along came Cliff Lee, the left-hander who had starred on City Island for the Senators in 2002 before becoming part of the prospects-for-magic-beans trade that Expos general manager Omar Minaya made with Cleveland.

Lee went on to become a Cy Young Award winner in Cleveland and an All-Star selection for three different teams in a four-season span from 2008 to 2011.

In between, Lee made some history. He needed only the 2009 and 2010 postseasons to not just match the double-digit strikeouts, no-walk performances of Phillippe, Newcombe, Seaver and Hitchcock but to surpass each of them.

Four times over.

On Oct. 18, 2009, Lee struck out 13 in eight innings of an 11-0 victory over the Dodgers in Game 3 of the NLCS in Philadelphia.

Ten days later, Lee – a midseason acquisition by the Phillies from Cleveland that summer – struck out 10 in a 6-0 shutout of the Yankees in Game 1 of the World Series in New York.

Pitching for Texas less than a year later, the well-traveled Lee opened the 2010 American League Division Series with a seven-inning, 10-strikeout performance in the Rangers' 5-1 victory Oct. 6 at Tampa Bay.

Lee returned to Tropicana Field six days later to close out the ALDS by striking out 11 in a 6-1 complete game victory.

That pair of games in 2010 left both his Texas teammates and the beaten Rays calling Lee a "warrior." Lee eschewed such comments.

"A warrior is someone that is like a gladiator ... when I think warrior, it sounds like a fighter. I am not really that," said Lee, whom the Expos selected out of the University of Arkansas with the 105th overall pick of the 2000 amateur draft.

"I'm a professional athlete. I am a pitcher. But I'm competitive. I hate to lose. ... If that goes under 'warrior,' I guess I'm that. But I am just extremely competitive is how I would phrase it."

Mark Grudzielanek during his MVP season with the Senators in 1994

Best of Show

The Senators won Class AA Eastern League championships in 1987, 1993 and then four straight from 1996 to 1999.

Individually, the Senators had six Eastern League most valuable players in an 11-season span from 1989 to1999. Beyond the island, Senators' alumni entering the 2012 season have collected Gold Gloves, Silver Sluggers, a Cy Young Award and an American League MVP trophy.

Overall, not a bad haul.

EASTERN LEAGUE MVPs
1989 – Wes Chamberlain, right fielder
1991 – Matt Stairs, infielder
1993 – Cliff Floyd, first baseman
1994 – Mark Grudzielanek, shortstop
1996 – Vladimir Guerrero, right fielder
1999 – Andy Tracy, third baseman

MAJOR LEAGUE GOLD GLOVES
2001 – Orlando Cabrera (Senators Class of '97), shortstop, Montreal Expos
2006 – Mark Grudzielanek (1994), second baseman, Kansas City Royals
2007 – Orlando Cabrera (1997), shortstop, Anaheim Angels
2008 – Brandon Phillips (2001-2002), second baseman, Cincinnati Reds
2009 – Ryan Zimmerman (2005), third baseman, Washington Nationals
2010 – Brandon Phillips (2001-2002), second baseman, Cincinnati Reds
2011 – Brandon Phillips (2001-2002), second baseman, Cincinnati Reds

COMEBACK PLAYER OF THE YEAR, AMERICAN LEAGUE
2008 – Cliff Lee (2002), pitcher, Cleveland Indians

CY YOUNG AWARD, AMERICAN LEAGUE
2008 – Cliff Lee (2002), pitcher, Cleveland Indians

MOST VALUABLE PLAYER, AMERICAN LEAGUE
2004 – Vladimir Guerrero (1996), designated hitter, Anaheim Angels

SILVER SLUGGER AWARDS
1994 – Moises Alou (1989-1990), outfielder, Montreal Expos
1998 – Moises Alou (1989-1990), outfielder, Houston Astros
1999 – Vladimir Guerrero (1996), outfielder, Montreal Expos
2000 – Vladimir Guerrero (1996), outfielder, Montreal Expos
2002 – Vladimir Guerrero (1996), outfielder, Montreal Expos
2003 – Jose Vidro (1995-1996), second baseman, Montreal Expos
2004 – Vladimir Guerrero (1996), outfielder, Anaheim Angels
2005 – Michael Barrett (1998), catcher, Chicago Cubs
         Vladimir Guerrero (1996), outfielder, Los Angeles Angels
2006 – Vladimir Guerrero (1996), outfielder, Los Angeles Angels
2007 – Vladimir Guerrero (1996), outfielder, Los Angeles Angels
2009 – Ryan Zimmerman (2005), third baseman, Washington Nationals
2010 – Vladimir Guerrero (1996), designated hitter, Texas Rangers
         Ryan Zimmerman (2005), third baseman, Washington Nationals
2011 – Brandon Phillips (2001-2002), second baseman, Cincinnati Reds

8th Inning

When a Can't-Miss Kid Misses

The writers and editors at *Baseball America*, savants of all things in the minor leagues, have projected starting lineups for years. Not for the current season – that would be too easy – but for a few summers down the road.

The projections are based on how well prospects have performed in the minor leagues and how they may fare in the majors. Like most predictions, they are entertaining, if not entirely accurate.

As the 21st century was getting under way, the national publication projected Scott Hodges to be the starting third baseman for the 2005 Montreal Expos. Made sense, particularly after the light-hitting Shane Andrews lost the job and was released in 1999, and after Michael Barrett, the shortstop-turned-catcher-turned-third baseman was turned back into a catcher. Third base in Montreal became a refuge for utility players such as Geoff Blum and Jamey Carroll, as well as sporadically brilliant stopgaps such as Tony Batista and Fernando Tatis.

Hodges was an upgrade over all of them, both with the bat and the glove. By 2002, he had been anointed as the Expos' third baseman of the future. Just needed another season or two in Class AA and AAA.

That was the perfect scenario, both for the Expos and for Hodges. Life, though, has precious few perfect scenarios as both the Expos and Hodges were soon to learn.

By the time 2005 arrived, Montreal no longer existed in Major League Baseball; the cash-strapped franchise had been taken over by commissioner Bud Selig in 2002 and relocated to Washington, D.C., after the 2004 season.

Hodges did not make the trip with them to Washington.

As the Nationals gathered for their first spring training in the still-developing town of Viera on Florida's Atlantic Coast, Hodges was in Baton Rouge, Louisiana, for yet another doctor's appointment. He had already seen plenty of doctors over the previous four years.

In 2001 with the Senators, Hodges had his first full season on the island cut short by Crohn's disease. An infected right quadriceps from a spider bite in 2002 kept him out of the Senators' playoff run that ended against Norwich in the Eastern League finals.

Hodges recovered in 2003 to bat .288 at Class AAA Edmonton, ending the season with 12 homers, 66 runs batted in and a renewed hope that he would be the Expos' third baseman of the immediate future. Edmonton was just another stepping stone on his way to the majors, just as places like Burlington, Vermont, and Fayetteville, North Carolina, had been after Hodges had turned pro in 1997 out of Henry Clay High School in Lexington, Kentucky.

What followed in 2004 was the beginning of the most difficult time in Hodges' life. A woeful .212 batting average in Edmonton made him suspect the Crohn's disease that ate away at his intestines in 2001 was returning.

The Expos reacted to Hodges' lackluster performance in 2004 by taking him off their 40-man roster and cutting him loose as a minor league free agent.

Hodges, though, had more immediate concerns after he discovered some lumps along his spinal column. He began to wonder not about his future on the field but his future, period.

Being told you have cancer can make you think that way.

During the first week of February 2005, when Hodges should have been wowing the Nationals in spring training, he was waiting in Baton Rouge for a biopsy to determine the extent of the cancer that doctors had come across four months earlier.

Being poked and prodded by doctors looking for cancer was something Hodges didn't envision in 1997, when he was named Kentucky's "Mr. Baseball" before being selected by Montreal with the 38th pick of the amateur draft. The Expos paid him a signing bonus of $487,500 and – as *Baseball America* would later do – quickly projected him as their third baseman come the new millennium.

"I thought I would have been there (in the majors) for a few years by now," Hodges said between one of his dozen rounds of chemotherapy in 2005.

Instead, he was back on City Island in 2005, trying to get through the chemo and its side effects while working to revive his now-teetering career.

"Stuff happens," Hodges said.

Stuff.

That's quite the euphemism for the personal hell Hodges had endured, from the debilitating Crohn's disease during the summer of 2002 to the cancer that was confirmed on Feb. 1, 2005, when Hodges officially went from can't-miss prospect to one of 60,000 Americans diagnosed annually with Hodgkin's disease.

Hodges' cancer was confirmed after countless blood draws, scans and biopsies to determine why he was waking up in the middle of the night drenched in sweat and spiking temperatures of 104. Doctors found more than 30 tumors in his body, including one of the size of a golf ball embedded near his spine.

The thought of playing in the majors, let alone becoming an All-Star there as Hodges had once envisioned suddenly became secondary.

"Death," he said, "is what really came to my mind first."

His second thought was finding a phone. He needed to call his teammates. He needed to tell his family. Mostly, he needed to break the news to Cristyn, his bride of only a few weeks.

"My heart dropped. You hear 'cancer' and you immediately think you're going to die," Hodges said. "I just got married in November and I'm thinking, 'What am I going to tell my wife?' "

As chemotherapy sessions were being arranged, Hodges made plans to travel to Florida to talk with his teammates, some of whom he had known for nearly a decade. In time, they would see his shaved head, and a body that no longer was a solid 190 pounds. They also would see a softening in Hodge's persona. No longer was he an ultra-cocky Alpha male jock.

"When I had the Crohn's, I wondered 'Why?' and 'How good could I have been,' " Hodges said. "The first day I found out I had cancer I said, 'Why?' But then, I thought I couldn't pout about it; I just had to beat it."

If doctors and family didn't remind Hodges of his goal – live first, play later – then the words of singer-songwriter Tim McGraw surely did.

"You know what's weird?" Hodges said. "The day I get the call about the cancer, that whole day I was hearing the Tim McGraw song, that 'Live

Like You Were Dying' song. I must have heard the song 10 times that day."

McGraw wrote the song in memory of his father, Tug McGraw, the free-spirited relief pitcher for World Series winners in New York and Philadelphia who died of brain cancer in January 2004.

Nine days after he heard his own bad news and after McGraw's lyrics first filled his head, Hodges walked into the Mary Bird Perkins Cancer Center in Baton Rouge to receive the first of 12 bi-weekly treatments. There, Hodges saw others like him waiting to receive drugs so toxic that some oncologists are fond of saying they will kill the cancer just before they kill the patient.

"You wonder why some things happen the way they do," Hodges said. "I've met some people and it's sad to know that some of them aren't going to beat it."

Hodges told himself he was going to beat the disease.

Shortly after the 2005 season began, Hodges quietly – and with the Nationals' blessing – started working out with Washington's Class AAA affiliate in New Orleans, a mere 90-minute drive from Baton Rouge, where he had his chemo. Hodges quickly regained not just his enthusiasm, but the 10 pounds he lost during the initial treatments.

By May 15, Hodges had signed a minor league contract with the Nationals.

By May 22, he was on his way back to Harrisburg to play in Class AA for the first time since 2002.

"I would have played in rookie ball," Hodges said as he rejoined the Senators. "Three months ago, if you would have seen me laying on that bed, getting a procedure done … nobody would have believed I would be where I'm at now."

Hodges already had completed nine of his 12 treatments before returning to City Island. Two more treatments were scheduled in Harrisburg, with the final one planned for Baton Rouge during the All-Star break in July.

The semi-regular injections to boost Hodges' white blood cell count ran $5,500 per shot. The costs for everything totaled well into six figures, but were covered by Major League Baseball's insurance plan and the philanthropic Baseball Assistance Team.

The Nationals covered Hodges' spirits by giving him a chance to re-connect with the game he admittedly once took for granted.

The injections to boost the immune system allowed Hodges to play. An anti-nausea medication called Anzemet allowed him to keep his food down.

"I can take the Anzemet," Hodges said, "and ride a roller coaster the same day."

None of the medications, though, could help the left handed-hitting Hodges recover his bat speed. What once was a sneaky quick bat that sprayed doubles from gap to gap had slowed considerably after the treatments.

During his comeback, Hodges played 10 of his 11 games with the Senators at first base, flawlessly handling all of his 96 chances at a position he had not played since 2000. His bat, though, was nowhere near what it was in 2000, when he hit .306 in 111 games at Class A Jupiter with 14 homers and 83 runs batted in.

Hodges' return trip to Harrisburg in 2005 produced only five singles in 38 at-bats before the Nationals sent him to finish the season at Class AAA New Orleans. The results there were no better as Hodges managed only a single and double in 14 at-bats.

Hodges never played pro ball again. He was finished four months shy of his 27th birthday.

He left the game a different person, though. The failures so indigenous to the game – lineouts, strikeouts, runners left on base – no longer nagged at Hodges as they once did. Failure on the field became acceptable. Getting healthy – and staying that way – was more important than the game, a perspective that had eluded Hodges until he was diagnosed with cancer.

Instead of becoming a major leaguer, Hodges became a mortgage broker in Baton Rouge, where he lives with Cristyn and their two children.

"The world is a different place now from the one I was living in," Hodges said.

"It's the same world, but I appreciate things more, things that I didn't appreciate before. That's not to say I would go back and do things differently, but I have learned some lessons in life."

Five O'Clock Thunder

When Jim Tracy managed the Senators in 1993, he knew two things for certain before each night game on City Island.

One was that he would be fielding one of the most impressive teams in the history of the minor leagues. The Senators won 100 of 147 games on their way to the Eastern League championship.

TYRONE WOODS

The second? He would unfailingly place Tyrone Woods with the last group of hitters during batting practice – a spot usually reserved for the Senators' best prospects.

Cliff Floyd, Shane Andrews, Rondell White and Glenn Murray all took turns in that last group.

They were seen by the Montreal Expos as front-line prospects; Woods was not.

By 1993, the 23-year-old outfielder from Brooksville, Florida, was considered an "organizational player," code words in baseball for a minor league lifer.

Nonetheless, Tracy included the 6-foot-1, 200-pound Woods in that final BP group at 5 p.m., because Tracy knew the other team would be watching.

While opposing players did their pregame stretches in left field before their own BP, Woods routinely hit long, towering drives over their heads, well beyond the left-field wall.

"We demoralize a lot of teams that way," Tracy said, remembering how visiting players scrambled out of the way of Wood's BP show.

Come game time, Woods was back on the bench. There was little playing time for him in an outfield that included four future major leaguers – Floyd, White, Murray and Curtis Pride.

"Prospects play," Woods lamented, "and suspects sit. ... I just didn't carry it over to 7 o'clock, and that's when it counted."

The Island's "Major League" Moment

The palm trees in the players' parking lot were a sign of things to come on City Island. Palm trees simply don't exist in Harrisburg. Yet there they were, lining the players' lot beyond the right-field bleachers near the end of the 1993 season.

Actor Dennis Haysbert on the island

As soon as the Senators finished their final home playoff game on Sept. 12, production crews began repositioning the palms around the ballpark to give RiverSide Stadium the look of a Florida spring training site. This became the backdrop for the characters from the fictitious Cleveland Indians for scenes in "Major League II."

With the Senators on the road to finish the playoffs, actors Charlie Sheen, Tom Berenger, Dennis Haysbert, James Gammon and Corbin Bernsen arrived in Harrisburg to film their make-believe spring training on a City Island made up to resemble the Indians' spring training home in Winter Haven, Florida.

Observant moviegoers from the Harrisburg area can find plenty of RiverSide Stadium in the movie, including outfield fence signs advertising the East Mall, Sutliff Chevrolet and Wolf's Bus Line. Also remaining in the film was the billboard down the left-field line emblazoned with then-mayor Stephen R. Reed's welcome to Harrisburg. There was one slight alteration – the sign identified Reed as the mayor of Winter Haven.

While the cameras rolled on the island, the Senators rallied in Canton, outscoring the real Indians' Class AA affiliate 23-4 in three games to win the Eastern League title. The Senators were back from Ohio with the championship trophy long before filming finished on the island. Director David S. Ward kept his cast and crew in Harrisburg for two weeks, but ended up using the local scenes for only 15 minutes or so in the 105-minute film.

213

Role Reversal

After watching pitcher T.J. Tucker launch three balls off the pavilion roof beyond RiverSide Stadium's wall in left-center field on April 29, 2000, Senators manager Doug Sisson came up with an idea for Tucker's next start.

For the following afternoon's game against the Reading Phillies, Sisson listed Tucker seventh in the batting order rather than ninth, where every other manager not named Tony LaRussa would have put him.

Batting ninth is what pitchers do, according to the oft-quoted but never-seen "book" of baseball strategy, axioms and other absolutes.

And who would argue with the book of Mack, McGraw and Murtaugh? The iconoclastic Sisson.

"Until I find out who wrote the 'book,' " Sisson said, "I'm not going to worry about the 'book.' "

Besides, Sisson liked Tucker's lifetime .286 batting average – albeit in only 14 at-bats – so he batted his pitcher ahead of catcher Jaime Malave, a .251 hitter in 740 at-bats as a pro, and third baseman Garret Osilka, who at that point had not had a hit in three weeks.

While the Senators won the game 8-5, Tucker contributed nothing at the plate with only a weak infield pop-out and an even weaker strikeout.

Malave and Osilka were a combined 0-for-4 with two strikeouts and two flyouts. As if batting two spots behind the pitcher was not embarrassing enough, Osilka was demoted after the game to Class A Jupiter.

"I thought Tucker was the seventh-best hitter in the lineup," Sisson said, "but I told him that if he swings the bat like that again, he'll hit ninth for the rest of his life."

Batting last is exactly what Tucker did during his five seasons in the majors. Tucker, though, rewarded Sisson for his initial confidence in him. Just over a month after batting seventh in the Senators' order, Tucker stepped up to the batter's box in Montreal's Olympic Stadium and singled off Baltimore's Pat Rapp in his first at-bat in the majors. He added nine more hits in 35 other at-bats over the next four seasons to finish with a lifetime major league batting average of .278.

> *"We wanted them to stay aggressive, to swing at the first pitch. I guess it paid off."*
>
> *Manager Luis Dorante*

Threepeat

Early in the 2001 season, while the Senators tried to get above .500, the middle of their batting order – Valentino Pascucci, Matt Cepicky and Scott Hodges – struggled just to put the ball in play.

Then they met Altoona relief pitcher Geraldo Padua.

Padua was trying to protect the Curve's 2-1 lead in the bottom of the eighth inning on April 23, 2001. But on this night the right-hander's slider didn't slide very much and his fastball wasn't very fast.

The result: Three pitches, three swings, three baseballs flying over the outfield fence at RiverSide Stadium.

After recording two quick outs, Padua jumped ahead of Pascucci 0-2 with a pair of not-so-fast fastballs. Pascucci worked the count to 2-2 on a pair of sliders off the plate. After fouling off another slider, Pascucci pummeled the next pitch – a fourth straight slider – off the third tier of billboards in left field to tie the score at 2.

"When Val hit his home run, I thought their pitcher was going to want to get ahead in the count," Cepicky said. "Nine out of 10 times, he's going to want to put one in there, because he doesn't want to get behind. You're looking for something to drive there."

Padua's next pitch was a straight, four-seam fastball that Cepicky drove over the fence in right-center. Padua stayed with his fastball against Hodges, who promptly lined the first pitch he saw over the wall in right-center for a 4-2 lead.

The back-to-back-to-back homers gave the Senators a 4-2 victory before a crowd of 3,233. They also gave Pascucci, Cepicky and Hodges the distinction of being the only players in the first 25 years of the franchise's modern era to homer in three consecutive at-bats.

"We wanted them to stay aggressive, to swing at the first pitch," Senators manager Luis Dorante said. "I guess it paid off."

Moonlight madness

There wasn't much of a crowd by the time the game drifted into the 13th inning.

There was, however, a full moon over City Island on May 24, 2002 – and that was enough to turn the night from weird to wacky.

Having already used three relief pitchers to get through the 10th inning against Binghamton, Senators manager Dave Huppert had to make a decision. Lacking better options, Huppert called on Jeff McAvoy, a right-hander with an 8.37 earned-run average.

> *"I could get one more out with half a foot."*
>
> *Jeff McAvoy*

McAvoy worked three perfect innings. Even better, he ended the game himself by driving a 2-1 pitch over the wall in left-center for a solo homer that gave the Senators a 5-4 victory. Losing pitcher Rene Vega was subjected to the shame of not just of serving up a game-winning homer to another pitcher, but of doing so to one who batted just three times in a three-year career.

"The home run was good, but those three innings were better," said McAvoy, whose ERA dropped nearly a run that night to 7.43.

McAvoy's renaissance was brief.

Two days after his homer, the 25-year-old McAvoy suffered a fractured bone in his right foot when he was struck by Aaron McNeal's ninth inning grounder up the middle.

Huppert and trainer Rich Ramirez went to the mound to assess the damage, but McAvoy was not about to willingly leave the game. He needed just one more out to pick up the save in a 4-2 victory for starter Cliff Lee.

"I needed all the innings I could get," McAvoy said. "I could get one more out with half a foot."

McAvoy needed only two more pitches to get Virgil Chevalier to fly out and end the game. But there were not many pitches left in his career; McAvoy was demoted shortly thereafter to Brevard County in the Class A Florida State League. The 2002 season was his last as a player.

One of a Kind, Kind of

With the exception of the 29 games he played for the Angels and Tigers in the late 1970s, Dave Machemer spent all or parts of the last five decades riding buses in the minor leagues.

Statistically, those 29 games in the majors didn't amount to much. The middle infielder from St. Joseph, Michigan, batted .229 in 48 at-bats for California and Detroit over the 1978 and '79 seasons.

Historically, though, Machemer left his mark on June 21, 1978, leading off the top of the first inning of his first major league game with a home run.

A quarter-century before becoming the Senators' manager in 2003, Machemer was wearing the uniform of the California Angels when he made his major league debut a memorable one, lining Geoff Zahn's 3-2 pitch just inside the left-field foul pole at Minnesota's old Metropolitan Stadium.

The stadium's scoreboard flashed a message noting the hit was the first in the majors for the Angels' 27-year-old shortstop. No mention, though, was made of its uniqueness, so it's doubtful any of the 10,801 fans realized what they had witnessed.

Three other players – Heinie Mueller (Phillies, 1938), Jose Offerman (Dodgers, 1990) and Jon Nunnally (Royals, 1995) – started their careers with leadoff homers – but in the bottom of the first.

"Really? I didn't know that," Machemer said the day before starting his second season as Harrisburg's manager in 2004. "Are you sure about this? Really, are you sure?"

Yes. Really.

"I've got to go tell my players," Machemer said. "They won't believe it."

Armed with the knowledge and bragging rights, Machemer gave his players the news, even if it was 26 years old.

Then the baseball gods played a cruel trick. Within three hours of learning about his one-of-a-kind moment, Machemer had to share it.

At 7:36 p.m. on April 6, 2004, Kaz Matsui from Osaka, Japan, stepped into the batter's box to start the Mets' game at Atlanta's Turner Field.

Like Machemer in 1978, Matsui was making his major league debut and, just like Machemer, Matsui was a shortstop.

Unlike Machemer, Matsui came to the majors as a highly touted player, a switch-hitter and seven-time Japanese All-Star signed by New York a few months earlier.

Unfortunately for Machemer, the left handed-swinging Matsui drove a first-pitch fastball from right-hander Russ Ortiz over the center-field wall.

Matsui's achievement was quickly noted by the 50 members of the Japanese media in Atlanta who had been assigned to document his every spit, scratch and swing.

Machemer learned of Matsui's homer the next morning, when Senators pitcher Luke Lockwood told him he had seen it on ESPN.

"I got sick to my stomach," said Machemer, who still wanted to cling to history – his history – if only for a few more seconds.

"I asked Lockwood, 'Luke, was it in the bottom half of the inning?' He said no. I went, 'Geez, then I guess I'm the only American-born player who's ever done it.' I'm OK with that."

Running Smack Into History

No one recalled seeing anything quite like it before on the island.

So, when 5-foot-7 Josh Labandeira sprinted from the on-deck circle to the plate for his first ever at-bat in Harrisburg on June 28, 2003, observers simply presumed he was tapping into his inner Pete Rose.

But then Labandeira did it again. And again. He kept on running to home plate before each of his at-bats that season.

Nearly everybody enjoyed his ritual, except Josh McKinley, who came to loathe the Labby Dash.

Not that Labandeira cared much about McKinley's feelings. The diminutive, oft-overlooked shortstop would reach the majors; the once ballyhooed McKinley, the Expos' first-round pick in the 1998 draft, would never play above Class AA.

Labandeira made his debut in the majors on Sept. 17, 2004, joining the Expos in their final days before the team relocated to Washington, D.C.

Labandeira wore No. 1, which unfortunately for him was one digit higher than his career hit total during his two-week major league career. An ignominious 0-for-14 is how Labandeira's batting line will forever read in the *Baseball Encyclopedia*. Only eight other position players in history had more at-bats in the majors without a hit:

> Larry Littleton, outfielder, 0-for-23 for the Indians in 1981.
> Mike Potter, outfielder, 0-23, Cardinals, 1976-77.
> Harry Redmond, second baseman, 0-19, Dodgers, 1909.
> Cy Wright, shortstop, 0-18, White Sox, 1916.
> Ramon Conde, third baseman, 0-16, White Sox, 1962.
> Mike Gulan, third baseman, 0-15, Cardinals and Marlins, 1997-2001.
> Dutch Lerchen, shortstop, 0-15, Red Sox, 1910.
> Roy Luebbe, catcher, 0-15, Yankees, 1925.

Bo McLaughlin, the Senators' pitching coach in 1995 and '96, finished his career second among pitchers – and, subsequently, second all-time – for most at-bats without a hit. McLaughlin went 0-for-37 for Houston, Atlanta and Oakland from 1976 to 1982. The use of the designated hitter during McLaughlin's final two seasons with Oakland denied him the chance to shatter Randy Tate's all-time record for futility of 0-for-41 with the Mets in 1975.

No. 1 in Your Program

Shortstop Josh Labandeira, an Eastern League All-Star for the Senators in 2004 who ended that summer in the majors, made sure to grab "a couple of bags of stuff" as the Expos closed out their 36-year run in the majors.

Among the stuff Labandeira grabbed was his first major league jersey with the No. 1 stitched on the back.

Only one other former Senator wore No. 1 with the Expos during their 36 seasons – outfielder Yamil Benitez in 1995.

Taking his jersey home to Fresno, California, was a no-brainer for Labandeira.

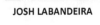

JOSH LABANDEIRA

"Nobody," he said, "is going to wear one of those again."

Neither did Labandeira. He never returned to the majors.

The Silly, Stupid and Scandalous

Not everyone who plays on City Island is been a choir boy. Some are strange in their behavior, others downright criminal in theirs. Here's a lineup of players who made some truly knuckleheaded decisions:

CATCHER: Gary Hymel

With two weeks left in the 1995 season, Hymel announced he wanted to be known as Lou Hymel, opting to be recognized by his middle name. "I'm having a bad season. I want to start over," Hymel said on Aug. 15, while hitting .198 with 88 strikeouts in 82 games. "I'm trying to get something going." Life as Lou was no better. Hymel's batting average dipped to .189 over the final 13 games of his fifth – and last – season of pro ball.

FIRST BASEMAN: Izzy Alcantara

Enigmatic would be the polite adjective to describe Alcantara, whose tantalizingly great power came as a package with an inability to make consistent contact and maddeningly poor defense. In three seasons with the Senators from 1995 to 1997, Alcantara collected 45 homers in 222 games, but he also struck out 227 times in 832 at-bats. Defensively, he struggled at both corners of the infield, committing 55 errors in 196 games for Harrisburg. Alcantara earned his moment of infamy four years after leaving the island. Playing then for Boston's AAA team from Pawtucket, Alcantara reacted to being hit with a pitch by kicking Scranton/Wilkes-Barre catcher Jeremy Salazar in the face before charging pitcher Blas Cedeno.

SECOND BASEMAN: Mike Hardge

Eighteen months after helping the Senators win the 1993 Eastern League title, the slick-fielding Hardge was out of work when the Montreal Expos suspended him for insubordination following a profanity-laced altercation with then-field coordinator Dave Machemer.

"Mike made a mistake and now he's paying the price," said Bill Geivett, the Expos' director of player development. "I told him I'd be in touch."

Good to his word, Geivett called Hardge a few days later at his home in Killeen, Texas, to tell him he was being released.

THIRD BASEMAN: Ofilio Castro

After an unremarkable seven seasons in the minors with the Expos and Nationals, Castro was batting a career-high .296 in his first 96 games of the 2009 season. He never played a 97th game. He was suspended for 50 games by Major League Baseball on Aug. 6, along with Senators outfielder Edgardo Baez, after testing positive for using amphetamines. Castro returned to the island in 2010, but batted only .209 in 69 games before disappearing from the minors.

SHORTSTOP: Ramon Castro

Major League Baseball was busy in 2005 trying to clean up its image as a sport littered with performance-enhancement drugs. MLB officials handed out 15-game suspensions to 75 minor leaguers in the season's first three months. Player No. 76 – Castro – received a lot more. Castro was batting .285 for the Senators with nine homers and 30 RBIs in 34 games when he was given a record 105-game suspension on June 20. MLB gave Castro the standard 15-game suspension for possessing amphetamines, then tacked on 90 games for allegedly trying to distribute those illegal pick-me-ups to players at Class AAA New Orleans.

Manager Doug Sisson restrains Milton Bradley during Gumgate in April 1999

LEFT FIELDER: Garrett Guzman

Winning a Player of the Week award will always get the attention of your bosses. So will getting arrested for having a dalliance with a minor. Unfortunately for the 25-year-old Guzman, he achieved notoriety in 2008 for the latter distinction. He admitted to having sex with a 15-year-old girl he met on the island. Guzman tried to explain to police that he did nothing wrong since the girl told him she was 16. In turn, Guzman's bosses with the Washington Nationals told him to find another job.

CENTER FIELDER: Milton Bradley

So gifted and yet so troubled. In the fall prior to arriving on the island in 1999, Bradley received national publicity for poking an umpire in the face. He received even more attention for his myriad problems while he was in the majors. In between, Bradley earned himself a seven-game suspension for helping incite a bench-clearing brawl against Altoona and then putting an exclamation point on his ejection by spitting gum on umpire Tim Pasch.

RIGHT FIELDER: Jake Powell

Powell had the power and speed to play in the majors, but nothing inside his granite-like head to guide him through the world. He hated Jews and liked blacks even less. Three years after playing for the Senators in 1933, Powell – then in the majors with Washington – deliberately ran into Hank Greenberg, fracturing the left wrist of Detroit's great Jewish first baseman. Then, during a live radio interview in 1938, Powell said he spent his offseasons as a police officer who enjoyed staying in shape by "cracking (blacks) over the head" with his nightstick. Ten years later, Powell shot himself to death in a Washington, D.C., police station, where he was being booked for writing bad checks.

DESIGNATED HITTER: Archie Gilbert

In seasons past, the Senators celebrated the clinching of a playoff spot by simply slapping teammates on the butt. They generally waited until after they won something big, such as a championship, before breaking out the champagne and beer. Not the 2011 Senators, who treated the mere clinching of a playoff berth as if they won the title. The chief partier was Gilbert, who at 28 was in the midst of reviving his career. He was one of the Senators' most dangerous threats in 2011, amassing 12 homers, 40 runs batted in, 27 stolen bases and a .313 batting average in only 98 games. But in the wee hours of the morning after the Senators clinched a playoff spot, Gilbert made himself dangerous off the field before police arrested him on DUI charges. According to the police report, Gilbert was speeding along a closed section of road on the West Shore, and nearly ran down a nine-man overnight construction crew. He never played another game for the Senators. Without Gilbert, Harrisburg was swept by second-place Richmond in the first round of the playoffs.

STARTING PITCHER: B.J. Wallace

Wallace's career peaked before he reached the Senators in 1994. He was Montreal's first-round draft pick out of Mississippi State University in the spring of 1992, an Olympian that summer and an 11-game winner for Class A West Palm Beach in 1993. The left-hander made only eight starts for the Senators in 1994, going 1-3 with a 4.81 ERA before being sidelined by a sore shoulder he claimed had been aching since the Olympics. He was out of the game by 1997. Not much more was heard from Wallace until late August 2011, when he was arrested in Loxley, Alabama, for allegedly running a methamphetamine lab out of the house he shared with his wife and three children.

MIDDLE RELIEF: Anthony Ferrari

The diminutive left-handed relief pitcher never seemed to say much during his three seasons on the island from 2003 to 2005. Perhaps that was because Ferrari spent much of that time with a blow-gun in his mouth. The real kind, not some dollar store knockoff, equipped with darts, really sharp darts. On a mid-August night in 2004, Ferrari gave an impromptu postgame demonstration of his newest blowgun. Aiming for the clubhouse door 15 feet from his locker, Ferrari fired a shoulder-high dart into the wall to the right of the door – just as prized left-hander Mike Hinckley walked through from the other side. Had Ferrari's dart landed just three inches to the left Hinckley would have gone from prospect to prey.

ANTHONY FERRARI

CLOSER: Ugueth Urbina

Urbina was a dominant starting pitcher on the island during the 1993 and '94 seasons before becoming an All-Star closer in the majors, where he saved 237 games during an 11-year career that ended in 2005. The right-hander was just 31 when he last pitched for the Phillies, but despite his notoriously combustible personality he seemed to have a few more seasons left in him. Instead, Urbina spent 2006 in a Venezuelan jail before being sentenced in March 2007 to 14 years in prison for attempting to murder five workers at his home in Caracas.

Top of the 9th

Why They Play the Game

The car ride from Reading to Harrisburg is usually uneventful, unless you crack open the window approaching, say, the Myerstown exit.

Then the ride sometimes stinks.

Literally.

That would be thanks to the smell of methane gas – courtesy of the local bovine population – mixing with who-knows-what chemicals the local farmers use to fertilize their crops.

As midnight approaches, I'm doing 65 on I-78, traveling an all-but-empty stretch of road toward Harrisburg. Not even the car's overworked air conditioner can hold back the odor emanating from the fields that line each side of the highway.

Jamey Carroll looks out the passenger side window and sees nothing but darkness.

A sigh comes first, then a decision.

That's it. I quit. I'm going home.

Carroll tells me that as soon as we reach City Island in 40 minutes he will retrieve his car from the players' parking lot next to the stadium and leave Harrisburg behind.

Instead of going to Class AAA Ottawa, where he had been promoted earlier in the day, Carroll says he will drive home to Evansville, Indiana, where he feels appreciated both as a ballplayer and a person.

Carroll no longer feels respected by the Montreal Expos, who had selected the former University of Evansville infielder in the 14th round of the 1996 amateur draft.

Now, six years later, Carroll is tired of the BS being fed to him by the organization. To him, the promotion from Class AA Harrisburg to AAA

Ottawa – more specifically, how it was handled – is the final affront in a litany of insults that started a month earlier at spring training in Florida.

Carroll, who played all or parts of three seasons with the Senators from 1998 to 2000, had spent all of 2001 in Triple-A before being placed on Ottawa's disabled list to start the 2002 season.

Except Carroll isn't hurt.

Not now in 2002, nor any other year.

The Expos simply want to keep him around as a spare part, just in case something happens to one of the Triple-A infielders they value more.

JAMEY CARROLL

To Montreal, sticking the 28-year-old Carroll on the disabled list with a bogus injury is better than releasing him.

Carroll has been reduced to that, to being a widget in the minor leagues, waiting for someone else to break down so he can get another chance to play.

Now, he is stuck in the netherworld of the phantom DL. Carroll knows how the politics of the game work, having seen it done before in the minors.

Back in 1998, the year Carroll reached Class AA with Harrisburg, the Expos needed a roster spot for the Senators when power-hitting first baseman Fernando Seguignol came off the DL, where he legitimately had been placed with an ankle injury.

With Seguignol – a prospect – ready to play again, the Expos placed backup outfielder Ed Bady – a non-prospect – on Harrisburg's DL with what they called a "strained right hamstring."

Bady was no more hurt in 1998 than Carroll is in 2002, but since the easy-going Bady was an "organizational player" – baseball-speak for roster filler – he was an easy choice to end up on the phantom DL.

While Rick Sweet, the Senators' manager in 1998, didn't publicly expose the phantom DL for the sham it was, he didn't exactly hide Bady in the trainer's room, either.

Instead, Sweet used Bady as his bullpen catcher, as well as his catcher on another occasion for a pregame hitting contest featuring former National League MVP George Foster. You would think squatting behind the plate

The Expos left Jamey Carroll feeling lost and alone early in the 2002 season

would not be such a good thing for a strained hamstring. Of course, Bady never complained about his "injury."

The Expos rewarded Bady's loyalty by releasing him two weeks before the 1999 season opened. He was 26 then, only a year older than the Senators' starting second baseman that season – Jamey Carroll.

Now, three years later, Carroll finds himself traveling the Bady Road to Nowhere and he doesn't like the scenery.

Less than 60 hours before his impromptu retirement while riding westbound on Interstate 78, the Expos had reassigned Carroll from Ottawa's disabled list to the Senators' active roster after determining Carroll had sufficiently recovered from an injury he had never sustained.

In those hours, Carroll played in three games, reached base seven times in 12 plate appearances and took a road trip to Reading only to be told to make a U-turn to Harrisburg and then on to Ottawa.

This infuriated Carroll. Not the promotion – who doesn't want one of those? – but how he received the news from manager Dave Huppert.

Carroll said Huppert had told him of his pending return to Ottawa as the Senators were beginning batting practice late that afternoon in Reading, even though the Expos knew they were sending Carroll back to Ottawa before the Senators had boarded their bus hours earlier for Reading.

If the Expos knew then, Carroll thought, why not allow him to make the eight-hour drive during the day from Harrisburg to Ottawa? Especially since Huppert was not planning to play him that night in Reading?

Or, at the very least, allow him to drive his own car to Reading so he could have cut down on travel time after the game rather than return to Harrisburg only to head back out for the red-eye drive to Ottawa.

And, oh, by the way, Carroll was told in Reading, you'll need to find your own way back to City Island after the game.

"They found out this morning and they tell me now," an uncharacteristically irate Carroll said before taking his turn in the batting cage at Reading. "Why didn't they me *before* I got on the bus?"

Because they were the Expos, who by then no longer cared for their minor leaguers as they had before Major League Baseball took over the franchise a few months earlier.

That stewardship began when Expos owner Jeffrey Loria orchestrated a deal prior to spring training to sell his franchise to Major League Baseball for $120 million and turn around to buy the Florida Marlins for $158 million.

Once Loria took over the Marlins, he began firing nearly everyone in the organization and replacing them with personnel he had known with the Expos. Managers, coaches and scouts, majors and minors. It didn't matter to Loria, who was content to abandon his old franchise, making it a virtual ward of the state for Major League Baseball to handle.

After stealing away more than 50 of the Expos' minor league managers, coaches, roving instructors and scouts, Loria left his old franchise with nothing but assistant farm director Adam Wogan, Class AAA manager Tim Leiper and his pitching coach, Randy St. Claire.

They were the only ones who knew Jamey Carroll. Unfortunately for Carroll, none of them was around much when the Expos opened camp for their minor leaguers in early March at Jupiter, Florida.

Leiper and St. Claire were busy in major league camp helping new Expos manager Frank Robinson, while Wogan was inundated with sorting through work visas, airfares and the other 612 items on his daily to-do list.

The minor leaguers were entrusted to a staff that out of necessity ended up being comprised mostly of the same managers, coaches and instructors whom Loria had just fired from the Marlins.

The 2002 camp was Carroll's sixth on the back fields, and easily his most humbling, embarrassing and perplexing in a career that now seemed destined for oblivion.

The new staffers barely knew their way around the Expos' minor league complex as they started sorting out work groups for the four practice fields behind Roger Dean Stadium.

Class AAA players over here ... Double-A go there ... Class A guys on those two other fields. ... Let's go!

The new coaches thought Carroll looked too young and – at 5-foot-9 and 165 pounds – too small, so they told him to go to the Class A fields.

Dumbfounded, Carroll just looked back at the coaches.

"They didn't even know me," Carroll said, shaking his head.

Finally some older players mentioned that Carroll had spent the previous season-plus at Class AAA Ottawa.

Good God, the players thought, *don't those coaches know anybody in camp?*

The coaches eventually shifted Carroll to the Triple-A work group.

"It makes you look in the mirror and try to figure out what your future is," Carroll said. "There were times when I was trying to figure out what I was going to do. Would going to another organization be any better? And where would I go? But as long as I had the uniform on, I realized there was a chance."

A small chance, at least at the start of the 2002 season when Carroll was placed on Ottawa's disabled list. The only thing truly hurting Carroll at that point was his pride, which would be further pricked two weeks later when he was sent back to Harrisburg.

For the fourth time since 1998, Carroll was heading to Class AA, and for the first time in his life he was ready to quit the game.

So he did.

For all of 10 minutes along Interstate 78, somewhere between the Myerstown and Lebanon exits. For those few moments, the thought of going home to load boxes onto UPS trucks didn't seem all that bad.

Then again, the thought wasn't all that appealing, either.

At least one person had been keeping tabs on the increasingly disgruntled Carroll – his manager with the Senators in 1999. Doug Sisson, who in 2002 was managing the Angels' Class AA team in Arkansas, called Anaheim to give his bosses a scouting report on his old second baseman.

"When Jamey started on the phantom DL in Triple-A, I told the people in Anaheim – because they're the same guys who pulled David Eckstein off waivers from Boston – that 'Eckstein's clone was in Montreal,' " Sisson said.

"And I told them if the Expos released Jamey or if he asked for his release, we needed to snatch him up, because you can win with a guy like that on the field every day in the major leagues."

But nothing happened, at least not right away.

Shortly after midnight near the Grantville exit, Carroll reconsidered his words and decided not to quit the game. He quietly returned to the island, picked up his car and drove on to Ottawa, where he batted .280 in 117 games before the Lynx's season ended over Labor Day weekend.

Hitting .280 in Class AAA would be fine for a 22-year-old prospect. Not so for Carroll, who at 28 was finishing his seventh season in the minors with a career .270 average over 785 games.

Carroll returned home to Indiana that first week of September wondering how he would spend his offseason. He needed to do something for money. He knew he always could go back to clearing restaurant tables or loading boxes into those oversized brown trucks.

Then the phone rang, and Carroll's life never again would be the same.

The call came from the Expos. The conversation was short.

Uh, Jamey, have any plans for today?

Kind of, Carroll told them. He was planning to drive to Wrigley Field with his younger brother, Wes, score a couple of tickets and watch the Expos play the Cubs.

Terrific ... can you get there a little early today?

Sure.

And, oh, bring your gear.

Just like that Jamey Carroll was a major leaguer, a reward not so much for his perseverance in the minors as it was for his proximity to Chicago.

Jose Macias' wrist injury had left the Expos without a utility player for the rest of their series against the Cubs. The injury also left the Expos looking at the map to see which of their minor league infielders lived near Chicago. The front office, still being frugally run by Major League Baseball, was keenly aware that any money they spent belonged to the game's 29 other owners and booking flights on short notice for backup infielders can be expensive.

Since he was only 300 miles from Wrigley Field – a relatively straight shot from Evansville – the call went to Carroll on Sept. 10.

Carroll did not play that day, but he was in the starting lineup the next day, batting second and playing third. He went 2-for-3 with a walk, and soon emerged as one of manager Frank Robinson's favorite players.

Robinson was old school. He knew the fundamentals of the game, and he had played it with passion. His Hall of Fame career was marked as much by his toughness running the bases as it was for his home run power.

Carroll was just like his new manager, only without the power.

Reaching base three times in his major league debut – not to mention a penchant for getting his uniform dirty – would give Carroll more opportunities to play.

At 28, Carroll became the oldest position player to make his major league debut with the Expos since 29-year-old Coco Laboy played third base for them in their inaugural 1969 season.

After seven seasons in the minors, Carroll finished the 2002 season in the majors batting .310 in 16 games. He either had a hit, walk or moved along a runner with a sacrifice bunt in 30 of his 79 plate appearances.

"Coming up here changed things for the good for me," Carroll said. "Hopefully, it added more years to my career, where before I didn't know how many years I had left."

How could he know? Especially after starting the season five months earlier as little more than an afterthought in the Expos' plans.

"I use that as a reminder when things are tough and I'm struggling," Carroll said years later. "It keeps me going. It tells me to enjoy the time I have while I'm here in the majors, because I never know how long it's going to last."

Carroll stayed with the Expos for two more seasons before moving with them to Washington in 2005. He remained gainfully employed as a utility player with the Colorado Rockies, Cleveland Indians and Los Angeles Dodgers through the 2011 season.

"I was so happy for him," said catcher Michael Barrett, who was among the first to greet Carroll when his Harrisburg teammate from 1998 joined the Expos in 2002. "He's worked so hard and given so much to the game. It's fun to see him get a return on it."

Along the way, Carroll became an integral part of the 2007 Rockies' run to the World Series. His 13th-inning sacrifice fly off Trevor Hoffman scored Matt Holliday and beat the San Diego Padres – with Barrett as their catcher – in a one-game tiebreaker to reach the National League playoffs.

That one swing provided more than enough return for the Rockies, who prior to the 2006 season purchased Carroll from the Nationals for just $300,000. A rookie making the major league minimum would have been paid more than what Washington received for its best utility player.

Nationals general manager Jim Bowden ditched Carroll because he had just signed journeyman infielder Damian Jackson, who eight years earlier had played for Bowden in Cincinnati.

Carroll ended up batting .300 in 136 games for the Rockies that season. Bowden ended up releasing Jackson, who was hitting .198, with five weeks left in the 2006 season and eating the rest of his $700,000 contract.

"He's as solid a player as you can find," Sisson said of Carroll. "His instincts, his effort … he has all the intangibles. He's the hardest-working guy in the organization. He can flat out play the game.

> *"There were times when I was trying to figure out what I was going to do. ... But as long as I had the uniform on, I realized there was a chance."*
>
> *Jamey Carroll*

"I firmly believe he's going to play in the major leagues for a decent period of time," Sisson predicted three years before Carroll reached the majors. "He's the type of guy that helps your team win."

Carroll has been able to do that because he always did the little stuff – the game's scut work – that never shows up on ESPN's SportsCenter.

Instead of hitting home runs, Carroll bunted. Instead of stealing bases, Carroll hit behind runners to put them in scoring position.

George Kissell, the longtime St. Louis Cardinals coach, instructor and guru, referred to players like Carroll as "spare tires."

"George knew the value of those players," said longtime major league scout Ben McLure. "George would always say, 'Now, would you drive from New York to California without a spare tire? Of course not.' "

Carroll began 2012 with the Minnesota Twins, who signed him to a two-year, $6.5 million contract after the Dodgers – their ownership in flux – let Carroll go as a free agent after the 2011 season.

"He's been a great story, hasn't he?" another scout said of Carroll. "Sometimes, it's just getting that chance to play, and he got that chance."

Carroll's chance came after 20 of his teammates from the Senators' 1999 championship team had already reached the majors. Just two of them – pitcher Jake Westbrook and catcher Brian Schneider – were still playing in the majors in 2012.

But only Carroll, who turned 38 before spring training 2012, had a contract guaranteed for 2013.

"I don't think you can ever really forget what got you here," Carroll said. "It motivates you to stay here. I think about that every day.

"When you tell the story, you laugh about it and you laugh about where you once were. But that's also the frustrating part of baseball. A lot of guys end up having to go through it, but they don't always make it."

Bottom of the 9th

The Grand Finale

At times, the Montreal Expos' minor league coaching staff openly questioned the maturity of Brad Fullmer, who was known to show up for a morning workout wearing shower shoes instead of spikes.

There were questions about his lack of respect, about the way he challenged authority. Some coaches wondered if his abilities to swing a baseball bat on the field were worth the headaches he created off of it.

"Who me?" Fullmer playfully asked in the final days of spring training in 1997.

Fullmer then lowered his voice as he looked around the Expos' nearly deserted minor league complex.

"Let me tell you about somebody else," he said. "Do you know Milton Bradley?"

Bradley? No, not yet.

"You think they have problems with me?" Fullmer said. "Just wait until you see this guy's act when he gets to Harrisburg."

That was still a couple of years away. Turned out that Fullmer, the catalyst of the Senators' offense in 1997, was quite the prognosticator.

By the spring of 1999, Fullmer had established himself as the Expos' everyday first baseman. As a major leaguer, he could wear his shower shoes anywhere he wanted and nobody would yell at him. What Fullmer said of Bradley two years earlier was, to him, a forgotten throwaway line.

The moment Fullmer had foreseen, though, was nearing fruition.

Bradley started the 1999 season as the Senators' center fielder, the focal point of their offense and also their leading candidate to implode at a moment's notice.

Being the Senators' most gifted athlete, however, did not always keep the enigmatic Bradley on the field.

He had injuries to his shoulders, knees and ankles.

He had issues with umpires over the strike zone.

He had a bad reputation with umpires after being kicked out of the prospect-oriented Maryland Fall League in 1998 for poking an umpire in the face during an argument.

Less than two weeks into the 1999 season with Harrisburg, Bradley ignited a bench-clearing brawl with Altoona and received a seven-game suspension for spitting his gum at umpire Tim Pasch after the melee.

The suspension started the next day, on the eve of Bradley's 21st birthday.

Senators manager Doug Sisson, who had worked with Bradley at Class A Jupiter in 1998, was undeterred by the antics. He went so far as to make an even bolder proclamation than the one Fullmer offered in 1997.

In the moments after Gumgate on April 13,1999, Sisson said, "I would be surprised if Milton Bradley is going to be remembered for this."

Bradley ended up playing in only 87 of the Senators' 142 games during the regular season, batting .329 with 12 homers and 50 runs batted in.

He played another nine games in the postseason.

He will be best remembered for one of those games. The last game.

And Bradley nearly missed the moment.

After each of their first eight playoff games against Erie and Norwich had been decided by one run, the Senators trailed Norwich by four runs, 11-7, entering the bottom of the ninth on City Island in Game 5 of the best-of-5 Eastern League finals.

As his teammates made their way into the dugout for their last at-bat, Bradley ducked through a steel door at the end of the dugout and stormed into the clubhouse.

And he stayed there.

Bradley did the math. Six teammates were ahead of him in the batting order with Norwich closer Joe Lisio looming in the bullpen on the rainy Monday night of Sept. 20, 1999.

"I didn't think the game was over," Bradley said, "but I was too nervous to watch it."

So Bradley stood alone near his locker as the clubhouse radio followed a game that was taking place only a cinderblock wall away.

Bradley wasn't really listening as Senators radio announcer Brad Sparesus returned from the between-innings commercial break. It was just background noise as he brooded over a season he expected to end in a few minutes with a loss to a Norwich team with lesser talent.

Then came another voice. This one belonged to batting coach Steve Phillips, who a moment earlier had realized all of his hitters were in the dugout except for one: Bradley.

"I went in there and said, 'Hey, what's up?' " Phillips said. "He said he couldn't watch right now. I said, 'Well, we're going to get some baserunners and you never know what's going to happen.' "

The time was shortly before 9:39 p.m. as Andy Tracy, the Senators' top power hitter with 37 homers during the regular season, led off the bottom of the ninth against Norwich reliever Oswaldo Mairena.

Some thought Mariena was a curious choice to close out the game for the Navigators rather than Lisio, who led the EL with 33 saves.

Lisio, though, was right-handed and Mairena was a lefty, and the first three Senators batters in the ninth – Tracy, Jon Tucker and Brad Wilkerson – were left-handed hitters.

Tracy, slowed by a swollen right elbow, began the inning with a single to center before Mairena walked Tucker and Wilkerson to load the bases. Finally, Lisio came in to face Jeremy Ware, a right-handed hitter.

The time was 9:40 as Bradley returned to the dugout to watch.

Phillips was right: The Senators had some baserunners, although it seemed like a moot point as Lisio retired Ware on a pop-up to shortstop Les Dennis before striking out Brian Schneider on three pitches.

Lisio and the Navigators still had a commanding four-run lead with Jason Camilli, the No. 9 hitter coming to bat.

Champagne was waiting.

Camilli, though, was a dangerous hitter here. He already had been on base three times in the game and scored three runs. His three-run homer off Craig Dingman in the sixth inning briefly gave the Senators a 6-4 lead.

As Camilli walked toward the plate, Bradley emerged from the dugout and into the on-deck circle.

The rain continued as Camilli drilled a 3-1 fastball off the upper body of third baseman Donny Leon to score Tracy and cut the Navigators' lead to 11-8.

No. 9 hitter Jason Camilli reaches on infield single in the ninth inning of Game 5

Shaken on the play, Leon stayed down on the infield dirt near third base, unable to continue. A couple of minutes passed before he was replaced by Brian McLamb.

Lisio never moved on the mound, opting not to throw any warm-up pitches to catcher Victor Valencia. Meanwhile, Bradley stood alone by the Senators' dugout, keeping his bat dry with a towel.

"I think that was to my advantage," Bradley said. "He was in a groove, throwing good. He was getting batters out. He was making good pitches. He had his rhythm going. Then the injury breaks it. Now (Lisio) has to stand out there, holding the ball with the rain coming down on him. He's probably thinking about me coming up and what he has to do."

And Bradley's thoughts?

"Me? I'm trying not to think about it. I have to go up there and hit. I'm doing anything I can to ease my mind."

The crowd of 3,171 was loud, but Bradley said he heard only the voice of a single fan standing above the Senators' dugout.

He was shouting at Bradley.

"You can do it! We believe! You can do it!"

Bradley busied himself by either looking out toward Lisio or toweling off his bat. He never glanced above him to see the man behind the voice.

"I had a lot of time to walk around and think," Bradley said. "I was cleaning out my spikes, grabbing my bat to make sure it was nice and dry.

I got a good grip with the pine tar. You hear a lot of things, but that guy's voice … it just struck a nerve. That's all I could hear."

Finally, with Leon helped from the field, public address announcer Chris Andree called out Bradley's name. The time was 9:43 when the switch-hitter settled into the left side of the batter's box.

To this point, Bradley had done little in the finals.

After batting .316 in the semifinals against Erie, Bradley had only two hits in 15 at-bats before starting Game 5 with three strikeouts and a flyout.

He had already left nine runners on base during the finals. He was now looking at three more of them as he waited on Lisio, who was intent on throwing nothing but fastballs.

"They had been throwing fastballs at me the whole series," Bradley said. "They would start off away, but if they got behind in the count, they always came back in. He started out 2-0 in the count and I wasn't sure if he was going to go fastball away. I was going to take it to make sure he was going to throw a strike, because he's wild a lot."

Lisio could pitch himself into trouble that way. While the 26-year-old closer led the league in saves, his 4.13 earned-run average was a concern. He had walked 27 batters in only 56 innings during the regular season.

Walking more now could be a problem.

Bradley took Lisio's next pitch for a strike before swinging through a pitch to even the count at 2-2. Lisio came back with another fastball away, running the count full.

The time on the outfield clock in deep left-center read 9:44.

Lisio, who had been a closer in the New York Yankees' system since they selected him in the 25th round of the 1994 amateur draft, was preparing to make his 17th pitch since replacing Mairena.

"I thought this was a spot where they like to come back in," Bradley said. "I was waiting for something in."

Bradley had spent the entire postseason hoping for inside fastballs. Batting left-handed, he knew this was the only pitch he could lift deep to right or right-center. A fastball away was a pitch he tended to drive, but not lift, toward left and left-center.

"Not being a power hitter, that pitch middle-away is just a pitch I can hit for a line drive into the gap," Bradley said. "To be able to handle it and drive it far, I want it inside a little."

Trying to stay away from Bradley's power, catcher Victor Valencia signaled for another fastball on the outer half of the plate.

Lisio's pitch, though, came in toward Bradley, not away from him.

"I picked it up early out of his hand," Bradley said. "You don't want to guess there. You want to clear your head of any distractions and just go off instincts. My instinct was to react to the fastball in; anything else, just work with it."

Bradley pummeled the pitch, hitting the ball so hard that Norwich right fielder Chip Glass could do little more than watch.

"I thought it was going to be a line drive toward (Glass)," Lisio later told Norwich broadcaster Mark Leinweaver. "It was a rocket that went out so fast. ... I thought, 'Oh, shit.' "

The time was 9:45.

More than 1,100 miles to the south in West Palm Beach, Tommy Phelps was waiting on tables at Big City Tavern when he was beckoned by the kitchen to serve another plate of stuffed tortellini, the house special.

Phelps instead let the order cool on the counter as he sat down at the restaurant's computer.

Phelps, a starting pitcher with the Senators before his release in June, had been an integral member of Harrisburg's three previous championship teams. He needed to know if his former teammates could win another one.

Tortellini be damned.

"It was weird," Phelps said. "I kept going on the computer, trying to find out how they were doing."

Everyone was about to find out.

"When I let go of the pitch, I knew it was a mistake," Lisio said. "I just missed my spot."

As Bradley swung at Lisio's 3-2 pitch, Jeremy Salyers was standing nearby in the Senators' bullpen. He had been warming up, hoping his teammates could somehow tie the score and force extra innings.

Salyers had temporarily stopped throwing and became a spectator for Bradley's at-bat. Then he saw the drive. No one had a better vantage point to watch the ball's trajectory.

"I thought, 'No way.' I said, 'This ball is off the wall; we're going to extra innings and I'm in there,' " Salyers said.

More than 100 yards away from Salyers was Doug Sisson, the Senators' first-year manager who was standing in the third-base coach's box.

As Lisio prepared to make his 3-2 pitch to Bradley, Sisson looked toward first base, knowing Camilli would be running on the pitch.

"I was just hoping we'd get to a full count because the runners were starting and Camilli was on first, and he can run," Sisson said. "Jamey Carroll's coming up next. I'm thinking worst-case scenario and that if Milton singles, the tying run is going to be at third base and you have a pretty good chance with Carroll."

But Bradley's drive carried farther than Sisson had anticipated. He knew Bradley hit the ball hard enough to go off the wall, but perhaps not high enough to clear it.

"When Milton hit the ball, I knew we were going to tie the game because I knew Camilli could score on it," Sisson said. "I saw Chip Glass going back. … I thought it was going to be a double because the trajectory was too low. It was so foggy and the rain was coming, and you can never tell with those lights out there."

While his teammates from the dugout shouted at him to run, Bradley momentarily stood at the plate after the swing.

He then gently dropped his bat at Valencia's feet as the Navigators' catcher peered around him to see Glass run toward the wall in right-center and abruptly stop, slumping to the grass.

"I was just frozen at home watching Glass and the ball and thinking, 'Get up, get up. *Stay up, stay up,*'" Bradley said. "A lot of times when I hit a ball like that it will just die off all of a sudden, but this one stayed up.

"I was watching Glass and he gave up, and dropped his shoulders," Bradley said. "Then I saw (first baseman) Nick Johnson drop his shoulders, too. And I realized then it was gone. … I don't remember the rain or anything else; just that guy's voice saying, 'You can do it! You can do it!' I hit the ball and then it seemed real quiet. Kind of like 'The Twilight Zone.'"

This episode ended with Bradley's line drive clearing the first wall of billboards in right-center for a grand slam, giving the Senators an improbable 12-11 victory and their Eastern League-record fourth straight title.

In context, Bradley's two-out, two-strike grand slam is arguably the greatest homer ever hit on any level.

Greater than Bobby Thomson's one-out, three-run homer in the bottom of the ninth off Brooklyn's Ralph Branca that gave the New York

A grand way to end a game: Milton Bradley's championship-winning swing

Giants the National League pennant in 1951, The Giants had a pretty fair hitter – Willie Mays – coming up next if Thomson had made the second out of the inning.

Greater than Bill Mazeroski's leadoff homer off the Yankees' Ralph Terry in the bottom of the ninth of Game 7 of the 1960 World Series, because the game would have gone on if Mazeroski had made an out.

Greater still than Joe Carter's three-run homer off the Phillies' Mitch Williams with one out in the bottom of the ninth of Game 6 in the 1993 World Series. Had Carter made an out, Toronto's at-bat would have continued. Had the Blue Jays lost the game, they still had Game 7 to play.

Had Bradley made an out against Lisio, Harrisburg's season would have been over. One of the most talented teams in the Senators' modern era would have fallen short of a fourth straight title and the sixth overall since pro baseball returned to the island in 1987.

"Somehow," Salyers said, "that ball got over fence. It's the most amazing thing I've ever seen."

And for another the most anguishing.

"My heart went down to my stomach," Lisio said, "because I knew we had just lost the game. ... To this day I still think about it. It was the worst experience I ever had in baseball, in life, by far."

As Bradley circled the bases, 12-year-old Cory Swartzlander left his spot in the picnic area down the right-field line, ran toward the back of the fence in right-center and retrieved the ball.

The noise picked up as Bradley reached Sisson at third base and grew louder as he continued toward the plate, where he was swarmed under by his teammates.

Sisson, celebrating his 36th birthday that day, watched as Bradley disappeared in the pile only to see him re-emerge as he was hoisted in the air.

"You know, it's like when you're playing Wiffle Ball in the backyard when you're a kid," Sisson said as he struggled to remove the cork from a postgame bottle of champagne. "This is how you played every day with your buddies. 'It's a 3-2 count, two outs, bottom of the ninth, down by three.' And then you hit a grand slam to win it. Milton just made a dream come true. … It's a miracle."

Eventually the Senators' victory shower of champagne and beer spilled out of the clubhouse and onto the public concourse. Along the way, Swartzlander, the boy from Northumberland County who was attending his first game of the summer, asked Bradley to autograph the baseball.

Bradley not only signed the ball, he added "Grand Slam 9th Inning" by his name. Harrisburg mayor Stephen R. Reed approached Swartzlander about trading the ball for a pair of season tickets.

Crossing the plate somewhere in the pile is Milton Bradley, author of "The Slam"

> *"I hit the ball and then it seemed real quiet.*
> *Kind of like 'The Twilight Zone.' "*
>
> *Milton Bradley*

As Reed's offer was rejected, word of Bradley's blast rapidly made its way through the Expos' organization.

Among the first to know was Brent Strom, the Expos' minor league pitching coordinator. He had been waiting – literally – by the phone to learn of the outcome. Strom had been calling the island throughout the night, getting updates from staffers in the front office.

"Then in the ninth inning I was talking to somebody there who just said, 'I have to go see this, we have two runners on base,' " Strom said.

Instead of hanging up on Strom, the employee thoughtfully propped the phone next to an office radio, which had been tuned to the broadcast.

"Suddenly," Strom said, "you thought you were listening to Bobby Thomson's home run again. It was so surreal; I couldn't believe it."

Neither could his boss, at least not at first.

Donnie Reynolds, Montreal's director of player development and the man responsible for assembling the 1999 Senators, thought about traveling to City Island for the winner-take-all Game 5 but couldn't make it.

He had hoped to listen to the broadcast over the Internet, but could not get a signal. So he hunkered down in his office in Jupiter, Florida, and waited for a call from somebody, anybody.

"I couldn't listen to it live anyway," Reynolds said. "What a mess I would have been."

Reynolds joked that he didn't know if he could ever return to City Island to see another game. What would be the point? What else could top "The Slam," the quintessential moment in one city's long baseball history.

"I don't know if I ever want to come back to Harrisburg," Reynolds said. "It's an interesting area; it's like the Bermuda Triangle. Weird stuff happens there."

Indeed, it does.

It has.

And it will again.

All of it on one patch of grass.

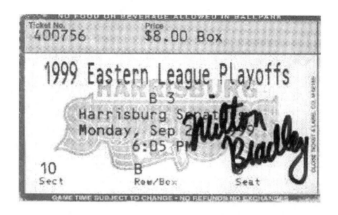

Extra Innings

A Blast From The Past

Maybe you were there in the crowd of 3,171; maybe you weren't.

Either way, you can close your eyes now, grab some snacks and have someone read to you the inning-by-inning details. Here's your ticket to the wildest game ever played on City Island: The Slam Game.

Sept. 20, 1999 at RiverSide Stadium
Final score: Senators 12, Norwich Navigators 11

STARTING LINEUPS

Norwich	Senators
Donzell McDonald, cf	Milton Bradley, cf
Vick Brown, 2b	Jamey Carroll, ss
Nick Johnson, 1b	Talmadge Nunnari, 1b
Donny Leon, 3b	Andy Tracy, 3b
Chip Glass, rf	Jon Tucker, dh
Marcus Thames, lf	Brad Wilkerson, lf
John Rodriguez, dh	Carlos Adolfo, rf
Les Dennis, ss	Brian Schneider, c
Victor Valencia, c	Jason Camilli 2b
Francisco DeLaCruz, p	Jake Westbrook,p
Lee Mazzilli manager	Doug Sisson, manager

FIRST INNING

Norwich: McDonald reaches on infield single to pitcher; Brown grounds out, short to first, moving McDonald to second; Johnson grounds out, second to first, moving McDonald to third; Leon pops out to short. **No runs, one hit, one error.**

Senators: Bradley strikes out; Carroll pops out to shortstop; Nunnari grounds out, short to first. **No runs, no hits, no errors.**

SECOND INNING

Norwich: Glass grounds out, first unassisted; Thames doubles to left; Rodriguez singles to center, scoring Thames; Dennis grounds into double play, short to second to first. **One run, two hits, no errors.**

Senators: Tracy grounds out, first to pitcher; Tucker walks; Wilkerson pops out to third; Tucker steals second; Adolfo walks; Schneider pops out to short. **No runs, no hits, no errors.**

THIRD INNING

Norwich: Valencia doubles to left-center; McDonald flies into double play to center, Valencia out at third, center to third; Brown grounds out, third to first. **No runs, one hit, no errors.**

Senators: Camilli singles to center; Bradley flies out to center; Carroll reaches on fielding error at third, moving Camilli to second; Camilli scores on fielding error in left, Carroll moving to second; Carroll moves to third on wild pitch; Nunnari walks; Tracy flies out to left; Tucker singles to center, scoring Carroll and moving Nunnari to second; Wilkerson singles to right, scoring Nunnari and moving Tucker to third; Wilkerson advances to second on fielder's choice; Adolfo strikes out, looking. **Three runs, three hits, two errors.**

FOURTH INNING

Norwich: Johnson hit by pitch; Leon grounds into double play, second to short to first; Glass walks; Thames homers to left field, scoring Glass; Rodriguez strikes out. **Two runs, one hit, no errors.**

Senators: Schneider singles to right-center; Camilli grounds into double play, short to first; Bradley strikes out. **No runs, one hit, no errors.**

FIFTH INNING

Norwich: Dennis grounds out, short to first; Valencia walks; McDonald strikes out, looking; Brown strikes out, looking. **No runs, no hits, no errors.**

Senators: Carroll singles to right-center; Nunnari flies out to left; Tracy flies out to left; Tucker strikes out. **No runs, one hit, no errors.**

SIXTH INNING

Norwich: Johnson walks; Leon singles to right, moving Johnson to second; Glass sacrifice bunts, pitcher to first, moving Johnson to third and Leon to second; Thames strikes out, looking; Johnson scores on wild pitch, Leon moves to third;

Rodriguez intentionally walks; Dennis grounds out, shortstop unassisted. **One run, one hit, no errors.**

Senators: *Pitching change, Craig Dingman replaces DeLaCruz.* Wilkerson walks; Adolfo pops out to second; Wilkerson steals second; Schneider reaches on fielding error at first, scoring Wilkerson; Schneider moves to third on fielding error in right; Camilli homers to left, scoring Schneider; Bradley strikes out, looking; Carroll flies out to left. **Three runs, one hit, two errors.**

SEVENTH INNING

Norwich: *Pitching change, David Moraga replaces Westbrook; Jeremy Ware replaces Adolfo, playing left; Wilkerson moves to right.* Valencia walks; McDonald singles to left-center, moving Valencia to second; Brown reaches on sacrifice bunt and error at third, loading bases; Johnson grounds into fielder's choice with Brown out second to short, scoring Valencia; Leon reaches on fielder's choice with Johnson out short to second, scoring McDonald; Glass homers to right-center, scoring Leon. *Pitching change, Rodney Stevenson replaces Moraga.* Thames homers to left-center; Rodriguez walks. *Pitching change, Christian Parker for Stevenson.* Dennis strikes out, foul tip. **Five runs, three hits, one error.**

Senators: Nunnari strikes out, looking; Tracy singles to right-center; Tucker strikes out; Wilkerson strikes out. **No runs, one hit, no errors.**

EIGHTH INNING

Norwich: Valencia strikes out, looking; McDonald out on bunt attempt, pitcher to first; Brown flies out to right. **No runs, no hits, no errors.**

Senators: Ware grounds out, pitcher to first; Schneider singles to center; Camilli reaches on fielder's choice with Schneider out, short to second; Bradley walks, moving Camilli to second; Carroll reaches on infield single to second, scoring Camilli and moving Bradley to third. *Pitching change, Oswaldo Mairena replaces Dingman.* Nunnari grounds out to first. **One run, two hits, no errors.**

NINTH INNING

Norwich: Johnson flies out to left; Leon homers to right-center; Glass singles to left-center; Thames pops out to short; Rodriguez singles to right, moving Glass to third; Glass scores on passed ball, moving Rodriguez to second; Dennis walks; Valencia grounds out, second to first. **Two runs, three hits, no errors.**

Senators: Tracy singles to center; Tucker walks, moving Tracy to second; Wilkerson walks, loading bases. *Pitching change, Joe Lisio replaces Mairena.* Ware pops out to short; Schneider strikes out; Camilli reaches on infield single to third, scoring Tracy, moving Tucker to third and Wilkerson to second. *Brian McLamb replaces Leon at third.* Bradley lines Lisio's 3-2 pitch over wall in right-center, scoring Tucker, Wilkerson and Camilli. **Five runs, three hits, no errors.**

Winning pitcher: Parker. **Losing pitcher:** Lisio. **Time:** 3:41. **Attendance:** 3,171

Postgame Buffet

What Happened When

Here is the meat-and-potatoes – tofu and lentils for the Vegans – timeline of what happened on the island since 1890 (with a couple of seasons at Harrisburg's West End Grounds thrown in):

1890: After flirtations with pro baseball in the city during the 1883, '84 and '89 seasons, Harrisburg places its first team on the island. The Ponies finish second in the independent Eastern Interstate League with a 39-24 record and jump to the Atlantic Association in midseason after the EIL folds. They go 31-26 in their new league. ... **James Farrington** manages the team in both leagues. ... Second baseman **Bill Egan** leads the Eastern Interstate League in hits (86), stolen bases (37) and runs scored (79), while infielder **Frank Grant** has a league-high five homers. ... The Ponies gain the distinction of being the first team in pro ball to have black and white teammates who eventually became Hall of Famers with Grant, who spent much of his career as a second baseman, and **Hughie Jennings**, a catcher with Harrisburg who was a longtime shortstop and manager in the majors. Grant would not get the same opportunity as Jennings, since the all-white majors would ban blacks from their leagues for another 57 years.

1891: Well that was a quick hello and goodbye as the Ponies fail to return in any league.

1892: The Ponies resurface in the Class B Pennsylvania State League, although not for long. Again managed by **James Farrington**, the team wins 25 of 44 games before disbanding on July 14. ... First baseman and Harrisburg native **Jake Drauby** is the Ponies' big hitter with a .325 batting average and a team-high – count 'em – two homers. He finishes the summer in the majors, batting .206 in 10 games for Washington.

1893: The Ponies return to the now-independent Pennsylvania State League with a new name, Senators, and a new manager, **Felix Marks**, who is replaced during the season by **Jack Huston**. ... The Ponies-turn-Senators also go by the name Hustlers as they finish 49-52, good for fifth place in the eight-team league. ... Infielder **John Meister** hits five homers to match Frank Grant's single-season franchise record.

1894: The Senators finish second in the independent Pennsylvania State League at 56-45 before losing to Pottsville in the championship game. ... **Jack Huston** remains as manager. ... Future Harrisburg mayor **George Hoverter** appears in three games and goes 4-for-11 at the plate. ... Outfielder **Dummy Stephenson**, a deaf player who precedes **Curtis Pride** to City Island by 99 years, sets a single-season franchise record with nine homers. ... Left-hander **Patrick Meaney** is the league's best pitcher, winning 23 of 30 decisions.

1895: The Senators drop out of the now-Class B Pennsylvania State League as they fold June 14 after compiling a 19-16 record with manager **Frank Seiss**. ... Third baseman **Heinie Kappel** leads the Senators in homers with one. ... The highlight of the season is the pro debut of 19-year-old **Vic Willis**, a right-hander who goes 4-4 with a 3.76 ERA in 11 appearances. Willis wins 20 or more games eight times in the majors before being elected to the Hall of Fame in 1995. ... **Henry Myers**, the manager and shortstop of Harrisburg's first pro baseball team in 1883, dies April 18 in Philadelphia. He is only 36.

1896: Oscar Charleston, the Hall of Fame player-manager for the Harrisburg Giants in the mid-1920s, is born Oct. 14 in Indianapolis ... At least there is some football on the island; the Carlisle Indian School hammers Penn State 48-5 on Nov. 21.

1897: Spottswood Poles begins playing organized baseball with a boys' league team called the Hello Bill Club. Within 10 years, he returns to the island to play for the semipro Harrisburg Black Giants.

1898: Glenn Killinger, who becomes Senators' second baseman and manager in the mid-1920s after an All-American football career at Penn State, is born Sept. 13 in Harrisburg.

1899: The only .400 hitter and Triple Crown winner in franchise history, outfielder **Joe Munson**, is born Nov. 6 in Renovo, Pa.

1900: The Ponies return to Island Park, sort of. The team begins in Philadelphia as the Athletics – no, not those Athletics – and is 10-11 before moving to Harrisburg for the final 10 days of the seven-week Class A Atlantic League season. The Ponies promptly lose all six of their games with manager **George Shoch**. ... In an amateur matchup of left-handers, **Harve Taylor** beats Gettysburg's **Eddie Plank** 3-1. Within a year, Plank starts his Hall of Fame career with the Philadelphia Athletics.

1901: Welcome back **Jake Drauby**! After nearly a decade bouncing from Johnstown to Buffalo to Reading and points in between, the first baseman returns to the Harrisburg, which briefly is part of the eight-team, Class D Pennsylvania State League. ... **Les Bell**, the future major league infielder and Senators manager, is born Dec. 14 in Harrisburg.

1902: No pro baseball on the island, although **Chief Bender** – an 18-year-old righty from the Carlisle Indian School and Dickinson College –

CONNIE MACK

summers on City Island with the semipro Susquehanna Athletic Club. He is paid $150 per month. Bender's best performance – at the least the one that most influenced his career – comes June 17 on the island in an exhibition game against the National League's Chicago Cubs, then known as the Orphans. Among those watching is **Connie Mack**, the manager of the Philadelphia Athletics of the fledgling American League. Mack is impressed enough to sign Bender for the 1903 season, doubling his monthly salary to $300. ... **Rap Dixon**, part of one of the game's great outfields with the Eastern Colored League's Harrisburg Giants of the 1920s, is born Sept. 15 in Detroit.

1903: No pro baseball on the island. No **Chief Bender**, either, as the right-handed pitcher joins the A's to start a 16-year career in the majors that leads to his election for the Hall of Fame in 1953.

1904: Back in business in the seven-team, independent Tri-State League, the Senators finish in third place at 58-51. ... **Peter Agnew** is the manager. ... **Rev Cannady**, who stars as a third baseman for the Harrisburg Giants of the mid-1920s, is born March 6 in Lake City, Florida.

1905: Once again in the eight-team, independent Tri-State League, the Senators finish 76-51 and end up in fourth place. ... The best player on the team also is the manager, 39-year-old outfielder **Billy Hamilton**, who retired from the majors in 1901 with a then-record 914 stolen bases. For the Senators, Hamilton bats .342 in 110 games with 15 doubles, eight triples and two homers. ... In a rematch from nine years earlier, the Carlisle Indian School's football team returns to the island and again beats Penn State – this time only 11-0 – on Oct. 7.

1906: Billy Hamilton returns for a second season as manager, but the Senators stumble to a 52-74 record and fifth place in the six-team independent Tri-State League. ... The 40-year-old Hamilton plays in only 43 games and hits just .277. ... **Spottswood Poles**, who soon acquired the moniker of "the black Ty Cobb," makes his semipro debut as an 18-year-old right fielder for the Harrisburg Black Giants. Poles plays three seasons in Harrisburg en route to becoming one of the greatest players – black or white – in the early 20th century.

1907: With the Tri-State League moving from independent status to a Class B league, the Senators finish 79-47, but that is only good enough for second place behind Williamsport. ... **George Heckert** replaces **Billy Hamilton** as manager, and remains in that role through 1909. ... Outfielder **Kip Selbach** leads the league with seven homers.

1908: Another great season in the Class B Tri-State League with an 80-47 record and a .630 winning percentage that eclipses the franchise record set the season before. Unfortunately for the Senators, their effort again is good enough only for second place, just two games behind Williamsport. ... Second baseman **Dick Egan** steals a franchise-record 93 bases. ... **Harry Krause**, a 19-year-old lefty who will pitch until he is 41, goes17-4 with a league-best .816 winning percentage.

1909: After finishing the previous two seasons 65 games over .500, the Senators drop to 49-65 and 26 games out of first place in the Tri-State League. ... First baseman **Merle Whitney** becomes the first Senator to reach double-figures in homers in a season, totaling 10 in only 65 games. ... **Jimmie DeShong**, who pitches for the Senators in 1929 and 1930 before spending seven years in the majors, is born Nov. 30 in Harrisburg.

1910: George Heckert leaves to become Trenton's manager in the eight-team, Class B Tri-State League, and is replaced by **Kip Selbach**, one of his outfielders on the 1907-1908 Senators. Selbach's first team finishes 52-59 in sixth place and 20 games behind league champion Altoona. ... **Buck Freeman**, Boston's first baseman when it won the first World Series in 1903, gives the Senators some star power, albeit a fading star. Freeman, whose 67 homers from 1899-1903 are the most in the majors, plays his last full season on the island and leads the Senators with 19 doubles, 12 triples and four home runs.

1911: Kip Selbach's second season as manager is worse than the first. The Senators, now called the Ponies, go 47-61 to finish seventh in the eight-team Class B Tri-State League. ... **Bob Shawkey**, a 20-year-old rookie pitcher out of Slippery Rock, makes his pro debut, going 10-10 for the Ponies with a 2.68 ERA. Two years later, Shawkey reaches the majors, beginning a 15-year career there that ends with 195 victories and five World Series appearances.

1912: The team changes names again, going back to Senators and winning its first league title with a 75-37 record and franchise-record .670 winning percentage in the eight-team, Class B Tri-State League. ... Steelton's **George Cockill** is the player-manager and bats .286 ... Right-hander **Rip Vowinkel** spends his final pro season on the island, going 5-5 in 12 appearances for the Senators before retiring for a nap at home in Oswego, New York. ... For the second time in three seasons, the Carlisle Indian School's football team plays Villanova on the island and, for the second time in three seasons, beats the Wildcats. Carlisle follows up its 9-0 victory in 1910 with a 65-0 rout on Oct. 2. The score would have been more lopsided had **Jim Thorpe** not been pulled from the game after scoring three touchdowns in the game's first 20 minutes.

1913: Steelton's **George Cockill** is back as player-manager and the Senators finish 59-52 and in a three-way tie with Allentown and York for second place in the six-team, Class B Tri-State League. ... Outfielder **Dutch Rudolph** is the Senators' best player, batting .330 with 29 doubles, 20 triples and five homers – and then retires at the age of 30.

1914: For the second time in three seasons under **George Cockill**, the Senators win the six-team, Class B Tri-State League title with a 78-32 record and a franchise-best .709 winning percentage. ... Harrisburg has its first home-run champion since **Frank Grant** in 1890 as catcher **Charles Miller** leads the league with seven. ... **Joe Chabek** wins a league-high 28 games while losing only three. ... Despite their success on the field, the Senators disband after the season.

1915: The season starts without a pro team on the island, but that changes when the 26-26 Newark Indians of the eight-team, Class AA International League relocate to Harrisburg on July 2. From there, the Indians become the Senators, but win only 35 of 85 games to finish in sixth place at 61-76 for managers **Eddie Zimmerman** and **Harry Smith**. ... The biggest draw on the island is outfielder **Jim Thorpe**, the 1912 Olympian from the Carlisle Indian School who bats .303 in 96 games with 13 doubles, seven triples and two homers. His island debut on July 25 attracts an overflow crowd of 5,822. ... One of team's pitchers is a clown. Really. Well, at least he would be one day as right-hander **Al Schacht** wins half of his 26 decisions. A sore arm in 1920 pushes him toward a second, more profitable career as the game's first "Clown Prince of Baseball."

1916: Harrisburg again fails to start the season with a team. That is remedied on June 20 as the terrible Troy Trojans from New York, losers of 27 of their first 35 games in the eight-team, Class B New York State League, move to the island and rename themselves the Harrisburg Islanders. From there, they go 48-47, but still finish the season in last place at 56-74 with three managers – **Louis Wachter**, **George Cockill** and **Walter Blair**.

1917: While Harrisburg remains with the name Islanders, the Islanders do not remain for long. After losing 30 of their first 41 games, they drop out of the eight-team, Class B New York State League on July 4. ... **Earle Mack**, the son of **Connie Mack**, is the manager, as well as the first baseman. His .198 batting average mirrors the team's success, or lack thereof. ... Shortstop **Joe Boley** bats only .244 for the Senators but later becomes an integral member of the Philadelphia Athletics' World Series teams from 1929 to 1931.

1918: The team remains disbanded as the United States enters its second year in World War I. Baseball on the island goes into a six-year hiatus.

1919: Harrisburg Tech's vaunted football team finishes 12-0 and outscores opponents 701-0. The so-called national championship game is played on the island in November and ends with a 56-0 rout of a team from Portland, Maine Among those watching on the island that day is a rising young baseball star named **Babe Ruth**. ... **Billy Cox**, who becomes one of the game's greatest fielding third basemen after playing on the island in the early 1940s, is born Aug. 29 in Newport, Pa.

1920: George Hoverter, a part-time outfielder with the Ponies in 1890 and the Senators in 1894, is elected the mayor of Harrisburg and stays in office until 1936. He is the city's longest tenured chief executive until **Stephen R. Reed** comes along in 1982 and stays for 28 years. ... **Max Patkin**, whose career as the new "Clown Prince of Baseball" starts on the island in 1946, is born Jan. 10 in Philadelphia.

1921: The ballfield, still unoccupied by a minor league team, is shifted slightly to the south as the city enlarges its water plant on the island.

1922: While the Senators, Ponies, Islanders or whoever they are remain idle, quality baseball returns to Harrisburg as the all-black Giants field an independent team. ... Serial criminal **Chick Meade** finishes out a wild career playing third base for the Giants, passing himself off as a black player. When Meade is arrested in 1931 for writing bogus checks, a police check reveals he is white.

1923: The Giants play their last season as an independent team before joining the Eastern Colored League in 1924. ... Seventeen years before returning to manage his hometown Senators, **Les Bell** makes his major league debut on Sept. 17. Bell plays 896 games in the majors and finishes in 1931 with a .290 career batting average.

1924: The Senators re-enter pro ball in the eight-team, Class B New York-Penn League, the forerunner of today's Class AA Eastern League. The Senators, though, do not come back right away to the island, instead playing the 1924 and '25 seasons at the West End Grounds in uptown Harrisburg. ... The Senators finish fourth at 70-60 while playing for four managers – **Steve Yerkes**, **Mickey LaLonge**, **Glenn Killinger** and **Frank Brannon**. ... First baseman **Freddy Leach** hits .346 in 115 games with a franchise-record 12 homers before batting .464 in eight late-season games for the Philadelphia Phillies. ... With future Hall of Famer **Oscar Charleston** in center field, the Giants are 26-28 in their first season in the Eastern Colored League. Charleston bats .380 with a league-high 13 homers.

1925: The Senators have one of the best players in the game with outfielder **Joe Munson**, but still finish 61-69 and sixth in the eight-team, Class B New York-Penn League. The manager is **Rankin Johnson**, whose son Rankin Jr. becomes Eastern League president in 1961... Munson becomes the league's first Triple Crown winner with a .400 batting average, 33 homers and 129 runs batted in. All three are franchise records. Munson also leads the league with 188 hits and 132 runs scored in 131 games. Munson leaves for Chicago at the end of the Senators' season and bats .371 in nine games for the Cubs. Munson is the last player – whether in the New York-Penn League or its successor, the Eastern League – to hit .400 in a season. ... The Giants finish second in the Eastern Colored League, winning 37 of 55 games. Player-manager **Oscar Charleston** again is the giant among Giants with a .451 batting average and a league-high 20 homers.

1926: With the West End Grounds razed in February, the Senators return to the island, but not without some preseason drama. On March 29, less than six weeks before their season opener, fire destroys four sections of the bleachers down the left-field line, as well as the team's equipment shed. In all, 700 seats are destroyed. ... Without **Joe Munson**, the Senators slip to 47-84 and last place in the eight-team, Class B New York-Penn League. **Rankin Johnson** splits time as manager with **Joe Lightner**. ... The Giants remain the best team in Harrisburg, winning 25 of 42 games to finish second in the Eastern Colored League.

1927: The Senators win their first title since 1914, going 87-51 under manager **Win Clark** in the Class B New York-Penn League. ... **Glenn Killinger**, the second baseman and Harrisburg native who had managed the Senators in 1924, hits a league-high 11 homers. ... No pitcher in the eight-team league tops the 18 games won by both **Louis Polli** and **Seymour Bailey**. Polli also leads the league with 109 strikeouts. ... The Giants play only 28 games, going 16-12 before the Eastern Colored League folds. Player-manager **Oscar Charleston** leads the ECL in homers with eight.

1928: Glenn Killinger, an All-American quarterback at Penn State in 1921, replaces manager **Win Clark** as the Senators finish 82-54 to repeat as champions in the eight-team, Class B New York-Penn League. ... Playing second base as well, Killinger leads the league with 82 RBIs. ... Outfielder **Ray Flood** leads the league in homers with 11. He also homers in an exhibition game against the New York Yankees on June 26 before a standing-room-only crowd of 4,200. The Yankees' **Babe Ruth** hits one that day, too, a drive into the second row of trees beyond the right-field wall. Ruth's homer is the second longest on the island, following one hit into the third row of trees a couple of years earlier by Harrisburg Giants player-manager **Oscar Charleston**. ... Right-hander **Clint Brown** is the league's best pitcher with 23 victories, 2.15 ERA and .742 winning percentage. ... Hall of Famer **Hughie Jennings**, whose pro career began on the island with the Ponies in 1890, dies Feb. 1 at the age of 58 in Scranton. ... **Charles Fleck**, a longtime policeman who in the 1880s became the city's first pro baseball player when the games were played on Allison Hill, dies May 17 in Harrisburg. He is 76.

1929: With **Glenn Killinger** joining Williamsport, former St. Louis Browns pitcher **Johnny Tillman** becomes the manager. The Senators finish 75-62, good enough for third place in the eight-team, Class B New

York-Penn League. Tillman ties Williamsport's **King Lehr** with a league-high 21 wins. ... Outfielder **Ray Flood** leads the league in homers with 18. ... The Senators sign **Robert "Lefty" Hefflefinger** on July 31, giving the 16-year-old junior from Harrisburg's John Harris High School a $200 bonus. Hefflefinger is 1-2 in six appearances and spends his entire pro career with the Senators, finishing in 1935 with a career record of 42-39.

1930: Johnny Tillman returns as manager, but the Senators slide to 70-69 and fourth place in the eight-team, Class B New York-Penn League. ... Outfielder **Horace McBride** – friends call him "Red" – leads the league with a .378 batting average. He also posts a franchise-record 198 hits and 40 doubles, along with 21 triples and 11 homers.

1931: The Senators begin a one-year affiliation with the Philadelphia Athletics and win their third Class B New York-Penn League championship in five years, going 83-56 for managers **Joe Cobb** and **Eddie Onslow**. ... Outfielder **Lou Finney** bats .347 in 128 games between Harrisburg and York. Nine years later, he becomes the first former Senator to play in the major league All-Star Game.

1932: The Senators switch affiliations to the Boston Braves. In their second season with **Eddie Onslow** as manager, the Senators finish second in the eight-team, Class B New York-Penn League at 74-66. ... Outfielder **Gene Moore** bats .322 in 49 games between Harrisburg and Elmira. In 1937, Moore becomes the first former Harrisburg player selected to the major league All-Star Game, but he would not play in the game at Washington. ... The Giants return as an independent team. That means playing not only in the shadows of the all-white majors and minors but also in the shadows of the Negro Leagues with which they were once affiliated.

1933: The Senators drop to 60-76 and seventh place in the eight-team, Class A New York-Penn League with **Eddie Onslow** in his final year as manager. ... Right-hander **Lew Krausse**, 5-1 for the Philadelphia Athletics over the 1931-1932 seasons, no-hits York 3-0 on Sept. 3. ... **Colonel C.W. Strothers**, owner and architect of the Harrisburg Giants, dies July 14 in Harrisburg. He is 65.

1934: The arrival of **Les Mann** as manager results in only one fewer loss, as the 60-75 as the Senators finish last in the eight-team, Class A New York-Penn League. ... First baseman **Elbie Fletcher** becomes – and remains through the 2011 season – the youngest position player ever on the island. Fletcher, less than a month past his 18th birthday when the season opens, bats .291 in 82 games.

1935: They have fewer wins and more losses, but at least the 59-77 Senators move up to sixth place in the eight-team, Class A New York-Penn League under manager **Art Shires**. ... Right-hander **Lew Krausse** accounts for 15 of the team's 59 victories. ... Third baseman **Bobby Estalella** hits a league-high 18 homers.

1936: A mid-March flood leaves the island and its ballpark under water, washing away pro baseball in Harrisburg for four years.

1937: Frank Grant, the first of seven Hall of Famers to play on the island for Harrisburg, dies penniless on May 27 in New York City. He is 71. His magnificent, if overlooked, career finally receives validation 69 years later with his induction into the Hall of Fame. ... **Andy Musser**, the Senators' bat boy in the early 1950s who becomes a nationally recognized broadcaster, is born Dec. 28 in Harrisburg.

1938: No ballpark, no team.

1939: Ditto.

1940: Pro ball returns to the island with a rebuilt stadium that seats 4,400. ... The Senators begin a three-year affiliation with the Pittsburgh Pirates. ... The home opener is postponed from May 1 to May 16 as workers hurry to install new bleachers, build outfield fences and put down sod. When complete, the ballpark would look eerily similar to the one erected 47 years later, when Pittsburgh's Class AA affiliate relocates from Nashua, N.H., to Harrisburg. ... Harrisburg's own **Les Bell** is the Senators' manager as the Senators finish 60-62 and fifth in the eight-team, Class B Interstate

LES BELL

League. ... First baseman **Arnold Greene** hits a league-high 21 homers in only 90 games. ... Creating the most buzz is the pro debut of **Billy Cox**, a 20-year-old shortstop from nearby Newport. He bats .288 in 120 games with 24 doubles, five triples and eight homers. ... Outfielder **Bill Embick** hits only .222 in 103 games, but has the distinction of being the first pro player selected in the United States' inaugural peacetime military draft. Embick never plays another pro game. ... **Billy Hamilton**, the Hall of Fame outfielder who was the Senators' player-manager in 1905-1906, dies Dec. 15 in Worcester, Massachusetts. He is 74.

1941: With **Les Bell** back as manager, the Senators win their first championship in 10 years, finishing 81-43 in the eight-team, Class B Interstate League before beating Reading and Trenton in the playoffs. ... In only his second pro season, shortstop **Billy Cox** leads the league in hitting at .363. He joins the Pirates for a 10-game audition at the end of the National League season. Cox never again plays in the minor leagues during a war-interrupted career that lasts until 1955.

1942: The Senators' first team in the World War II era goes 69-68 for third place in the six-team, Class B Interstate League before losing to Hagerstown in the first round of the playoffs. ... **Danny Taylor** is the manager. ... **Cot Deal**, a 19-year-old, switch-hitting outfielder, has 24 doubles, four triples and six homers before enlisting in the Army after the season. He spends the next three seasons playing for service teams and finally reaches the majors – as a pitcher – with the 1947 Boston Red Sox.

1943: York replaces the bankrupt Senators in the six-team, Class B Interstate League. ... Harrisburg returns as a member of the Negro National League. For a little while anyway, as the team, known as the Stars, splits its time and talent between City Island and St. Louis, winning five of nine games before dropping out of the league. The players then join a Midwest barnstorming tour featuring Pittsburgh Hall of Fame shortstop **Honus Wagner** to raise money for war bonds. ... Pittsburgh Pirates first baseman **Elbie Fletcher** becomes the first former Senator to start in an All-Star Game in the National League's 5-3 loss at Philadelphia's Shibe Park, which also is hosting the first All-Star Game to be played at night.

1944: Five days after his 18th birthday and five years before reaching the majors with Brooklyn, first-year pro **Don Newcombe** of the Newark Eagles beats **Josh Gibson** and the Homestead Grays 9-2 June 19 on the island. The Negro League game attracts a crowd of 2,500. ... Former Giants star outfielder **Rap Dixon** dies July 20 in Detroit. Dixon, only 41, is buried four days later in Steelton's Midland Cemetery.

1945: The Hall of Fame inducts the first player who once summered on the island as the Veterans Committee posthumously votes in **Hughie Jennings**, a catcher for the 1890 Ponies en route to becoming a star shortstop with the original Baltimore Orioles and then manager of the Detroit Tigers. ... **Harry O'Neill**, a catcher with the 1940 Senators, becomes the second – and last – former major leaguer killed during World War II when he dies March 6 on Iwo Jima.

1946: The Senators, in the first of six straight seasons affiliated with the Cleveland Indians, rejoin the eight-team, Class B Interstate League. ... With former major leaguer and native son **Les Bell** returning as manager, the Senators finish second in the regular season at 76-64 before beating Allentown and Wilmington in the playoffs for their first title since 1941. ... On July 9, the Indians come to the island for an exhibition game. The day also marks the formal debut of **Max Patkin** as the successor to one-time Senators pitcher **Al Schacht** as the "Clown Prince of Baseball." Patkin takes the act he first brings to the island and turns it into a half-century career with more than 4,000 performances at ballparks throughout North America. ... Catcher **Joe Tipton** bats .327 in 104 games. Three years later, Tipton is traded from the Chicago White Sox to the Philadelphia Athletics for a diminutive infielder whom manager **Connie Mack** didn't believe could succeed in the majors. That player is **Nellie Fox**, the Hall of Famer from nearby Franklin County.

1947: With manager **Les Bell**, the Senators return to the Class B Interstate League playoffs with a 71-69 record and fourth-place finish before losing to eventual champion Wilmington in the semifinals. ... First baseman **Herb Conyers** leads the league in batting with a .357 average. ... Pitcher **Vic Willis**, who spent the first season of his Hall of Fame career on the island in 1895, dies Aug. 3 in Elkton, Maryland. He is 71.

1948: With **Les Bell** still running the team, the Senators slip to 64-76 and sixth in the eight-team, Class B Interstate League. ... Among the outfielders is **Ed Musial**, brother of St. Louis Cardinals Hall of Famer **Stan Musial**. Unlike his older brother, Ed posts a skinny .219 batting average.

1949: Led by future American League All-Star outfielder **Jim Lemon** and manager **Les Bell**, the Senators finish at 74-64 and third in the eight-team, Class B Interstate League. They lose to Trenton in the playoff finals. ... The 21-year-old Lemon leads the league with 27 homers and 101 RBIs. ... **Stephen R. Reed** is born Aug. 9 in Chambersburg, Pa. Reed is elected Harrisburg's mayor in 1981 with an agenda that includes bringing baseball back to City Island. Three months later, **Marc Bombard**, who in 1990 becomes the second manager in the Senators' modern era, is born Nov. 15 in Baltimore.

1950: For the fourth time in five seasons under manager **Les Bell**, the Senators reach the playoffs. Their 77-62 record is good enough for a third-place finish in the eight-team, Class B Interstate League, but they lose to eventual champion Wilmington in the semifinals. ... **Willie Mays**, a 19-year-old center fielder in his first pro season, homers on the island Aug. 28 – one of just four homers he hits that summer with Trenton.

1951: The Senators struggle to finish within 30 games of first place at 55-84 and fall to sixth in the eight-team, Class B Interstate League. They start the season with **Les Bell** as manager, but finish with power-hitting outfielder **Harold Cox** running the team ... Cox, only 25 when he becomes player-manager, leads the league with 20 homers. ... For the first time since 1890, the island has an integrated pro team as pitcher **Brooks Lawrence** and outfielder **Joe Caffie** become Harrisburg's first black players since infielder **Frank Grant** and catcher **Clarence Williams** in 1890. ... The Cleveland Indians end their six-year affiliation with the Senators. ... **Dave Trembley**, the manager in the Senators' first three seasons of their modern era, is born Oct. 31 in Carthage, New York.

1952: The Philadelphia A's replace Cleveland as the Senators' major league affiliate. ... If the Senators were bad in 1951, they are dreadful in 1952 under managers **Buck Etchison** and **Woody Wheaton**. They finish last in the eight-team, Class B Interstate League and fold. The 46-94 record – a .329 winning percentage – remains the worst of any team to spend a full season on the island. ... Shortstop **Elbert Isreal** leads the league with a .318 batting average. Most of the attention goes to another infielder who never gets a chance to play in a game. Stenographer-turned-shortstop **Eleanor Engle** of Shiremanstown signs a contract on June 22, a first for a woman in affiliated baseball, but the deal is voided within 24 hours by minor league president **George Trautman**, as well as by major league commissioner **Ford Frick**. ... **Rick Sweet**, the manager of Harrisburg's 1998 EL championship team, is born Sept. 7 in Longview, Washington. ... The Senators attract only 30,592 fans for the summer. Just 301 attend the final home game. Presumably, someone closes the gate on the way out.

1953: Quiet summer with no pro baseball on the Island. More idle summers follow. ... Among the 1953 Hall of Fame inductees is **Chief Bender**, who pitched for the Harrisburg Athletic Club in 1902 before joining the Philadelphia Athletics and winning 208 of 320 decisions in the majors. ... **Ben Taylor**, the Hall of Fame first baseman and member of the 1925 Harrisburg Giants, dies Jan. 24 in Baltimore. He is 64. ... **Jim Thorpe**, an outfielder for the Senators three years after starring in the 1912 Olympics, dies March 28 in Lomita, California. He is 65.

1954: Chief Bender dies May 22 in Philadelphia. He is 70. ... The real Giant among the Giants of the 1920s – outfielder **Oscar Charleston** – dies on Oct. 5 in Philadelphia at 57.

1955: Pat Kelly, the Senators' manager during their worst-to-first finish in 1996, is born Aug. 27 in Santa Maria, California. ... **Jim Tracy**, who will manage the Senators to 100 victories and the EL title in 1993, is born Dec. 31 in Hamilton, Ohio.

1956: Right-hander **Brooks Lawrence**, a 10-game winner for Harrisburg in 1951, becomes the first former Senator pitcher selected for the major league All-Star Game, representing the Cincinnati Reds. Lawrence, though, does not pitch in the National League's 7-3 victory at Washington. ... **Andy Musser**, the onetime Senators bat boy from Lemoyne, is among nine winners of a high school broadcasting competition that puts him in the Phillies' radio booth for a game at Connie Mack Stadium. Twenty years later, he becomes a permanent fixture in the Phillies' broadcast booth. ...**Keith Bodie**, the Senators' manager in their first season as a Washington Nationals' affiliate in 2005, is born Feb. 16 in Brooklyn. ... **Rick Sofield**, the Senators' manager during their 1997 championship season, is born Dec. 16 in Cheyenne, Wyoming. ... **John Beckwith**, the power-hitting infielder of the Harrisburg Giants in the mid-1920s, dies Jan. 4 in New York City, three days shy of his 56th birthday.

1957: Another good year for the arrival of future Senators managers. **Dave Jauss**, who will lead Harrisburg to the 1994 Eastern League finals, is born Jan. 16 in Chicago. ... **Mike Quade**, the manager who would precede Jim Tracy on the island in 1991-92, is born March 12 in Evanston, Illinois. ...**Dave Huppert**, who will take the 2002 Senators to the EL finals, is born April 17 in South Gate, California.

1958: Chris Lein, the Senators' pitching coach in 1989, is born Oct. 23 in Staten Island, New York.

1959: Ten years after starring on the island, **Jim Lemon** hits his 100th career homer in the major leagues off **Jim Perry** during Washington's 8-2 loss to Cleveland on Aug. 4 at Griffith Stadium. ... Thirty-two years after leading the Senators to the New York-Penn League title, former manager **Win Clark** dies April 15 in Los Angeles. He is 84.

1960: Former Senators outfielder **Jim Lemon** represents the Washington Senators at the All-Star Game and goes 0-for-1 with a walk in the AL's 5-3 loss at Cleveland's Municipal Stadium.

1961: Twenty-one years after his death, former Senators player-manager **Billy Hamilton** is elected to the Hall of Fame.

1962: Spottswood Poles, the "black Ty Cobb" who starred for the Giants from 1906 to 1908, dies Sept. 12 in Harrisburg at age 72 and is buried at Arlington National Cemetery.

1963: Scott Little, who in 2007 becomes the first former Harrisburg player to manage the team in its modern era, is born Jan. 19 in East St. Louis, Illinois. ... **Doug Sisson**, who will manage the Senators during their wild 1999 championship season, is born Sept. 20 in Orlando, Florida.

1964: Johnny Tillman, the Senators' pitcher who served up Babe Ruth's homer during the 1928 exhibition game against the Yankees on the island, dies April 7 in Harrisburg. He is 70. ... **Jim Neidlinger**, who throws the first pitch to open RiverSide Stadium in 1987, is born Sept. 24 in Vallejo, California.

1965: Pitcher **Orlando Hernandez**, who in 2010 becomes the oldest player in franchise history at 44, is born Oct. 11 in Villa Clara, Cuba.

1966: Wes Chamberlain, the first of the Senators' six Eastern League MVPs in an 11-season span from 1989 to 1999, is born April 13 in Chicago. ... **Rip Vowinkel**, who pitched for the Senators in 1912, nods off for good, dying at his home in Oswego, New York, on July 13. He is 81.

1967: John Wehner, the Senators' third baseman in 1990 who in 2001 becomes the last player to homer at Three Rivers Stadium, is born June 29 in Pittsburgh.

1968: Matt Stairs, the second of the Senators' six league MVPs in the modern era, is born Feb. 27 in Saint John, New Brunswick, Canada. ... **Raymond "Bones" Boss**, who spent his life tending to the island's field, dies July 1 in Harrisburg. His ashes reportedly are scattered on the island. He is 73. ... **Fats Jenkins**, who in the mid-1920s joined **Oscar Charleston** and **Rap Dixon** to form one of the game's greatest outfields regardless of color, dies Dec. 6 in Philadelphia. He is 70.

1969: Oreste Marrero, the first position player from the prospect-filled 1993 Senators to reach the majors, is born Oct. 31 in Bayamon, Puerto Rico.

1970: Mark Grudzielanek, who joins **Cliff Floyd** as the Senators' back-to-back Eastern League MVP winners in 1993 and 1994, is born June 30 in Milwaukee.

1971: Glenn Killinger, the Harrisburg native who starred as a second baseman for the Senators in the mid-1920s, is inducted into the College Football Hall of Fame for starring as a quarterback for Penn State.

1972: Cliff Floyd, third of the Senators' six Eastern League MVPs from 1989 to 1999, is born Dec.5 in Chicago.

1973: Andy Tracy, the last of the Senators' six Eastern League MVPs in a 10-year span, is born Dec. 11 in Bowling Green, Ohio.

1974: Jamey Carroll is born Feb. 18 in Evansville, Indiana, three days after **Ugueth Urbina** is born in Caracas, Venezuela.

1975: Vladimir Guerrero is born Feb. 9 in Nizao, Peravia in the Dominican Republic. Twenty-one years later, he becomes the greatest prospect to ever play on City Island, as well as the Eastern League's MVP.

1976: The king of the Harrisburg Giants from the mid-1920s, outfielder **Oscar Charleston** is the seventh Negro Leagues player selected for the Hall of Fame on Feb. 9, following the previous inductions of Satchel Paige, Buck Leonard, Josh Gibson, Monte Irvin, Cool Papa Bell and Judy Johnson.

1977: Outfielder **Brad Wilkerson**, who in 1999 becomes the first Senator of the modern era to make his professional debut in Class AA, is born June 1 in Owensboro, Kentucky.

1978: Billy Cox, who made his pro debut on the island in 1940 before becoming one of major leagues' best third basemen, dies March 30 in Harrisburg. He is 58. ... **Milton Bradley**, author of City Island's quintessential baseball moment in 1999, is born April 15 in Harbor City, Calif.

1979: The water filtration plant that sits adjacent to the remnants of the Senators' old, wooden ballpark is destroyed by fire, leaving the weed-infested island with another blighted reminder of its once-proud past.

1980: Long before he becomes president of the Texas League, **Tom Kayser** buys the Holyoke Millers of the Class AA Eastern League for $35,000. Even though Holyoke wins its first title in any league since 1907, the Millers move to Nashua, New Hampshire, within two years and then on to Harrisburg in 1987. ... **Buck Etchison**, the Senators' manager in 1952 who said he would play **Eleanor Engle** only "when Hell freezes over," dies Jan. 24 in Cambridge, Maryland. He is 64.

1981: Stephen R. Reed is elected mayor of Harrisburg. Among his first goals: Overhauling the dump City Island had become after the old

Senators went out of business in 1952. ... Former Harrisburg Giants infielder **Rev Cannady** dies Dec. 3 in Fort Myers, Florida. He is 77.

1982: Jerome Mileur, a political science professor at the University of Massachusetts, and two other investors buy the Holyoke franchise from **Tom Kayser** for $85,000 – a tidy 240-percent return on Kayser's two-year investment.

1983: After only one season in Holyoke, **Jerome Mileur** moves his franchise to Nashua, New Hampshire, where attendance dwindles from 138,030 fans in his first season there to 78,103. He starts to look around for a new home. ... Not deterred by City Island's now seedy reputation, Harrisburg mayor **Stephen R. Reed** begins lobbying for more than $1 million to rebuild the island, starting with a new ballpark.

1984: Reed and Eastern League president **Charlie Eshbach** continue talks to bring baseball to City Island. ... **Ryan Zimmerman** is born Sept. 28 in Washington, North Carolina. ... **Al Schacht**, 91, who pitched for the 1915 Senators and was Max Patkin's predecessor as the "Clown Prince of Baseball," dies July 14 in Waterbury, Connecticut.

1985: Independent of Reed's pursuit of a team to fill his proposed stadium, Camp Hill sports legend **Brad Shover** and two partners, **Jeffrey Kirkus** and **Frederick Shulley**, purchase a team in the short-season, Class A New York-Penn League with the intent of relocating to Harrisburg. The league rejects the deal, saying moving a franchise to Harrisburg is not in its best interests since the closest team to City Island was 160 miles away in Elmira, New York. Shover's group unsuccessfully tries to buy the Class AA Eastern League franchise in Glen Falls, New York. ... **Les Bell** dies Dec. 26 in Hershey at 84.

1986: With his franchise failing at the gate in Nashua, **Jerome Mileur** decides to move his team out of New Hampshire, although Harrisburg is not his first choice. That is Springfield, Massachusetts, but that city is in no position to land his franchise since it has no stadium. Camp Hill's **Brad Shover** believes he has a deal to buy Mileur's team for $750,000 and move it to City Island, but Mileur decides instead to retain ownership, adding Texas banker **Scott Carter** as club president to run the franchise while Mileur stays home in Amherst, Massachusetts. Carter raids the Class AAA Richmond Braves for his first two hires – **Rick Redd** as general manager and **Todd Vander Woude** as the assistant GM. The pair quickly goes to work at makeshift offices inside City Hall. ... In the fall of 1986, the Pittsburgh Pirates hire **Dave Trembley** to be the Senators' manager in their first season back on the island in 35 years.

1987: The Senators finish in second place with a 77-63 record in the eight-team Class AA Eastern League before rallying to beat Reading in the playoff semifinals and then Vermont in four games of  the best-of-5 finals. **Tom Prince** saves the season in the ninth inning of Game 5 of the semifinals with a two-out, game-tying homer off Reading closer **Todd Frohwirth**. The Senators win the game in 13 innings, setting up the championship series with Vermont. … Right-hander **Jim Neidlinger** delivers the first pitch of the modern era at 2:09 p.m. on April 11. The Senators lose to Vermont

TOM PRINCE 11-5 before a crowd of 4,083 at newly minted $1.8 million RiverSide Stadium, which opens with a seating capacity of 5,300. … In only his third game on the island, first baseman **Ron Johns** goes 6-for-6 with three homers, three singles and nine RBIs during a 26-9 rout of Albany-Colonie on June 17. … Left fielder **Tommy Gregg** leads the EL in hitting with a .371 average. … In the first of four seasons as Pittsburgh's Class AA affiliate, the Senators endure an 11-game losing streak that remains a modern-franchise record entering the team's 25th anniver-  **TOMMY GREGG** sary season in 2012. … Attendance for the first season is 212,141. Another 2,878 turn out for the EL's all-star game June 27 on the island.

1988: The Senators, with **Dave Trembley** back as manager, cannot repeat their championship run, going 65-73 and falling to seventh place in the eight-team Class AA Eastern League. … Despite their struggles on the field, the Senators draw a league-high 216,940 fans, not including the 5,088 who turn out May 26 to watch an exhibition game against the Pittsburgh Pirates. … Former Senator and College Football Hall of Famer **Glenn Killinger** dies July 25 in Newark, Delaware. He is 89.

1989: In the third and final season with **Dave Trembley** as their manager, the 71-65 Senators finish second in the eight-team, Class AA Eastern League before losing to Albany-Colonie in the finals. … The Senators are second in attendance at 200,196. … Right fielder **Wes Chamberlain** bats .306 with 21 homers and a league-high 87 RBIs to become the first of six Senators named league's MVP over a 10-year span.

1990: In the last of their four seasons as Pittsburgh's Class AA affiliate, the 69-69 Senators under manager **Marc Bombard** fall to fifth in the eight-team, Class AA Eastern League. ... Despite missing the playoffs, the Senators lead the league in attendance at 223,033.

1991: The Senators switch major league affiliations from Pittsburgh to Montreal. ... With **Mike Quade** as their new manager, the 87-53 Senators post the best record in the eight-team, Class AA Eastern League before falling to Albany-Colonie in the finals. Their attendance of 233,423 is second in the league. ... Infielder **Matt Stairs** is the EL's MVP after leading the league with a .333 batting average and base hits at 168. With 30 doubles, 10 triples and 13 homers, Stairs becomes the first Senator since **Joe Munson** in 1927 to post such a triple double. Stairs' MVP season begins only six weeks after Munson – Harrisburg's last .400 hitter and its only Tri-

MATT STAIRS

ple Crown winner – dies Feb. 24 in Drexel Hill, Pa. He is 91. ... Stairs also becomes the first Senator in the modern era to hit for the cycle Aug. 23 on the island in a 7-4 loss to New Britain. The Red Sox's victory is fueled by the first and last Class AA homer hit by light-hitting catcher **Luis Dorante**, who 10 years later becomes the Senators' manager.

1992: The Senators go 78-59 in their second year under manager **Mike Quade** to finish third in the eight-team, Class AA Eastern League. They reach the EL playoffs, but lose to Binghamton in the first round. Their attendance of 209,159 ranks third in the league. ... General manager **Rick Redd** resigns in midseason and is replaced by his assistant, **Todd Vander Woude**.

1993: Built by the Expos to win early, often and by wide margins, the prospect-packed Senators win 100 games between the regular season and playoffs for their first Eastern League title since 1987. ... **Jim Tracy** is named the EL's manager of the year after the Senators' 94-44 regular season. ... After eliminating Albany-Colonie in the first round of the playoffs, the

CLIFF FLOYD

Senators fall behind Canton-Akron 2-0 in the best-of-5 finals before outscoring the Indians 23-4 to sweep the final three games on the road for the championship. The franchise also receives the Bob Freitas Award given by Baseball America to the best-run Class AA operation. ...

Attendance of 250,476 ranks third in the eight-team league. ... Outfielder-first baseman **Cliff Floyd** is named the Senators' second EL MVP in three seasons after batting .329 with league-highs with 26 homers and 101 RBIs – all in just 101 games. ... **Rondell White** becomes the second player in the team's modern era to finish with a triple-double, amassing 16 doubles, 10 triples and 12 homers, and a .328 batting average in only 90 games. ... In July, owner **Jerome Mileur** agrees to sell the franchise to **Van Farber** for $4 million, but the deal is voided when the National Association questioned Farber's finances.

1994: Following a record-breaking team, the Senators under manager **Dave Jauss** finish 88-51 and return to the Eastern League finals, where they fall in four games to Binghamton. Despite his success, Jauss – the league's manager of the year – is told during the finals by Expos general manager **Kevin Malone** that his contract will not be renewed for 1995. ... With the proliferation of new teams and new ballparks in the league, the Senators slip to seventh in attendance at 234,774. ... Shortstop **Mark Grudzielanek** is the league's MVP after batting .322 with 37 doubles, 11 homers, 32 stolen bases and 92 runs scored. ... Right fielder **Kevin Northrup** leads the league with a .331 batting aver-

DAVE JAUSS

age. ... Binghamton left-hander **Bill Pulsipher** no-hits the Senators 2-0 in Game 2 of the EL finals on Sept. 12 on the island. ... In July, owner **Jerome Mileur** agrees to sell the team to **William Collins III** for more than $3.5 million, but Mileur decides in September to sell the team for $4.1 million to four investors from suburban Philadelphia.

1995: Major League Baseball's strike ends late in spring training, but that does not keep teams from dumping would-be replacement players onto their minor league affiliates. The island turns out to be the destination for 10 such players. The influx of mediocrity leaves the Senators with a league-worst record of 61-80. ... Attendance of 240,488 is seventh in the 10-team, Class AA Eastern League. ... At times, the best prospect on the field before the game is **Casey Kelly**, the 5-year-old son of manager **Pat Kelly**. In 2008, Casey would become the 30th overall pick of the amateur draft. ... Only months after talking about "conquering" the local market, co-owner **Steven Resnick** and his partners clandestinely plan to relocate the franchise after the 1996 season. Their preferred destination is the

Lehigh Valley. After state funding dries up for a stadium there, Resnick and his partners turn to Springfield, Massachusetts, where **Jerome Mileur** initially wanted to move the franchise in 1986. As Resnick signs a 10-year lease in Springfield, Harrisburg mayor **Stephen R. Reed** implores the National Association to allow his city to purchase the team. After the NA gives its OK, the city buys the Senators for $6.7 million, a record sum for a Class AA team. ... **Vic Willis**, whose pro career started in 1895 on the island and finished in 1910 with 249 victories in the majors, is elected to the Hall of Fame.

1996: Manager **Pat Kelly** is rewarded for surviving 1995 with a team that finishes 74-68 during the regular season, reaches the Class AA Eastern

League playoffs and wins the first of its league-record four straight championships. ... Attendance of 230,744 is only good enough for seventh in the 10-team league. ... The lineup features **Vladimir Guerrero, Brad Fullmer** and **Jose Vidro**. The trio – with Guerrero still playing through 2011 – goes on to combine for nearly 4,900 hits, 700 homers and 2,600 RBIs in the majors.

BRAD FULLMER Little wonder they dispose of Portland in four games in the EL finals after beating Trenton in the semifinals. Guerrero goes directly from the finals to the join the Expos in the majors. ... After spending April in the gentle climes of the Class A Florida State League, Guerrero joins the Senators on May 1 and ends up batting a league-high .360 in 118 games with 19 homers and 78 RBIs, and is the team's third league MVP in four seasons. ... **Elbert Isreal**, the 1952 Interstate League batting champion and the best player on the Senators' worst team, dies Oct. 22 in Rockville, Maryland. He is 68.

1997: Of the Senators' EL-record four straight championship teams from 1996 to 1999, the '97 team under manager **Rick Sofield** is the only one to finish the regular season in first place in the Southern Division. They post the league's best record at 86-56 before beating

RICK SOFIELD

Bowie and Portland in the playoffs. ... Attendance of 242,431 ranks seventh in the 10-team league. ... Infielders **Jolbert** and **Orlando Cabrera** become the first set of brothers to play for the Senators in the modern era; they miss by only a few days of playing together on the island. ... Right-

266

hander **Javier Vazquez** leads the EL in oohs and aahs, going 4-0 with a 1.07 ERA in six starts to end the regular season and 2-0 in the playoffs.

1998: Manager **Rick Sweet** follows up the titles won by **Pat Kelly** and **Rick Sofield** with a team that finishes 73-69 during the regular season before beating Akron and New Britain in the Eastern League playoffs. ... Attendance of 259,381 is sixth in the 10-team league. ... Infielder **Geoff Blum** records one of baseball's rarest single-game feats Aug. 3 as he hits for a natural cycle with a single, double, triple and homer in only four at-bats of a 3-2 victory over New Haven.

1999: The Senators' 76-66 record is good enough to qualify for the Class AA Eastern League playoffs, where each of Harrisburg's nine games is decided by one run. The last of those games – a 12-11 victory over Norwich on Sept. 20 – brings a league-record fourth straight championship. ... Attendance of 253,399 ranks seventh in the 12-team league. ... The Senators are 10 games under .500 on May 25 and nine games out of a playoff berth on July 1 before winning 33 of 51 games after the All-Star break to move from last place in the Southern Division to the EL playoffs. In the postseason, they beat Erie in four games before stunning Norwich 12-11 in the fifth and deciding game of the finals Sept. 20 on the island as **Milton Bradley** launches a two-out, two-strike, bottom-of-the-ninth grand slam against the EL saves leader, **Joe Lisio**. ... Although loaded with prospects, the Senators become the first team in modern-franchise history to start a season with six straight losses. ... The wonderfully talented and equally incendiary Bradley ignites a bench-clearing brawl April 13 against Altoona and receives a seven-game suspension for spitting gum on umpire **Tim Pasch** after being ejected from the game. ... Manager **Doug Sisson** abruptly quits the team July 5 to pursue a coaching career at the University of Georgia. He verbally slams both fans and media on his way out of town, only to rejoin the Senators a week later. The Expos allow Sisson to return after instructing him to give a mea culpa to anyone he has offended. Sisson needs the rest of the summer to complete his penance. ... Third baseman **Andy Tracy** sets an all-time franchise record with 37 homers. Tracy is named the league's MVP, the sixth time since 1999 that the award goes to a Senator. ... **Max Patkin**, who made his debut as the "Clown Prince of Baseball" on the island in 1946, dies Oct. 30 in Paoli, Pa. He is 79.

2000: For the fifth straight season, the Senators reach the postseason after beating Akron 8-1 at Canal Park in a one-game playoff after the teams finish the regular season tied for second at 76-66. The Senators fall short of a fifth straight Eastern League title, though, as they are swept by Reading in three games of the Southern Division finals. ... Harrisburg again ranks seventh in attendance in the 12-team league at 250,384. ... Manager **Doug Sisson** has the unenviable task of trying to reproduce 1999's drama both on and off the field.. Sisson tries, though, once tweaking his lineup to place pitcher **T.J. Tucker** seventh in the batting order. He also wants to use **Donnie Bridges**, his best pitcher, in the same spot as a designated hitter, but the Expos say no. Sisson's persistence on such matters eventually leads to his firing after the season for what Montreal general manager **Jim Beattie** calls "insubordination." ... Bridges goes 11-7 with a 2.39 ERA and emerges as the Expos' top pitching prospect. Unfortunately for Bridges, a 201-inning workload between Harrisburg and Class A Jupiter is too much for his right shoulder. He never recovers to have the career projected for him in the majors. ... **Brooks Lawrence**, who in 1956 became the first former Senator selected to an All-Star Game in the majors, dies April 27 in Springfield, Ohio. He is 75.

2001: After five straight playoff runs, the Senators drop to 66-76 under manager **Luis Dorante**. ... **Valentino Pascucci**, **Matt Cepicky** and **Scott Hodges** become the first Senators in the modern era to hit three home runs in a row. Their homers come on three straight pitches from Altoona reliever **Geraldo Padua** in the eighth inning of a 4-2 victory April 23 on the island. ... Right-hander **Ron Chiavacci** loses 11 of 14 decisions but ends up with a franchise-record 161 strikeouts. ... Even with a franchise-best 279,691 fans, the Senators rank eighth in attendance in the 12-team, Class AA Eastern League.

2002: After initially being hired to manage the Florida Marlins' Double-A team in Portland, Maine, **Dave Huppert** finds himself on the island after the Marlins' new owner – former Expos boss **Jeffrey Loria** – hires away nearly all of Montreal's staff as replacements for the Marlins' staffers he already has fired. With Huppert, the 79-63 Senators reach the Class AA Eastern League finals, where they lose to Norwich. ... Right fielder **Valentino Pascucci** tops the EL with 27 homers, while right-hander **Bryan Hebson** goes 10-1 with seven saves and a 1.72 ERA. ... The biggest headline of the season comes June 27, when Expos general manager **Omar Minaya** trades top prospects **Brandon Phillips**, **Cliff Lee** and **Grady Sizemore** to Cleveland for rent-a-pitcher **Bartolo Colon**. Phillips and Lee had spent the first half of the season in Harrisburg. ... The Senators remain stuck in the bottom half of the 12-team league in attendance at 266,808.

2003: After only two losing seasons in their first 12 as Montreal's Class AA affiliate, the Senators slump to 60-82 and a last-place finish in the 12-team Eastern League. ... Right-hander **Seung Song** is credited with the Senators' first no-hitter since 1952 as he beats Erie 2-1 April 28 on the island. Seung's no-hitter is preserved by a controversial scoring decision in the ninth inning. ... Manager **Dave Machemer** picks up his 1,000[th] career victory Aug. 22 in a 10-8 victory over Akron on the island. ... Center fielder **Brandon Watson** leads

DAVE MACHEMER

the team with a .319 batting average and a modern franchise record for hits with 180. ... Attendance of 257,989 ranks eighth in the league.

2004: With **Dave Machemer** back as manager, the Senators skid to a 52-90 record – their worst finish since the 1952 Senators went 46-94 and folded. The back-to-back losing seasons are the Senators' first since 1951-1952; the consecutive last-place finishes over a full season also is a first in franchise history. ... Once again, home attendance is eighth in the 12-team, Class AA Eastern League at 255,978. ... Shortstop **Josh Labandeira** sets a franchise record with six leadoff homers. He finishes the season with the Expos, becoming the last player they promote to the majors before relocating to Washington.

2005: The Senators begin their first season as a Washington Nationals affiliate, but their slide from 2003-2004 continues with a 64-78, fifth-place finish in the EL' Southern Division. The Senators match their predecessors from 1909-1911 and 1933-1935 as the only teams on the island with three straight losing seasons. ... Attendance falls to ninth in the 12-team league at 264,718. ... **Keith Bodie** is the manager. ... Third baseman **Ryan Zimmerman**, the fourth overall pick in June's amateur draft, bats .326 in 63 games for the Senators with 20 doubles, nine homers and a season-ending promotion to the majors.

2006: The Senators suffer their franchise-record fourth straight losing season, going 67-75 for manager **John Stearns** and finish 20 games out of first place. ... Attendance of 253,937 ranks ninth in the 12-team, Class AA Eastern League. ... After 10 years of claiming he did not want to be the team's de facto owner, mayor **Stephen R. Reed** announces in October that he wants to sell the franchise to someone who will promise to keep it on the island. … Onetime Senators outfielder **Jim Lemon**, who led the Interstate League in 1949 with 27 homers and 101 RBIs, dies May 14 in Brandon, Mississippi. He is 78.

2007: Scott Little becomes the first former Senator of the modern era to return to the island as a full-time manager. The 55-86 Senators finish their fifth straight losing season and in last place of the 12-team Eastern League. … Attendance of 229,241 ranks 10th in the 12-team league. … In May, **Michael Reinsdorf** – the son of Chicago White Sox owner **Jerry Reinsdorf** – heads a group that purchases the Senators for $13.25 million. As was the case in 1995, the sale price is a record for a Class AA franchise. … Assistant general manager **Mark Mattern**, who had been with the team since 1987, is fired in October with general manager **Todd Vander Woude**, the team's second hire in the fall of 1986, resigning a month later. Within a month, **Randy Whitaker**, an advertising executive for Harrisburg's local ABC affiliate, is hired as Vander Woude's replacement.

2008: With **John Stearns** back as manager, the Senators finish 73-69, ending their all-time franchise-record skid of five straight losing seasons in the Class AA Eastern League. … Longtime minor league operator **Kevin Kulp** is hired in July as team president as **Bill Davidson** is named CEO. … With new ownership vowing to drastically cut back on comp tickets, the Senators draw only 164,182 fans – marking the first time they attract fewer than 200,000 since their return to the island in 1987.

2009: Construction begins in January on a two-year, $45 million stadium renovation. Even with renovations going on around them, 228,741 fans turn out to watch a 70-72 team that misses the Class AA Eastern League playoffs for a seventh straight season. Attendance ranks ninth in the 12-team league. … Infielder **Ofilio Castro** and outfielder **Edgardo Baez** are enjoying career-rejuvenating seasons before being suspended in August for testing positive for using amphetamines. … Manager **John Stearns** leaves after the season to join the Seattle Mariners as a scout.

2010: Having been voted out of office in 2009 after seven terms, mayor **Stephen R. Reed** becomes Citizen Reed for the grand reopening of the ballpark – now a $45 million jewel that replaces the woefully outdated stadium that housed the team since 1987. … Manager **Randy Knorr** leads the Senators to a 77-65 record, good enough for second place in the Class AA Eastern League's Western Division and a playoff berth for the first time since 2002. The Senators do not last long, falling to Altoona in four games of the best-of-5 semifinals. ... A franchise-record 294,325 fans pack refurbished Metro Bank Park. The attendance ranks seventh in the 12-team league. ... Helping spike the attendance is the brief presence of **Stephen Strasburg**, the 21-year-old pitcher selected by the Nationals with the first overall pick of the 2009 amateur draft. Strasburg is 3-1 with a 1.64 ERA in five starts for the Senators before moving on to Class AAA Syracuse, his major league debut and – ouch – subsequent Tommy John surgery on his right elbow. ... Former World Series pitching hero **Orlando Hernandez** joins the Senators in mid-August, making him – at the reported age of 44 – the oldest player in all-time franchise history. He also is the oldest to pitch competitively on the island since the 50-something **Satchel Paige** brought his barnstorming team to town in the 1950s. As was the case with Paige, no one is truly sure of Hernandez's age.

2011: The Senators finish 80-62, reaching the Eastern League playoffs in consecutive seasons for the first time since their five straight appearanc-es from 1996 to 2000. The 80 victories under manager **Tony Beasley** are the Senators' most since 1997, when they won 86 games. ... The league-leading 80 victories also give the Senators their first division title since 1997. The Senators, though, do not get to enjoy the perks of home-field advantage in the EL playoffs as late-season flooding on the

The flood and mud of early September cost the Senators home-field advantage for the EL playoffs

island forces them out of town for the playoffs. The Senators travel to se-cond-place Richmond, where they are swept in three games. ... For the second straight summer, baseball's most coveted prospect reaches the is-land. Left fielder **Bryce Harper**, the first pick in the 2010 amateur draft, hits .256 in 37 games with three homers and 12 RBIs before being side-lined with a strained hamstring. At 18, Harper is the youngest player in the

Senators' modern era. ... A record crowd of 8,637 turns out Sept. 1 to see **Stephen Strasburg** make his final injury rehab start on his way back from Tommy John surgery at the end of the 2010 season. His catcher this night

At only 18, left fielder Bryce Harper became the youngest player in the Senators' modern era

is **Ivan Rodriguez**, the future Hall of Famer also making an injury rehab appearance on the island. ... First baseman **Tyler Moore** leads the league with 31 homers and 90 RBIs, while right-hander **Brad Peacock** goes 10-2 with a league-best 2.01 ERA in 16 starts before being promoted to Class AAA Syracuse. ... Franchise-record home attendance of 291,248 is seventh in the 12-team league. In addition to drawing their 6 millionth fan to the island since their return in 1987, the Senators win their second Bob Freitas Award, given annually by *Baseball America* to the top organization in Class AA. ... **Joe Caffie**, the onetime Cleveland Indians outfielder who in 1951 became the first black position player for Harrisburg since infielder **Frank Grant** in 1890, dies Aug. 1 in Warren, Ohio. He is 80.

2012: The Senators and Nationals announce on March 16 a two-year extension to their player development agreement through the 2014 season. ... For the first time in team history, the Senators sell more than 100,000 tickets before the season even starts.

All-Time Roster

Jeremy Ware winced every time he was reminded he was moving up the Senators' charts for all-time leaders in this or that.

For the outfielder from Guelph, Ontario, those achievements only meant his career was stalling in Harrisburg. All-time records in the minors tend to be set by players who never reach the majors, let alone excel there.

"There are worse places to go," Ware said with a sigh before starting his sixth season on City Island in 2004. "This is my second home."

The same could be said of four other players who spent all or part of six seasons on the island – outfielder Horace McBride (1927-1932), and pitchers Lefty Hefflefinger (1929, 1931-1935), Dutch Schesler (1925-1926, 1928-1930,1941) and Zech Zinicola (2006-2011).

The longest lasting of any of the 52 managers on City Island was former major league infielder Les Bell, a native of Harrisburg who spent eight seasons with the Senators from 1940 to 1941 and 1946 to 1951.

From 1890 through Opening Day 2012, Harrisburg's teams – whether they were known as the Ponies, Hustlers, Indians, Islanders, Giants or Senators – had more than more than 1,600 players, managers and coaches.

Some, such as utility player Phil Wellman in 1987, lasted for one game. Some, such as first baseman Paul Thoutsis in 1996, played his few games as a Senator on the road. Some, such as the second baseman Lord in 1924, appeared in baseball's archives only by their last name.

An astounding 539 of 1,656 players reached the majors either before or after their stay in Harrisburg. Their names are listed in bold.

The list includes major leaguers such as Ivan Rodriguez and Dmitri Young who played with the Senators while on injury rehab assignments; it does not include players from semi-pro teams such as the Harrisburg Athletic Club with future Hall of Fame pitcher Chief Bender, or the turn-of-the-20th-century, all-black semipro Harrisburg Giants, whose players included outfielder Spottswood Poles.

HARRISBURG PLAYERS
Ponies, Hustlers, Indians, Islanders or Senators (1890-2011)

A

Abbott, Charles (1910)
Abner, Ben (1987)
Ackdt (1894)
Ackerman, Scott (2000, 2002-2003)
Adams, Mark (1914, 1917)
Adams, Steve (1988-1990)
Adams (1913)
Adams (1932)
Adler, Robert (1910)
Adolfo, Carlos (1998-1999)
Agamennone, Brandon (1999-2002)
Agnew, Sidney (1924-1926)
Alaniz, Adrian (2008-2010)
Albaladejo, Jonathan (2007)
Albin, Scott (2001)
Alcantara, Izzyl (1995-1997)
Allen, Matt (1995)
Alou, Moises (1989-1990)
Alvarez, Oscar (2006)
Alvarez, Tavo (1992, 1995)
Ambrosini, Dominick (2004)
Ames, Ed (1895)
Andersh, Kevin (1987)
Anderson, Charles C. (1946)
Anderson, Charles W. (1940)
Anderson, Dewey (1925)
Anderson, Thomas (1892)
Andrews, Jeff (2001)
Andrews, Shane (1993)
Ankiel, Rick (2011)
Ankoviak, Bill (1946)
Ankrum, Bob (1946-1947)
Anness, Earl (1942)
Anthony, Ed (1909)
Antonelli, Matt (2011)
Arata, Nick (2009)
Argeros, James (1952)

Armas, Tony Jr. (1999, 2006)
Armbrust, Orville (1935)
Armstrong, Sid (1894)
Arnesen, Erik (2009-2011)
Arthurs, Shane (2001)
Ashenback, Ed (1892)
Astacio, Pedro (2006)
Atilano, Luis (2008-2009, 2011)
Attreau, Dick (1928-1929)
Atzrott, Ed (1946)
Aucoin, Derek (1994-1995)
Ausanio, Joe (1990, 1993)
Avery, Matt (2009)

B

Bady, Ed (1997-98)
Baez, Edgardo (2008-2010)
Bailey, Jeff (2002-2003)
Bailey, Seymour (1924-1927)
Bain (1901)
Baker, Edward (1933-1934)
Baker, Jason (1998-1999)
Baker, Kerry (1987)
Baker, Lonny (1933)
Balester, Collin (2006-2007)
Balfe, Ryan (2003)
Ballard, Jerry (1948)
Banister, Jeff (1988-1990)
Bannon, Robert (1949)
Barczi, Scott (1990)
Barker, Tim (1993)
Barker, J. (1913)
Barnes, Luther (1917)
Barnett, Eddie (1942)
Barrett, Michael (1998)
Barron, Tony (1995-1996)
Barthmaier, Jimmy (2011)

Barthold, John (1910)
Batista, Miguel (1993-1994)
Battam, Larry (1900)
Baxter, Bob (1994)
Baxter, Frank (1890)
Baxter, Richard (1947-1948)
Beard, Ted (1942)
Beasley (1932)
Beaster, Harvey (1942)
Belcher, Jason (2004-2005)
Belen, Lance (1987-1988)
Belinda, Stan (1989)
Bell, Juan (1994)
Bell, Bob (1950)
Bell, Les (1933, 1940-1941)
Bellar, Lamar (1935)
Belliard, Rafael (1987)
Belliard, Ronnie (2008)
Benitez, Yamil (1994)
Bennett, Chris (1991)
Bennett, Shayne (1996-1997)
Benson, Allen (1935)
Bentley (1912)
Bentz, Chad (2003-2004)
Benz, Jake (1996-1998)
Benzel, Herbert (1948)
Bergeron, Peter (1998-1999)
Bergmann, Jason (2004-2005)
Bergolla, William (2008)
Bernadina, Roger (2007-2008)
Berresford, Bob (1952)
Berryhill, Robert (1900)
Billingsley, Brent (2001-2002)
Bibby, Frank (1908)
Bisenius, Joe (2010)
Bittner, Tim (2008)
Black, Edward (1940)
Black, William (1940)
Black (1910)
Blair (1916)

Blanco, Tony (2006-2007)
Blank, Matt (1999)
Blatnik, Johnny (1946)
Blodgett, Alton (1925)
Blum, Geoff (1996, 1998)
Bobzean, Eugene (1949-1950, 1952)
Bocachica, Hiram (1997-1998)
Bochtler, Doug (1992)
Bock, Leonard (1952)
Bold (1917)
Boley, Joe (1917)
Bonner, John (1906)
Bonness, Bill (1946)
Bonthrom, Harry (1901)
Borgmann, Benny (1930)
Boselo, George (1948)
Botkin, Allan (1995)
Boucher, Dan (1996)
Bouknight, Kip (2005-2006)
Bournigal, Rafael (1995)
Bowie, Micah (2005)
Bowman, Duke (1951)
Bowman, Joe (1930)
Bowman, Summer (1890)
Boyle (1895)
Boynton (1924)
Bradbury, Miah (1993)
Bradley, Milton (1999)
Bradley, William (1892)
Brady (1930)
Braham, Thomas (1893-1894)
Bramhill (1932)
Brandt, Bill (1941)
Bravo, Danny (1999)
Bray, Bill (2005)
Bream, Jess (1927)
Breckenridge, Clinton (1916)
Brehm, Maurice (1926)
Brennan, James (1907-1908)
Brennan, William (1991)

Brenner (1931)
Bressler, Rube (1913)
Brewer, Billy (1992)
Bridges, Donnie (2000-02, 2004-05)
Bridges, Marvin (1908)
Brinkley, Josh (1997)
Briscoe, Albert (1932)
Brito, Eude (2008)
Brito, Mario (1992-1993)
Broadway, Larry (2003-2005)
Bronson, Evan (2011)
Broskie, Sig (1942)
Brotherton, Paul (1946)
Broukal, Bill (1950-1951)
Brown, Clint (1925-1926, 1928)
Brown, Craig (1987)
Brown, Dee (2007)
Brown, Dermal (2005)
Brown, Elmer (1915)
Brown, Jason (2002-2004)
Brown, Walter (1935)
Brown (1901)
Brown (1916-1917)
Brownlee, Harry (1930)
Brownlie, Bobby (2008)
Bruce, Mo (2001)
Brydle, Harold (1950)
Buckles, Jess (1916)
Buckley, Travis (1992)
Buckley, Troy (1995)
Budura, Victor (1946)
Buell, Donald (1947)
Bullinger, Kirk (1995-1997)
Bunch, Melvin (1997)
Burdick, Kevin (1988-1989)
Burgess, Michael (2010)
Burke, Edward (1927, 1929-1930)
Burke, J. (1928)
Burke, Mike (1892)
Burke (1917)

Burns, Jim (1946-1947)
Burns (1916)
Burson, Donald (1951)
Bushing, Chris (1991)
Butler, Maynard (1950)
Butler, Otis (1926)
Buvid (1931)
Buyer, Robert (1946)
Bybee (1926)
Byers, Bill (1900)
Byers, John (1914)
Byers (1925)
Bynum, Freddie (2009)
Bynum, Seth (2006-2009)

C

Cabrera, Jolbert (1994-1997)
Cabrera, Orlando (1997)
Cacciola, James (1952)
Caffie, Joe (1951)
Cain, Sugar (1931)
Cairo, Sergio (1995)
Caldwell, Bruce (1932)
Calhoun, Jack (1906-1908)
Callahan, Leo (1915)
Calloway, Ron (2001-2002)
Camilli, Jason (1998-2000)
Camilo, Juan (2004)
Camp, Norm (1949)
Campbell, Billy (1906-1907)
Campbell, Brett (2006-2007)
Campos, Jesus (1996-1998)
Capes, Del (1930)
Cardner, Ralph (1940)
Carey, Lee (1949)
Carithers, James (1934)
Carlonas, George (1942)
Carman, George (1890)
Carney (1911)
Carpenter (1894)

Carr, Adam (2007-2010)
Carreno, Jose (2001-2002)
Carrigan (1925)
Carroll, Jamey (1998-2000, 2002)
Carroll, Wes (2003-2004)
Carrow, Rexford (1949-1951)
Carter, Steve (1988)
Carvajal, Jhonny (1996-1998, 2000)
Casadiego, Gerardo (2002-2004)
Casey, John (1935)
Casey (1926)
Cassels, Chris (1991)
Castiglione, Pete (1942)
Casto, Kory (2006)
Castro, Ofilio (2007-2010)
Castro, Ramon (2005)
Cepicky, Matt (2001-2002)
Chabek, Joe (1912-1915)
Chalfant, John (1950)
Chamberlain, Wes (1989)
Chance, Tony (1988-1989)
Chandler, John (1935)
Chaney (1925)
Chapman, Jake (2000-2002)
Chapman, Mark (1992)
Chappelle, Bill (1906)
Charbonnet, Mark (1995)
Charlton, Joseph (1895)
Chavez, Ender (2006)
Chellew, R. (1901)
Chervinko, George (1934)
Chiavacci, Ron (2001-2003)
Chick, Bruce (1995)
Chico, Matt (2006, 2009-2011)
Childs, Pete (1895)
Chlan, Charles (1948)
Church, Ryan (2005-2006)
Cianfrocco, Archi (1991)
Cicero, Joe (1935)
Cihocki, Ed (1931-1932)

Clay, Bill (1906)
Clark, Dick (1950)
Clark, Robert (1924)
Clark, Walter (1940-1941)
Clark (1917)
Clermont (1916)
Cleveland, Russ (2006)
Cloude, William (1948)
Coats, Buck (2011)
Cobb, Joe (1930-1931)
Cochlin, David (1925, 1927-1928)
Cockill, George (1912-1914)
Cole, Jason (1997-1998)
Coleman, Frank (1932-1933)
Coleman, Jim (1946)
Coleman, John (1893)
Collins, Pat (2002-2003)
Collins (1892)
Colone, Joseph (1948)
Coma, Albert (1950)
Comstock, Warwick (1925-1926)
Concepcion, Onix (1987)
Conklin, Howell (1933)
Conn, Bert (1900)
Connaughton, Frank (1905)
Conroy, Ben (1892)
Conroy, Ray (1948)
Conroy, Tim (1989)
Conyers, Herb (1946-1947)
Coogan, Thomas (1942)
Cook, Jeff (1987-1990)
Cook, Walter (1917)
Cook (1916)
Cooke, Fred (1893)
Coon, Brad (2010)
Cooper (1917)
Copp, Bill (1987-1988)
Copple, Addis (1940)
Coquillette, Trace (1997-1998)
Corbin, Archie (1992-1993)

Corcoran, Roy (2003, 2006)
Cordero, Wil (2005)
Cornelius, Reid (1991-1993)
Costello, Andrew (1893)
Cotton, John (2001)
Coughlin, David (1892)
Cousins, Tim (1999)
Covington (1925)
Cox, Billy (1940-1941)
Cox, Harold (1949-1951)
Cox, John (1890)
Cox, Wesley (1941)
Coyne, Joe (1895)
Cramer, Edward (1935)
Crane, Anthony (1909)
Crawford, Tristan (2008)
Crimmel, Robert (1940)
Crist, Brook (1913-1914)
Crist, HJ (1912)
Cristall, Billy (1906)
Cronin (1900)
Crosby, Mike (1996)
Crowley, Terry Jr. (1988-1990)
Cruikshank, Frank (1913-1914)
Crump, Harold (1925)
Crumpton, Chuck (2000-2004)
Cuccurullo, Cookie (1942)
Cummings, John (1935)
Curtis, Mike (1988)
Czajkowski, Jim (1990)

D

Dailey, Vince (1895)
Daniel, Clay (1987-1988)
Daniel, Mike James (1993)
Daniel, Mike John (2008-2010)
Daniels, Alexander (1947)
Darrell, Tommy (2001)
Dash, Walter (1925-1926)
Dasilva, Fernando (1997)

Dauphin, Phil (1994-1995)
Davis, Allen (2001-2002)
Davis, Charles (1948)
Davis, Erik (2011)
Davis, Fred (1893)
Davis, Glenn (2002-2003)
Davis, Harry (1924)
Davis, Ira (1890)
Davis, Kevin (1988)
Davis, Leonard (2008-2011)
Daviu, August (1926)
Day, Zach (2005)
Deal, Cot (1942)
Deasley, John (1890)
DeCaster, Yurendell (2008)
Dedrick, Jim (1997)
Deeds, Robert (1950)
Dehaney, Frank (1925)
DeHart, Rick (1993, 1995-1996)
DeLaRosa, Tomas (1999)
DeMent, Dan (2005-2007)
Demoe (1930)
Dempsey, Lee (1925-1926)
DePillo, George (1951)
DePriest, Derrick (2000)
DeQuin, Benji (2003)
DeShong, Jimmie (1929-1930)
Desmond, Ian (2006-2009)
Dessau, Rube (1906)
Detwiler, Ross (2009-2010)
Dezik, John (1940)
Dials, Zach (2010)
Diaz, Felix (2003)
Diaz, Frank (2006-2007)
Diaz, Ralph (1993-1995)
Dietrich, Bill (1931)
Dietz, Paul (1913)
Diggs, Reese (1935)
Ditter, Brad (2005)
Dixon, Eddie (1994)

Dixon, Tim (1997-1999)
Dodson, Frank (1927-1929)
Doherty, Walter (1948)
Dolphin (1894)
Doran, John (1895)
Dorlarque, Aaron (1996)
Dorner, Gus (1911)
Dorta, Melvin (2004-2007)
Doscher, Jack (1906-1908)
Dotzler, Michael (1987)
Dougherty, Patrick (1926)
Douglass, Ryan (2004)
Downey (1916-1917)
Drauby, Jake (1892, 1901)
Drese, Ryan (2006)
Driscoll, John (1930)
Duggleby, Bill (1900)
Duginski, Philip (1947)
Dukes, Elijah (2009)
Dumford, Wilbur (1932)
Dundon, Gus (1912-1913)
Dunn, John (1894)
Dunterman, Albert (1950)
Duran, Roberto (1999)
Durocher, Jayson (1998-1999)
Duval (1926)
Dwyer (1892)
Dyer, William (1906)

E

Eagan, Bill (1890, 1892)
Eagan, Pete (1894-1895)
Eagan, Roland (1942)
Easterday, Henry (1892)
Ebert, John (1925)
Echols, Justin (2004-2006)
Eckert, Charlie (1932-1933)
Edge, Greg (1990)
Edwards, Robert (1935)
Egan, Dick (1908)

Egbert (1924, 1926)
Ehrler, Clifford (1951)
Eichberger, Charles (1910)
Eischen, Joey (1993)
Eisemann, William (1933)
Eisenberger (1909)
Elliott, Hal (1935)
Elliott (1916-1917)
Ellis (1909)
Embick, William (1940)
Emerson, Chester (1912, 1914)
Emery, Zigmond (1947-1948)
Emmer, Frank (1932)
Emmerick, Josh (2005-2006)
Enzmann, Johnny (1915)
Escobar, Alex (2006-2007)
Eslinger, Ray (1940)
Espinosa, Danny (2010)
Esrang, Ron (1952)
Estalella, Bobby (1935)
Estrada, Jesse (2009)
Estrada, Johnny (2008)
Estrada, Marco (2008)
Estrada, Oscar (1934)
Etchison, Buck (1952)
Eustace, Frank (1900)
Evans, Keith (1998-1999)
Evans, William (1900)
Everson, Darin (1995)
Everts, Clint (2009)

F

Faber, Joe (1924)
Fagg (1916)
Fairhurst, John (1894)
Falteisek, Steve (1995-1996)
Fansler, Stan (1988)
Faulk, Jim (1991)
Fee, Jack (1892)
Feeney, Charles (1893)

Felfoldi, Jon (2006)
Feliciano, Jesus (2005-2006)
Feori, Joseph (1925)
Ferguson, Frank (1900)
Fermaint, Charlie (2009)
Fermin, Felix (1987)
Fernandez, Jose (1997-1998)
Ferrari, Anthony (2002-2005)
Ferrell, Hugh (1930)
Fesler (1892)
Fick, Robert (2006)
Field, Jim (1900)
Fields, Jocko (1893)
Figueroa, Bien (1994)
Figueroa, Luis (2002)
Filkins, Leslie (1950)
Fink, Clarence (1910)
Finn, James (1950)
Finn (1909)
Finney, Lou (1931)
Fischer, Babe (1931-1933)
Fish, Hamilton (1926)
Fitch, Frank (1925)
Fittery, Paul (1910-1912)
Fitzgerald, Gerald (1933)
Fitzpatrick, Rob (1993-1995)
Flanagan, Steamer (1913)
Flannery, William (1890)
Fleetham, Ben (1994, 1996-1997)
Fleming, Tom (1900)
Fleming (1906)
Fletcher, Elbie (1934)
Flood, Ray (1928-1930, 1934-1935)
Flores, Jesus (2009)
Flournoy, John (1906)
Floyd, Cliff (1993)
Foley (1900)
Foli, Dan (2006-2007)
Forbes, William (1949-1950)
Ford, Gabriel (1893)

Fordham, Willie (1952)
Forster, Scott (1996-1999)
Fortier, Chester (1924)
Foster, Eddie (1907)
Foster, Quincy (2002-2003)
Foulk (1893)
Foulkrod, Frank (1890)
Fox, Adam (2010-2011)
Fox, Jack (1912-1914)
Fox, Jason (2002)
Frazer, Bill (1952)
Frebel, Roger (1949-1950)
Freed, Dan (1991)
Freed (1926)
Freeman, Buck (1910)
Freeman, James (1951)
Friday, Ray (1930)
Fuentes, Javier (2001)
Fuller, Joseph (1951)
Fullmer, Brad (1996-1997)
Fulse, Sheldon (2007)
Fulton, Greg (1991-1993)

G

Gaffney (1917)
Gagain, Henry (1940)
Gagen, Matt (1893)
Galarraga, Armando (2005)
Gallagher, Gil (1927-1929)
Gallagher, Jackie (1924)
Gallagher, James (1892)
Gallagher, Shawn (2000)
Galvin, Jim (1932)
Gamble, Bob (1890)
Garate, Victor (2010)
Garcia, Carlos (1989-1990)
Garcia, Miguel (1990)
Gaskell, Prince (1910)
Gates (1926)
Geissberger, Harry (1934)

Gelbert (1892)
Gentile, Gene (1987)
Gentile, Scott (1994-1996)
Gettinger, Tom (1890)
Geygan (1932)
Gibney, Russell (1940)
Gibson, Whitey (1890)
Gibson (1906)
Gideon, Brett (1987-1988)
Gil, David (2005-2006)
Gilbert, Archie (2011)
Gilmartin, Gil (1952)
Gimpel, Henry (1940)
Gingrich, Troy (2001-2003)
Girdley, Raymond (1946)
Gladfelter, Armand (1935)
Gleason, Harry (1909)
Gleason, Joe (1930)
Glenn, Joe (1928)
Glessner, William (1951)
Goff, Frank (1927-1928)
Gohon (1914)
Golden, Thomas (1895)
Goldstein, Sidney (1942)
Gonzalez, Edgar (2005)
Gonzalez, Gabe (2000)
Gonzalez, Somer (2005)
Goodale, Charles (1940)
Goodbred, Richard (1915)
Goodhart, George (1892)
Goostree, Eddie (1925)
Gordon, Kevin (1987)
Gordon, Sid (1908)
Gough, Irwin (1916)
Grabowski, Reggie (1932)
Gracey, Richard (1940-1942)
Grady, Mike (1909)
Grant, Frank (1890)
Grant, Harold (1934)
Graulich, George (1892)

Gray, Dennis (1996)
Greene, Arnold (1940-1942)
Greene, June (1932-1933)
Gregg, Tommy (1987)
Greifzu, Henry (1947)
Gressett, Charles (1927)
Griffin, Marc (1993-1994)
Grissom, Antonio (1995)
Grott, Matt (1991)
Grove, James (1893)
Grudzielanek, Mark (1994)
Gruenewald, George (1934)
Guerrero, Cristian (2005-2007)
Guerrero, Vladimir (1996)
Gulian, Edward (1930-1931, 1933)
Gunkel, Frank (1946)
Gunson, Joe (1900)
Gutierrez, Dimas (1987-1988)
Gutierrez, Victor (2003)
Guzman, Garrett (2008)
Guzman, Joel (2009)

H

Haas, Matt (1997)
Haines, Hinkey (1933)
Haines, Russell (1930)
Hairston, Jerry Jr. (2011)
Hall, Andy (1989)
Hall, Josh (2007-2008)
Hall, Noah (2000, 2003)
Hall (1895)
Haller, Frank (1893)
Hamburg, Charlie (1894)
Hamilton, Billy (1905-1906)
Hammonds, Jeffrey (2005)
Hancock, Lee (1990)
Haney, Chris (1991)
Hanrahan, William (1895)
Hansen, Doug (1949)
Hanson, Ollie (1927)

Hardge, Mike (1993-1994)

Hardy, Harry (1908)

Harned, Warren (1924)

Harper, Bryce (2011)

Harr, Walter (1951)

Harris, Robert (1990)

Harrison, Edward (1916-1917)

Harrison, Phil (1991)

Hart, Bill (1935)

Hartley, Chick (1909)

Hartman, Ed (1989)

Hartman, Fred (1906)

Hartman, William (1906)

Harvey, George (1952)

Hauser, Emil (1910)

Hayes (1931)

Haynes, Dee (2005)

Haynes, Heath (1992-1993)

Head, Ralph (1927)

Hearn, Bunny (1930)

Hebson, Bryan (2000-2002)

Hechinger, Mike (1915)

Hecht, Steve (1992)

Hefflefinger, Lefty (1929, 1931-35)

Helfrich, Gus (1916)

Heller, Fred (1910)

Heltzel, Heinie (1935)

Hemperly, Walt (1940)

Henderson, Rodney (1993-1995)

Henley, Bob (1996-1997)

Hennessy, George (1935)

Henriquez, Ralph (1951)

Henry, Clark (1952)

Henry, Snake (1931, 1933)

Herman, Sam (1952)

Hernandez, Cesar (1991)

Hernandez, Orlando (2010)

Herrell (1929)

Herrera, Javi (2007-2009)

Hess (1894, 1901)

Hibbs, Norm (1935)

Higgins, Thomas (1893)

Hildebrand, Richard (1949-1950)

Hill, Orsino (1988)

Hill, Shawn (2003-2004, 2006)

Hill (1924)

Hinckley, Mike (2004-05, 2007-08)

Hinton, Steve (1995)

Hintz, Harry (1952)

Hires, Tim (1992)

Hirsch, Chris (1991)

Hirtensteiner, Rick (1992)

Hmielewski, Chris (1996)

Hoch, Harry (1908-1909)

Hodges, Scott (2000-2002, 2005)

Hodson, George (1893)

Hoeme, Steve (1994)

Hofleit, Richard (1951)

Holden, William (1925)

Holman, Shawn (1987)

Holmes, Russell (1917)

Holsman, Richard (1991)

Homan, William (1940-1941)

Hoppe, Melvin (1940)

Horne, Tyrone (1992-1995)

Horton, Huron (1940)

Horvath, Julius (1940)

Householder, Charlie (1890)

Hoverter, George (1890, 1894)

Huelsman, Frank (1908, 1910)

Huenke, Al (1916)

Hughes, Dick (1926-1930)

Hughes, Edward (1906)

Hughes, John (1932)

Hummel, Lewis (1940)

Hummel (1924)

Humphrey, Charles (1925)

Hurley, Jerry (1911)

Hurst, Jonathan (1991)

Huston, Jack (1893-1895)

Hutton, Major (1935)
Huwer, Charles (1949)
Huyler, Mike (1990)
Hymel, Gary Lou (1994-1995)
Hynes, William (1894)

I

Imholtz, George (1952)
Inglis, John (1916)
Irving (1924)
Isreal, Elbert (1952)
Ivany, Devin (2007-08, 2010-2011)

J

Jacklitsch, Fred (1900)
Jackson, John (1934, 1946)
Jacobs, Frank (1995)
Jacobs, Michael (1909)
Jacobsen, Robert (2010)
Jadwin, James (1951)
James, Chuck (2010)
James, Kenny (1999-2001)
Jamison, Walter (1946)
Jarlett, Al (1941-42)
Javet, Lloyd (1935)
Jennings, Hughie (1890)
Jennings, Robin (2007)
Jessup, Carl (1911)
Jewitt, Trent (1990)
Jimenez, Luis Antonio (2008)
Johannes, Todd (1999)
Johns, Ron (1987-1988)
Johnson, Carl (1930)
Johnson, Chris (1991-1993)
Johnson, Harvey (1941)
Johnson, Josh (2010-2011)
Johnson, Mike (1998)
Johnson, Rankin (1925-1926)
Johnson (1928-1929)

Jones, Alex (1893)
Jones, Brian (1987)
Jones, Joseph (1890, 1892)
Jones, Jason (2010)
Jones, Justin (2007-2009)
Jones, K. (1931)
Jones, Sam (1932)
Jorgens, Orville (1931-1932)
Julian, Alvin (1924)

K

Kamp (1928)
Kappel, Heinie (1895)
Karakul, Joseph (1946)
Karlon, Bill (1933)
Karp, Josh (2002-2003, 2005)
Karst (1916)
Katzaroff, Rob (1991)
Kearns (1916)
Keefe, Dave (1917)
Keener, Harry (1900)
Kelchner, Pop (1909)
Keliipuleole, Carl (1991)
Keller, Bob (1935)
Kelley (1895)
Kelly, Kenny (2005)
Kendrena, Ken (1995-1996)
Kennedy (1900)
Kerley, Collin (1995)
Kern, Frank (1932-1933)
Kerr, McDonald (1940, 1942)
Ketick, Larry (1892)
Keyes, John (1914)
Khalifa, Sam (1988)
Kilgo, Rusty (1991)
Killinger, Glenn (1924, 1927-1928)
Kilpatrick (1925)
Kimball, Cole (2010)
King, Don (1940-1941)
King, Jeff (1987-1988)

King, Ray (2007)
King, Stephen (2011)
Kinnere, Martin (1925-1926)
Kipila, Jeff (1994)
Klarman, Walter (1934)
Klepacki, Ed (2002)
Kline, Benjamin (1926)
Kling, James (1910)
Kling (1916)
Klinger, Joe (1934)
Kneisch, Rudy (1929-1930)
Knotts, Joe (1908)
Koerner, Al (1947-1948)
Koeyers, Ramsey (1996)
Kolb, Dan (2006-2007)
Komatsu, Erik (2011)
Konnick (1930)
Koons, Harry (1890)
Kosco, Bryn (1991-1992)
Kotrany, Joe (1948)
Kounas, Tony (1995)
Kown, Andrew (2008-2010)
Kraft, Clarence (1915)
Kramer, Randy (1987)
Kramer (1901)
Krasovich, Tony (1933)
Kratzer, Joe (1952)
Krause, Harry (1908)
Krause, Ron (1993)
Krausse, Lew (1933-1935)
Kuzmic, Craig (2005)

L

Labandeira, Josh (2003-2005)
Lahti (1931)
Lake, Bernard (1933-1935)
Lake, Ken (1991)
Laker, Tim (1991-1992)
LaLonge, Mickey (1924)
Lane, Dan (1994-1995)

Lane, Rich (2003-2006)
Lannon, John (2007, 2010)
Lansing, Mike (1992)
Lapp (1901)
Lara, Yovanny (1999-2000)
Larkin, Robert (1948)
Larson, Brandon (2007)
Latimore, Tacks (1906)
Lawrence, Brooks (1951)
Lawson, Al (1890)
Layden (1916)
Leach, Frank (1935)
Leach, Freddy (1924)
Leach, Jalal (1996)
Leary, Frank (1906-1907)
Leatherman, Dan (2009-2010)
Lee, Cliff (2002)
Lee, Harold (1940)
Lee, Watty (1909, 1915)
Lefave, Andrew (2008)
Lehman, Pat (2011)
Lehr, Norman (1931)
Leid, Fred (1916)
Lemon, Jim (1949)
Letrick, Albert (1946-1947)
Levi, John (1925-1926)
Lewan, Stanley (1931-1932)
Lewis, Craig (2002)
Lewis, Richie (1991)
Lewis (1893)
Lewis (1925)
Lightner, Joseph (1926)
Lind, Orlando (1987-1989)
Links, Eugene (1950)
Lint, Royce (1941-1942)
Liriano, Pedro (2004)
Litschi, Lou (1908)
Little, Scott (1988)
Lloyd, Tom (1942)
Lockwood, Harry (1948)

Lockwood, Luke (2003-2004)
Logan, Brett (2007)
Lombardozzi, Steve (2010-2011)
Longmire, Tony (1988-1990)
Looney, Brian (1993)
Lopez, Pedro (2010)
Lord (1924)
Lorenzo, Juan (2005)
Love, Ruel (1931)
Lowrance, Marvin (2008-2010)
Lucia, Fred (1906)
Lucke, Ed (1931)
Lukachyk, Rob (1996-1997)
Luzansky, William (1941)
Lynch, Dale (1946)
Lyons, Eddie (1952)
Lyston, John (1893)

M

Machado, Albenis (2001-2003)
Machado, Alejandro (2004)
MacDougal, Mike (2010)
Mace, Harry (1893)
Mack, Earle (1917)
Mackey, C (1894)
Madjeski, Ed (1931)
Magrane, Jim (2007)
Mahady, Jim (1924-1925, 1928)
Mahaffey, William (1900)
Mahon, Frank (1942)
Maisel, George (1912)
Malave, Jaime (1999-2000)
Malinoski, Chris (1992)
Malmberg, Harry (1949)
Manarik, Ken (1947)
Mandel, Jeff (2009-2011)
Mangum, Mark (2001-2002)
Manning, Jerry (1946)
Manon, Julio (2000-2002)
Manriquez, Salomon (2004, 2006)

Maple, Howard (1934)
Marabella, Tony (1995)
Marchok, Chris (1991-1992)
Marquez, Robert (1998-1999)
Marquis, Jason (2010)
Marrero, Chris (2009-2010)
Marrero, Darwin (2002, 2004)
Marrero, Oreste (1993)
Martin, Billy (2005)
Martin, Chris (1991-1993)
Martin, Joe (1906-1907)
Martin, Rafael (2010-2011)
Martineck, Mike (1926-1927)
Martinez, Anastacio (2006-2007)
Martinez, Carlos (2007-2009, 2011)
Martinez, Michael (2009-2010)
Martinez, Ramiro (1996-1998)
Martinez, Ray (1995)
Martis, Shairon (2006, 2008, 2011)
Masteller, Dan (1996)
Mata, Gustavo (2003-2004)
Mateo, Henry (2000-2001, 2005)
Mathile, Mike (1992)
Mattes, John (1951)
Mattes, Troy (1999-2000, 2003)
Mattheus, Ryan (2011)
Matthews (1925)
Mattox, Cloy (1930-1931)
Matz, Brian (2000-2001)
Matzer, Ralph (1946)
Maust, David (2003-2006)
Maxwell, Justin (2008)
Mayo, Todd (1991-1992)
Mays, R. (1911-1912)
Maysey, Matt (1991)
Mazurek, Arnold (1948)
McAleese, Jack (1906)
McAvoy, Jeff (2002)
McBride, Horace (1927-1932)
McCabe, Ralph (1942)

McCann, John (1894)
McCarthy, Arch (1908)
McCarthy, Bill (1909)
McCarthy, James (1914)
McCarthy, Thomas (1929, 1931-32)
McCarthy (1892)
McCommon, Jason (1996-1998)
McConnell, Chris (2011)
McCormick, Edward (1924)
McCormick, Frank (1910)
McCormick, Jerry (1890, 1892)
McCormick (1911)
McCoy, Art (1893)
McCoy, Pat (2011)
McDonald, Chad (1992)
McDonald (1892)
McGee, Dan (1934-1935)
McGovern, Red (1916)
McGiffin (1901)
McGilvray, Bill (1908)
McGlynn, Stoney (1901)
McGuire (1900)
McHenry, Arthur (1935)
McHenry (1932)
McKay (1932)
McKinley, Dan (2000, 2002)
McKinley, Josh (2002-2004)
McKinley, Tim (1989)
McLean, Al (1935)
McMillan, Drew (2004-2005)
McNally, Sean (2002)
McPhee (1926)
McQuaid, Mart (1894)
Meaney, Patrick (1894-1895)
Meanor (1925)
Meister, John (1893)
Melendez, Jose (1987-1988)
Melo, Juan (2007)
Melton, Larry (1987-1989)
Melucci, Lou (2001)

Melvin, Duane (1950)
Menefee, Thomas (1893)
Mensor, Ed (1915)
Merced, Orlando (1989)
Mercedes, Victor (2005)
Merejo, Domingo (1990)
Merville, Lawrence (1933)
Metro, John (1946)
Meyers, Brad (2009-2011)
Meyers, Chief (1906)
Michaels, Ralph (1933)
Mikkelsen, Linc (1995)
Micklejohn Matthew (1890)
Milan, Horace (1926)
Miller, Charles (1912, 1914, 1917)
Miller, Doggie (1893)
Miller, George (1906)
Miller, Henry (1893)
Miller, John (1946)
Miller, J. (1932)
Miller, Kohly (1892)
Miller, Paul (1990)
Mills (1916)
Milone, Tom (2010)
Mimbs, Michael (1994)
Minor, Blas (1990)
Mitchell, Scott (1997-1999, 2001)
Mock, Garrett (2006-07, 2010-11)
Mohr, Roger (1941)
Molina, Albert (1988)
Montague, Dick (1934)
Montoyo, Charlie (1996)
Montz, Luke (2007-2009)
Moore, Gene (1932)
Moore, Trey (1997)
Moore, Tyler (2011)
Moraga, David (1998-2000)
Morales, Alex (2006-2008)
Morales, Francisco (1997-1998)
Morales, Ricardo (2006)

Morales, Ysmael (1934)
Moran, Hiker (1934-1935)
Morgan, Cy (1931-1933)
Morgan, G. (1926)
Morgan, R. (1926)
Morrell, Bill (1933)
Morrow, Ben (1987)
Mortimer, Steve (2007)
Moss, Charlie (1893-1894)
Mota, Guillermo (1998)
Mowe, Ray (1915)
Mowen, Roger (1941)
Mueller, Art (1926)
Mueller, Ray (1932-1934)
Munn (1932)
Munoz, Arnie (2008)
Munoz, Omer (1991)
Munson, Joe (1925)
Murphy, Pete (1989-1990)
Murray, Glenn (1993)
Murray, Jim (1905)
Murray, Meredith (1949)
Musante, Ted (1925)
Musial, Ed (1948)
Musselman, Harry (1952)
Musser, Danny (1935)
Mutryn, Ed (1946)
Myers, Chris (1992)
Myers, Joseph (1908-1912)
Myers, Tootie (2001)
Myers (1925)

N

Nall, T.J. (2007)
Nanita, Ricardo (2009)
Naragon, Hal (1948-1949)
Natal, Rob (1991)
Navarret, Paul (1940)
Neal, Scott (1987)
Nebinger (1913)

Neely, Jeff (1990)
Neidlinger, Jim (1987-1988)
Nelson, Dan (2010)
Nelson, Jerome (1992)
Nerei, Yugi (2000)
Nettles, Marcus (2005)
Nichols, Pat (2008)
Nicol, Sean (2011)
Niebla, Ruben (1998-1999)
Niederkorn, Norman (1929)
Nieves, Melvin (2005)
Nist, Charles (1940)
Noblitt (1931)
Nolan (1892)
Norderum, Jason (2005-2006)
Norris, Derek (2011)
Norris, Shawn (2004-2005)
Norrito, Joe (2008)
Northrup, Kevin (1994-1995)
Novoa, Yunior (2008-2010)
Nunez, Johnny (2008)
Nunnari, Talmadge (1999-01, 03)
Nyquist, Brett (2006)

O

O'Brien, Charlie (2000)
O'Brien, Dink (1927)
O'Brien, James (1890)
O'Brien, Jerry (1892)
O'Brien, Patrick (1941)
O'Connell, John (1933)
O'Connor, Edward (1911-1913)
O'Connor, Mike (2007, 2009)
O'Hara, John (1892, 1894)
O'Neil, Edward (1893)
O'Neill, Harry (1940)
O'Neill, Mike (1907)
O'Neill, Pat (1914)
O'Rourke (1892)
Odom (1925)

Ogiltree, John (2005)
Okleson, Rudy (1946)
Ollinger (1924)
Onslow, Eddie (1931)
Ortiz, Bo (1997)
Ortiz, Nick (1998)
Osborne, Jeff (1989-1990)
Osilka, Garrett (2000)
Ovalles, Juan (2006)
Owens, Frank (1912)
Owens, Red (1909)

P

Pacheco, Alex (1995-1996)
Pachot, John (1997)
Padilla, Jorge (2008)
Pahuta, Tim (2010-2011)
Paniagua, Jose (1995-1996)
Pardon, Bill (1947-1948)
Parker, Christian (1998-1999)
Parker, Clark (2005)
Parks, Thomas (1940-1941)
Parkes, Chant (1928-1929)
Parson, Jiggs (1916)
Pascucci, Valentino (2001-2002)
Pattee, Harry (1907)
Patterson, John (2004)
Patton, Fuller (1929)
Paxton, Darrin (1994-1995)
Peacock, Brad (2010-2011)
Peacock, Brian (2011)
Pearson, Alex (1906)
Pedro (1946)
Peerenboom, Clarence (1951)
Peguero, Julio (1989-1990)
Pena, Hassan (2010-2011)
Pennington, Walt (1947)
Pennye, Darwin (1990, 1992)
Peploski, Henry (1931-1933)
Pepper, Jerry (1934)

Perdy, Purdy (1901)
Perez, Beltran (2006-2008)
Perez, Carlos (1994)
Perez, Miguel (2011)
Perez, Oliver (2011)
Perez, Pedro (1988-1990)
Perez, Yorkis (1993)
Perlmutter, Dan (1949)
Perrault, Josh (2007-2008)
Perrin, Devin (2006-2007)
Peters, Floyd (1942)
Peterson, Nate (1997)
Peticolas, Frank (1935)
Phelps, Tommy (1996-1999)
Phillips, Andy (1926)
Phillips, Brandon (2001-2002)
Phillips (1914)
Piatt, Doug (1992)
Pickrel, Clarence (1933)
Picota, Len (1992)
Piercey, Knowles (1947, 1949)
Pillar, Len (1948)
Pinto, Lerton (1924-1926)
Pipgras, Ed (1934)
Pisciotta, Scott (1996)
Plank (1925)
Plasencia, Francisco (2009)
Pleiss, Eddie (1910)
Plexico, Jeremy (2006-2007)
Plummer, Jake (1935)
Pollack, Chris (1991-1992)
Pollard, Damon (1994-1995)
Polli, Lou (1927)
Pond, Simon (1998)
Poole, Jim (1932)
Porter, Ned (1935)
Posner, Julius (1892)
Post, David (1997-1999)
Pote, Lou (1995-1996)
Pounds, William (1907-1908)

Powell, Brandon (2007)
Powell, Jake (1933)
Powell, Jeremy (1998)
Powers, Terry (1994)
Preston, Brian (1999)
Pride, Curtis (1993)
Prince, Tom (1987)
Puello, Ignacio (2003-2004)
Puig, Benny (1993, 1995)

Q

Qualben, Luther (1951)
Quezada, Edward (1999-2000)

R

Radsavage, Alfred (1948-1949)
Rahl, Chris (2011)
Raines, Tim Jr. (2006)
Rakar, Raymond (1948)
Ramirez, Ismael (2008)
Ramos (1931)
Ramsey, Buck (1917)
Randozzo, Joseph (1951)
Rangnow, Milton (1926)
Rase, Irvin (1931-1932)
Rasner, Darrell (2004-2005)
Rauch, Norcum (1931)
Raymundo, G.J. (2004)
Reamer, Alexander (1892)
Reboulet, Jim (1987)
Reding, Josh (2000-2002)
Redman, Prentice (2006)
Reed, Rick (1988)
Reed (1916)
Reeder, Joseph (1906)
Reeser, Wilbur (1940)
Reichle, Ed (1917)
Reid, William (1942)
Reilly, Herbert (1949)

Reilly (1895, 1900)
Reitz, Al (1933)
Remorenko, Edward (1935)
Rendina, Mike (1996)
Renteria, David (1996)
Reyes, Al (1994)
Reynolds, Bill (1915)
Reynolds, Harry (1942)
Reynolds (1926)
Rhinehart, Bill (2008-2011)
Rice, Lance (1993-1994)
Richardson, Keith (1989-1990)
Riddle, Chase (1948)
Riegel, George (1946)
Riel, Frank (1930-1931)
Rigos, John (1988)
Rijo, Fernando (2004)
Ritter, Chris (1987-1988)
Ritter (1916)
Rivera, Saul (2002, 2004-2005)
Roark, Tanner (2010-2011)
Roberts, Ross (1925-1926)
Roberts (1894)
Robinson, Wade (2007)
Roca, Gilberto (1988)
Rodemoyer, Howard (1951)
Rodriguez, Cristobal (2003)
Rodriguez, Henry (2011)
Rodriguez, Ivan (2011)
Rodriguez, Robert (2006)
Rodriguez, Ruben (1988)
Rodriguez, Wilfredo (2004)
Roesler, Mike (1990)
Rofile (1892)
Rogelstad, Matt (2007-2008)
Rogers, Buck (1935)
Rogers, Eddie (2008)
Rollins, Pat (1890, 1893)
Roman, Mike (1929)
Rombley, Danny (2004)

Roneberg, Brett (2002)
Rooi, Vince (2004-2005)
Rook, William (1947)
Rooker, Dave (1987)
Rooney, Sean (2009-2010)
Roseboro, Jamie (1992)
Rosenbaum, Daniel (2011)
Roser, Bunny (1930, 1932)
Rossy, Rico (1989)
Roth, Andy (1895)
Rothermel, Bobby (1892)
Rothfuss, Jack (1906)
Roussey, Elmer (1892)
Rowland (1926)
Ruan, Wilkin (2001)
Rudolph, Dutch (1913)
Rueckel, Danny (2004-2007)
Rueter, Kirk (1993)
Rundels, Matt (1993-1995)
Rundles, Rich (2004-2005)
Runge, Scott (1988)
Rush, Andy (1931-1932)
Ruskin, Scott (1988-1989)
Russell, Rob (1987-1989)
Rutherford, Austin (1910-1911)

S

Sabo, Ernie (1934)
Sabrinsky, John (1942)
Saffer, Jon (1995-1996)
Sakas, Lou (1933)
Sales, Ed (1894)
Salyers, Jeremy (1999-2001)
Sampen, Bill (1988-1989)
Samuels, Scott (1997-1998)
Sanders, Harold (1948)
Sandusky, Scott (2000-2003)
Santangelo, F.P. (1991)
Sapp (1901)
Satterfield (1932)

Sauveur, Rich (1987)
Saylor, Ryan (1999)
Scanlon, Thomas (1911)
Schacht, Al (1915)
Schesler, Dutch ('25-26, 28-30, 41)
Schleicher, Robert (1932)
Schmidt, Curt (1994)
Schmidt, Jack (1924)
Schmidt, John (1946)
Schmoll, Steve (2008)
Schmutz, Charlie (1915)
Schnabel, Nick (2002)
Schneider, Brian (1999)
Schneider, George (1941)
Schreiber, Paul (1924)
Schriver, Pop (1906-1907)
Schroder, Chris (2003-2006)
Schubert (1924)
Schueler (1925)
Schwab, Chris (1998)
Schweitzer, John (1893)
Seale, Dustin (2002-03)
Searles, Jon (2004)
Sebring, Jimmy (1908)
Segovia, Zack (2008-2009)
Seguignol, Fernando (1998)
Selbach, Kip (1907-1908, 1910)
Seremba, Daniel (1931)
Serrano, Jimmy (2000-2001)
Sessions, Doug (2004)
Sequea, Jacobo (2005)
Severino, Atahualpa (2009)
Shaffer, Charlie (1893)
Shaner, Wally (1932)
Shannon, Spike (1900)
Shaw, Cedric (1995)
Shawkey, Bob (1911)
Sherlock, Brian (2000)
Shields, Tommy (1988-1989)
Shiffner, Ray (1952)

Shincel, Herman (1900)

Shires, Art (1935)

Shirk, Jacob (1940)

Shoch, George (1900)

Shuman, Harry (1941)

Sidddall, Joe (1991-1992)

Sierra, Andy (1935)

Sigmon, Jesse (1925)

Simons, Mitch (1993)

Sincock, Bert (1908)

Sinstack, Fred (1925-1926)

Sipple, Charles (1946-1947)

Sivinski, John (1947-1948)

Skrmetta, Matt (2004)

Slaten, Doug (2011)

Sloan (1892)

Sledge, Terrmel (2001-2002)

Smallwood, Walt (1915)

Smart, J.D. (1997-98)

Smink, William (1894)

Smith, Albert (1940)

Smith, Fred (1908-1909)

Smith, George (1893)

Smith, Hank (1892)

Smith, Joseph (1907-1908)

Smith, Robert (1951)

Smith, Thomas (1940)

Smith, Willie (1989)

Smith (1894)

Smith (1924)

Smoker (1901)

Smoyer, Henry (1912)

Snider (1930)

Snow (1915)

Snusz, Chris (1999)

Snyder, James (1913)

Snyder, Maynard (1946, 1951-1952)

Solano, Jhonatan (2009-2010)

Song, Seung (2002-2003)

Sorber, Duane (1952)

Southard, Henry (1892)

Spackman, Robert (1948-1949)

Sparra, Alex (1935)

Spearman, Jemel (2008-2009)

Speigner, Levale (2008)

Spell, Albert (1940)

Spencer, Stan (1991)

Spradlin, Jack (2008-2010)

Sprogell, Oliver (1893-1894)

Stachurski, Stan (1952)

Stading, Greg (1987)

Stairs, Matt (1991)

Stammen, Craig (2008)

Starr, Charlie (1906)

Starr, Chick (1935)

Stecher, William (1890)

Steese (1901)

Steffen, Dewey (1927)

Stein, Blake (2003)

Stephenson, Dummy(1893-94, '00)

Stevenson, Jason (2004-2005)

Stevenson, Rodney (1997-2000)

Stewart, Bill (1916)

Stockhausen, Milt (1947)

Stoltz, Marlin (1935)

Storen, Drew (2009-2010)

Storey, Eric (2004)

Stovall, DaRond (1996-1997)

Stowers, Chris (1997-1998)

Strait, Lee (1926)

Strasburg, Stephen (2010-2011)

Strickland, Scott (1999)

Stroh, George (1909-1910, 1913)

Stull, Everett (1995-1996)

Stutz, George (1910)

Stutzke, Alex (1940)

Sullivan, D. (1909)

Sullivan, Ed (1893)

Summers, Kid (1890)

Sunheim, John (1911-1913)

Suomi, John (2007)
Swacina, Harry (1909)
Swartman (1892)
Sweeney, Edward (1906)
Sweetland, Les (1933)
Swenson, Walter (1931)
Swift, Mart (1892)
Sylvester, Billy (2005-2006)
Szymanski, Joseph (1947)

T

Taaffe, Bert (1911)
Talanoa, Scott (1996)
Tamm, William (1915)
Tamsett, James (1906)
Tarr, Roy (1933)
Tatis, Bernie (1989)
Tatusko, Ryan (2010-2011)
Taylor, Danny (1941-1942)
Taylor, Dorn (1987)
Taylor, Robert (1940)
Taylor, Seth (2004)
Therre, George (1913)
Thissen, Greg (2006-2007)
Thobe, J.J. (1994)
Thoden, John (1991)
Thomas, Bill (1909)
Thomas, George (1929-1930)
Thomas, Herb (1933)
Thomas, Mike (1993)
Thomas, Tracy (1942)
Thomas, Walt (1909)
Thompson, Aaron (2009-2010)
Thompson, Chris (2006)
Thorpe, Jim (1915)
Thoutsis, Paul (1996)
Thrower, Jake (2003)
Thurman, Corey (2004)
Thurman, Mike (1996-1997, 2000)
Tibbetts, Edward (1940)

Tickey, Edward (1925)
Tierney, Daniel (1915)
Tillman, Johnny (1928-1930)
Tipton, Joe (1946)
Tirado, Aris (1995)
Todd, Kyle (1987)
Tomaso, Daniel (1940-1942, 1946)
Tomlin, Randy (1989-1990)
Tomlin (1931)
Tooley, Bert (1915)
Torres, Luis (2003)
Tovar, Edgar (1993, 1995)
Tracy, Andy (1998-1999)
Tracy, Jim (1989-1990)
Trahan, David (2007)
Trout, Bob (1949)
Tubbs, Greg (1990)
Tucker, Jon (1998-1999)
Tucker, Jonathan (2011)
Tucker, T.J. (1999-2001)
Tuminelli, Joe (1952)
Twombly (1911)
Tyler, Johnnie (1933-1934)

U

Uht, Gerald (1951)
Ulloa, Enmanuel (2003)
Upp (1911-1912)
Urbina, Ugueth (1993-1994)
Urquhart, Derick (2003)

V

Vael, Rob (2000)
Valdez, Alex (2011)
Valdez, Edward (2007)
Valdez, Jesus (2010-2011)
Valdez, Trovin (1997-1998)
Valera, Yohanny (2000)
Vallee, Howard (1890)

VanAllen, Cory (2008-2011)
VanDyke, Frederick (1909)
Varanese, Louis (1933)
Vargas, Claudio (2002-2003)
Varhely, Edward (1950)
Vasquez, Javier (1997)
Veloz, Greg (2009)
Ventress, Leroy (1995)
Vidro, Jose (1995-1996, 2006)
Vigneaux, Sammy (1900)
Virgilio, George (1994-1995)
Vizcaino, Junior (1989-1990)
Voltz, Charles (1913, 1916)
Vorrell, George (1946)
Vowinkel, Rip (1912)
Voyles, Phil (1929)
Vroman, Doug (2005)
Vusich, Johnny (1935)

W

Wagenhurst, Howard (1941)
Wainhouse, David (1991)
Waldron, Joe (1994)
Walker, Mike (1987-1988)
Walker, Tony (1987)
Walker, Tyler (2010)
Wallace, B.J. (1994)
Walls, Charles (1933-1934)
Walsh (1892)
Wamback, Trevor (2001)
Wang, Chien-Ming (2011)
Ward, Piggy (1893)
Ward (1924)
Warden, Jim Ed (2008)
Ware, Jeremy (1999-2004)
Watson, Brandon (2002-03, 2005)
Watson, Matt (2002)
Watson (1932)
Wayne, Justin (2001-2002)
Webb, Ben (1989-1990)

Webb, Trey (2006)
Weber, Neil (1995-1997)
Weeks, Fred (1909)
Wehner, John (1990)
Wehrell, Fred (1911)
Weiser, Bud (1925)
Wellman, Phil (1987)
Wente, Jack (1894)
Westbrook, Jake (1999)
Westheafer, Charles (1946)
Westley, Jack (1940)
Wetzel, William (1893)
Whalen, Fenton (1914)
Wheat (1916)
Wheaton, Woody (1952)
White, Derrick (1992-1993)
White, Gabe (1993)
White, Rondell (1992-1993, 1996)
White (1892)
Whitesell, Josh (2006-2007)
Whiting, Jesse (1900)
Whitman, Rabbit (1933)
Whitney, Matthew (2009)
Whitney, Merle (1909)
Whitrock, Bill (1900)
Wilkie, Josh (2009)
Wilkerson, Brad (1999-2000)
Williams, Clarence (1890)
Williams, Dave (1900)
Williams, David (2009)
Williams, Jerome (2007)
Williams, Jimmy (1994)
Willis, Vic (1895)
Wilmet, Paul (1987-1988)
Wilson, Desi (2002)
Wilson, John (2004-2005)
Wilson, Morris (1940)
Wilstead, Randy (1993-1994)
Wiltse (1930)
Wineapple, Ed (1930)

Winston, Darrin (1993-1994)
Wirth (1892)
Wisneski, Richard (1946)
Witterstaetter, Leo (1915)
Wolfe, Maurice (1908)
Wollpert, Fred (1946-1947)
Wood, Arthur (1949-1950)
Woods, Tyrone (1992-1994)
Woodward (1926)
Wright, Joe (1894)
Wright, Pat (1932)
Wrightstone, Russ (1931)

XYZ

Yacopino, Ed (1988-1990)
Yepez, Marcos (2006-2008)
Yerkes, Stan (1906)
York, Mike (1988-1989)
Young, Chris (2003)
Young, Del (1934-1935)
Young, Dmitri (2008-2009)
Young, Pete (1991)
Young, Ralph (1911-1912)
Young, Tim (1997-1998)
Yount, Kenneth (1947-1948)
Yuhas, Robert (1950)
Zech, Scott (1999-2001)
Zetusky, Stanley (1941)
Zimmerman, Ed (1907-09, 1915)
Zimmerman, Ryan (2005)
Zimmermann, Jordan (2008, '10)
Zinicola, Zechry (2006-2011)

MANAGERS

Beasley, Tony (2011)
Bell, Less (1940-1941, 1946-1951)
Bodie, Keith (2005)
Bombard, Marc (1990)
Brannon, Frank (1924)
Burdock, Jack (1890)

Clark, Win (1927)
Cobb, Joe (1931)
Cockill, George (1912-1914, 1916)
Cox, Harold (1951)
Etchison, Buck (1952)
Dorante, Luis (2001)
Farrington, James (1890, 1892)
Hamilton, Billy (1905-1906)
Heckert, George (1907-1909)
Huppert, Dave (2002)
Huston, Jack (1894)
Jauss, Dave (1994)
Johnson, Rankin (1925-1926)
Kelly, Pat (1995-1996)
Killinger, Glenn (1924)
Knorr, Randy (2010)
LaCroy, Matt (2012)
LaLonge, Mickey (1924)
Lightner, Joseph (1926)
Little, Scott (2007)
Machemer, Dave (2003-2004)
Mack, Earle (1917)
Mann, Les (1934)
Onslow, Eddie (1931-1933)
Pulsifer, C. (1900)
Quade, Mike (1991-1992)
Seiss, Frank (1895)
Selbach, Kip (1910-1911)
Shires, Art (1935)
Shoch, George (1900)
Sisson, Doug (1999-2000)
Smith, Harry (1915)
Sofield, Rick (1997)
Stearns, John (2006, 2008-2009)
Sweet, Rick (1998-1999)
Taylor, Danny (1942)
Tillman, Johnny (1929-1930)
Tracy, Jim (1993)
Trembley, Dave (1987-1989)
Wheaton, Woody (1952)

Yerkes, Steve (1924)
Zimmerman, Eddie (1915)

HARRISBURG GIANTS
Independent (1922-24)
Eastern Colored League (1924-27)

PLAYERS
Banks (1924)
Barber, Bull (1923)
Barbour, Jess (1922, 1924-1925)
Battles (1924)
Beckwith, John (1926-1927)
Bell, Fred (1924-1925)
Branahan, Finis (1924)
Brigham (1924)
Britt, George (1922)
Brown, Earl (1924)
Brown, Malcolm (1922)
Burnett, Tex (1925)
Cannady, Rev (1925-1927)
Carter, Clifford (1924, 1926-1927)
Charleston, Oscar (1924-1927)
Chester, David (1926)
Cooper, Alex (1927)
Cooper, Dolly (1924-1927)
Cooper, Sam (1926-1927)
Corbett, Charles (1924-1927)
Craig, Charles (1927)
Curtis (1923, 1925)
Daniels, Pepper (1924)
Day, Connie (1926-1927)
Dixon, Rap (1922-1927)
Downs, Bunny (1925)
Eggleston, Mack (1925-1926)
Face (1924)
Fiall, George (1923-1925, 1927)
Fisher, George (1923)
Gamiz, Mazio (1926)
Gardner, Ping (1924-1927)

Garrett (1926)
Gaston (1926)
George, John (1924)
Gibbons (1923)
Gillespie, Henry (1926)
Gisentaner, Lefty (1925)
Gomez, Harry (1926-1927)
Goodrich, Joe (1926)
Grant, Art (1925)
Graves, Lawrence (1923)
Gurley, James (1927)
Harris, Ananias (1923)
Haynes, Willie (1924)
Henry, Charlie (1923-1925)
Jackson, Dick (1923-1926)
Jeffries, James (1924)
Jeffries, Harry (1924)
Jenkins, Fats (1924-1927)
Johnson, Bill (1925-1926)
Johnson, Claude (1924)
Johnson, Dan (1923)
Johnson, Heavy (1924, 1927)
Johnson, Hooks (1924)
Johnson, Nate (1923)
Johnson, Wise (1925-1926)
Jones, Edward (1925)
Jordan, Henry (1922-1925)
Kennedy (1927)
Lewis, Milton (1922)
Lucas, Pepe (1925, 1927)
Meade, Chick (1922)
Mitchell, Hooks (1926)
Mungin, Bill (1927)
Owens, William (1927)
Perez, Jose (1926-1927)
Perry, Don (1922)
Pettus, Zack (1923)
Poles, Possum (1924)
Pritchett, Wilbur (1925-1926)
Ransom, Joe (1926)

Raymond (1922)
Robbins, Slim (1926)
Robinson, Newt (1927)
Rogers, Nat (1924-1925)
Ross, Sam (1923)
Royce (1926)
Russell, E. (1924-1926)
Ryan, Red (1922)
Sanford (1925)
Scott, Robert (1927)
Shackleford, John (1925)
Smith, Cleo (1927)
Smith, H (1923)
Smith, J (1924)
Taylor, Ben (1925)
Taylor, Cyrus (1922, 1924)
Thompson, Wade (1923, 1926)
Treadwell, Harold (1923)
Weeks, E. (1922-1924)
Wesley, Edgar (1924)
White, Burlin (1923)
Williams, Fred (1924)
Wisher (1923)

McAllister, Chip
McCoy, Frank
Parker, Tom
Starks, James
Turner, James
Walker, Jim
Williams, Eddie
Williams, Harry
Wilson, Dan

MANAGER
Mitchell, George

MANAGERS
Beckwith, John (1927)
Charleston, Oscar (1925-1927)
Jordan, Henry (1924)

HARRISBURG-ST. LOUIS
Negro National League (1943)

PLAYERS
Armour, Buddy
Boone, Lefty
Calhoun, Walter
Carter, William
Ford, Jimmy
Gray, Chester
Jones, Collis

Selected Bibliography

ORGANIZATIONS and WEB SITES
Baseball Almanac (www.baseball-almanac.com)
Baseball in Wartime (www.baseballinwartime.com)
Baseball Reference (www.baseball-reference.com)
Dauphin County Library System (www.dcls.org)
Major League Baseball (www.mlb.com)
Negro Leagues Baseball Museum (www.nlbm.com)
Minor League Baseball (www.milb.com)
National Baseball Hall of Fame (www.baseballhall.org)
Society of American Baseball Research (www.sabr.org)

PUBLICATIONS
Harrisburg Patriot, Evening News, Telegraph, editions 1883-2011
Baseball America, editions 1993-2011
Los Angeles Times, July 23, 1996
Men's Journal, April 1994
New York Daily News, May 6, 2010
Sports Illustrated, August 12, 1991
The Sporting News, May 2, 1946

BOOKS
Baseball Goes to War, by William Mead (1978, Farragut Publishing)
Biographical Encyclopedia of the Negro Baseball Leagues, by James A. Riley (1994, Carroll & Graf Publishers)
Black Baseball's National Showcase: The East-West All-Star Game, 1933-1953, by Larry Lester (2002, Bison Books)
Chief Bender's Burden: The Silent Struggle of a Baseball Star, by Tom Swift (2008, University of Nebraska Press)
The Clown Prince of Baseball, by Max Patkin and Stan Hochman (1994, WRS Publishing)
Connie Mack, Grand Old Man of Baseball, by Fred Lieb (1945, G.P. Putnam's Sons)

Daguerreotypes, 8th edition (1990, The Sporting News Publishing Co.)

Ee-yah: The Life and Times of Hughie Jennings, by Jack Smiles (2005, McFarland)

Encyclopedia of Minor League Baseball, Third Edition, by Lloyd Johnson and Miles Wolff (2007, Baseball America)

Jim Thorpe, World's Greatest Athlete, by Robert W. Wheeler (1979, University of Oklahoma Press)

Minor Moments, Major Memories, by Mark Leinweaver with Ryan Bradley (2005, The Lyons Press)

Negro League Baseball, The Rise and Ruin of a Black Institution, by Neil Lanctot (2004, University of Pennsylvania Press)

New Bill James Historical Abstract, by Bill James (2001, Simon & Schuster)

Only The Ball Was White, by Robert Peterson (1999 edition, Gramercy Books)

The Negro Leagues Book, edited by Dick Clark and Larry Lester (1994, Society for American Baseball Research)

Willie Wells: "El Diablo" of the Negro Leagues, by Bob Luke (2007, University of Texas Press)

PHOTOGRAPHS

Every effort was made to determine the ownership of the photographs in this book, and receive permission from the copyright holders. Upfront apologies to anyone missed.

Dave Trembley headshot: Courtesy of the Harrisburg Senators; Dave Trembley and Rick Redd: Harrisburg Senators; Aerial view of RiverSide Stadium in 1987: Harrisburg Senators; Milton Bradley headshot: Harrisburg Senators; Stephen Strasburg pitching: Harrisburg Senators (Will Bentzel); Stephen Strasburg signing autographs : Harrisburg Senators (Will Bentzel); RiverSide Stadium, 1988: Harrisburg Senators; Metro Bank Park 2011: Harrisburg Senators (Ashley Grotte); RiverSide Stadium scoreboard: author's collection; Jerome Mileur headshot: Harrisburg Senators; First pitch at RiverSide Stadium 1987: Harrisburg Senators; Al Reyes headshot: Harrisburg Senators (Stephen Eddy); 1993 celebration: Harrisburg Senators; 1997 celebration: Harrisburg Senators (Stephen Eddy); Moises Alou batting: Harrisburg Senators; Jose Vidro in dugout: Harrisburg Senators (Stephen Eddy); Jimmy Sebring headshot: unknown; Kirk Rueter: pitching Harrisburg Senators; 1908 Harrisburg Giants team photo: Courtesy of Reid Poles; Spottswood Poles batting: Reid Poles; Chief Bender pitching: Courtesy of National Baseball Hall of Fame Library, Cooperstown, N.Y.; Oscar Charleston fielding: National Baseball Hall of Fame Library, Cooperstown, N.Y.; Fats Jenkins headshot: unknown; Rap Dixon headshot: unknown; Satchel Paige: author's collection; Brad Wilkerson headshot: Harrisburg Senators (Stephen

Eddy); 1987 celebration: Harrisburg Senators; Bryce Harper signing autographs: Harrisburg Senators (Will Bentzel); Matt Stairs batting: Harrisburg Senators; Ugueth Urbina pitching: Harrisburg Senators; Ugueth Urbina headshot: Harrisburg Senators; Wes Chamberlain headshot: Harrisburg Senators; Tommy John bobblehead: unknown; Art Mattingly headshot: Harrisburg Senators (Stephen Eddy); Valentino Pascucci headshot: Harrisburg Senators (Stephen Eddy); Carl Keliipuleole headshot: Harrisburg Senators; Hiram Bocachica headshot: Harrisburg Senators (Stephen Eddy); Javier Vazquez pitching: Harrisburg Senators (Stephen Eddy); Vladimir Guerrero headshot: Harrisburg Senators (Stephen Eddy); Jake Westbrook headshot: Harrisburg Senators; Miguel Batista headshot: Harrisburg Senators; Rondell White headshot: Harrisburg Senators; Bryce Harper batting: Harrisburg Senators (Will Bentzel); Jeff King headshot: Harrisburg Senators; Eleanor Engle fielding: Courtesy of Eleanor Engle; Eleanor Engle with teammates: Eleanor Engle; Eleanor Engle in press box: Eleanor Engle; Billy Cox fielding: author's collection; Max Patkin headshot: unknown; Max Patkin on bench: Harrisburg Senators; Chris Pollack headshot: Harrisburg Senators; Guillermo Mota headshot: Harrisburg Senators (Stephen Eddy); Jeff Cook headshot: Harrisburg Senators; Sugar Cain headshot (unknown); Bud Weiser headshot (unknown); Curtis Pride headshot: Harrisburg Senators; Glenn Murray headshot: Harrisburg Senators; Jeff Banister headshot: Harrisburg Senators; Vladimir Guerrero at batting practice: Harrisburg Senators (Stephen Eddy); Vladimir Guerrero signing autographs: Harrisburg Senators (Stephen Eddy); Vladimir Guerrero swinging at pitch: Harrisburg Senators (Stephen Eddy); Moises Alou headshot: Harrisburg Senators; Seung Song pitching: Harrisburg Senators (Stephen Eddy); No-hitter scoresheet: author's collection; Rich Sauveur headshot: Harrisburg Senators; Jim Tracy headshot: Harrisburg Senators; Mike Quade headshot: Harrisburg Senators; Ryan Zimmerman fielding: Harrisburg Senators (Stephen Eddy); Ryan Zimmerman signing autographs: Harrisburg Senators (Stephen Eddy); Joe Munson headshot: unknown; Ron Johns headshot: Harrisburg Senators; Andy Tracy headshot: Courtesy of Keith Wood; Geoff Blum in dugout: Harrisburg Senators (Stephen Eddy); Brandon Phillips fielding: Harrisburg Senators (Stephen Eddy); Cliff Lee: Harrisburg Senators (Stephen Eddy); Mark Grudzielanek batting: Harrisburg Senators (Stephen Eddy); Tyrone Woods headshot: Harrisburg Senators; Dennis Haysbert: Harrisburg Senators; Josh Labandeira headshot: unknown; Doug Sisson and Milton Bradley: Harrisburg Senators (Stephen Eddy); Anthony Ferrari headshot: Harrisburg Senators; Jamey Carroll headshot: Keith Wood; Jamey Carroll batting: Harrisburg Senators (Stephen Eddy); Doug Sisson and Milton Bradley: Harrisburg Senators (Stephen Eddy); Jason Camilli: Harrisburg Senators (Stephen Eddy); Milton Bradley grand slam swing: Harrisburg Senators (Stephen Eddy); Post-slam photo at home plate: Harrisburg Senators; Milton Bradley signed ticket: author's collection; Connie Mack headshot: unknown; Les Bell headshot: unknown; Tom Prince headshot: Harrisburg Senators; Tommy Gregg headshot: Harrisburg Senators; Matt Stairs headshot: Harrisburg Senators; Cliff Floyd headshot: Harrisburg Senators; Dave Jauss headshot: Harrisburg Senators; Brad Fullmer headshot: Harrisburg Senators (Stephen Eddy); Rick Sofield headshot: Harrisburg Senators (**Bruce Mervine**); Dave Machemer headshot: Harrisburg Senators (Stephen Eddy); Stadium flooding: Courtesy of Tony Wagner; Bryce Harper batting: Harrisburg Senators (Will Bentzel); back cover photograph: Harrisburg Senators (Stephen Eddy).

ANDREW LINKER

Acknowledgments

One Patch of Grass grew out of countless hours of research, hundreds of interviews and a few thousand newspaper stories from my 24 years at *The Patriot-News* in Harrisburg.

Twenty of those years were spent either covering the Senators fulltime or backing up a beat that allowed me to work with people throughout baseball. This book would not be possible without the moments those people created and the memories they made on a 63-acre island in the middle of the Susquehanna River.

Former Baltimore Orioles manager Dave Trembley wrote the book's foreword. There was no better person for the task. During his time on the island, Trembley worked tirelessly to teach his players the fundamentals of the game. He seemed to work even harder to help the community embrace a professional baseball team for the first time since 1952. His insights into that first magical championship season were invaluable.

Many thanks to Senators general manager Randy Whitaker for opening up the team's photo archives and sharing the outstanding work of Steve Eddy, Will Bentzel and Ashley Grotte.

Chris Andree and Jeremy Fagelman contributed lists for the book, while Dave Houseal and Ted Knorr filled my inbox with e-mails of cool stories that most have forgotten or never knew.

James Bailey, Jason Bristol, Casey Chambers, Ed Gruver and Ben McLure read portions of the draft, and offered advice and encouragement. The talented Jodie Morris created the front and back covers. I am grateful to all of them.

The thankless job of editing was provided by David Morris and Andy Young. Both possess a love of the game, a terrific feel for writing and a keen wit. They also have extraordinary patience and, Lord knows, I tested theirs with my typos, misplaced modifiers and fractured syntax. They did their best to save me from my literary bad self.

Bill Kratzer was the man behind the curtain who developed the website for the book, www.harrisburgbaseball.com. He handled all of the technical aspects of the project, including bringing me into the 21st century with Facebook, Twitter and the world of self-publishing. Bill made himself available 24/7 for any question, and I had a few hundred of them along the way. He did this selflessly while his 3-year-old son, Collin, was battling aggressive brain cancer. All Bill wanted in return for his help was a pizza.

Finally, special thanks to my wife, Michelle, and our daughter, Annie, for giving me the gift of time to write. Now that the task is complete I promise to clean up the hundreds of files, yellowed newspaper clips, faded faxes and dog-eared reference books that have been piling up around the house for far too long. Somewhere under all those piles is the honey-do list they gave me a couple of years ago.

ABOUT THE AUTHOR

Andrew Linker is an award-winning sports writer who has spent more than 30 years working for newspapers and magazines up and down the Susquehanna River. Most of that time has been spent covering the Harrisburg Senators since their return to City Island in 1987. He and his wife Michelle and their daughter Annie live 15 miles outside Harrisburg -- about the same distance some old-timers claim Babe Ruth hit his homer against the Senators in that 1928 exhibition game on the island. After more than 6,000 newspaper and magazine articles, this is his first book.

12369800R00161

Made in the USA
Charleston, SC
30 April 2012